MRF Shadow Troop

■ ■ ■

*The untold true story of top secret
British military intelligence
undercover operations in Belfast,
Northern Ireland, 1972-1974*

By Simon Cursey

This edition first published in 2013 by:
Thistle Publishing
36 Great Smith Street
London
SW1P 3BU

ISBN-13: 978-1909609020
ISBN-10: 1909609021

For security and legal reasons, all names of the surviving members of this undercover unit have been changed. Minor alternations, omissions and changes had to be made in this book to disguise, protect and secure the identity of all former MRF members.

It is not the critic who counts
Nor the man who points out how
the strong man stumbles.
Or where the doer of deeds
could have done better.
The credit belongs to the man
who is actually in the arena;
whose face is marred by dust
and sweat and blood;
Who knows great enthusiasm,
great devotion and triumph
of achievement.
And who, at the worst, if he fails
at least fails whilst daring greatly –
so that his place shall never be
with those odd and timid souls
who know neither victory nor defeat.
You've never lived until you've almost died.
For those who have had to fight for it
life has truly a flavour
the protected shall never know.

In memory of:

Ted Stuart - Len Durber - Richard Miller (Bob)

Together with all surviving members of the MRF, who cannot be
recognised while they are alive.

Table of Contents

Introduction by the editor

The existence of an elite, undercover military unit in Northern Ireland during the early 1970s was never officially acknowledged at that time by the British government, but neither was it ever denied. Not until its existence was confirmed in Parliament in 1994, some 23 years later. As a result, a rumour has persisted for almost four decades that speaks of a shadowy force which, released from the constraints of the regular Army, fought the IRA with lethal effectiveness and on their own terms. It was, so the rumour runs, a shoot-first, take-no-prisoners man-hunting squad, chasing IRA killers through the wet, dark and dismal streets of Belfast, as several querulous newspaper headlines of the time attest.

Over the years some claimed to have seen or served alongside these men, and have described their unkempt appearance – the long hair, moustaches and donkey jackets, the fast cars – in short, the utterly non-military demeanour of these ghost troops. Unfortunately, almost everything that has been written has either been marred by guesswork or mutilated by vainglorious claims and downright mendacious fictions. Nobody except those who served in it knew anything accurate about this shadowy force, until now.

Many titles for the unit have been appended to the rumour: somehow the initials 'MRF' made it into public discourse, and it was variously referred to as the Mobile Response Force, the Military Reconnaissance Force and the Mobile Reconnaissance force; all decent guesses, all as usual unconfirmed, and all wrong. The correct name, at least until 1974, was in fact the Military Reaction Force, and it was set up, experimentally in late 1971.

The military and intelligence disinformation seems to have worked only too well, for there has been no better-kept secret from the era of The Troubles than the true nature and operations of the MRF. It was said, out of the side of the official mouth, that some soldiers had gone wild and that their antics were swiftly closed down – that it had been an unsuccessful venture that got out of hand and was stamped on by the responsible authorities. Many things give the lie to this story, not least the fate of the unit's officer commanding who, early in 1972, joined the MRF as a captain from the Parachute Regiment. Had he been in charge of a disastrous rogue unit, such as has been described (he was also himself charged at one point with possession of an illegal weapon – an allegation that was subsequently dropped), his career would have ended in ignominy. The Army does not easily forgive those who overstep the mark or fail so conspicuously. In fact, this OC subsequently enjoyed rapid promotion and retired with the rank of brigadier, after a sparkling career.

Likewise, the careers of those members of the MRF who survived their spell in Ulster were unimpaired, and those who remained for many years in the forces – indeed, even men such as Simon, who didn't – were also successful and respected, not least for what they had achieved in Northern Ireland in helping to turn the tide against the IRA in the early, desperate years of The Troubles. Simon himself later continued for years with Military Reserves, and as a military and sometime Special Operations and Security trainer, through the Falklands war and into the period of the Balkans and early Gulf crisis. None of those who served in the MRF was penalised; indeed, the opposite. They were seen as valuable and highly experienced soldiers.

Operationally, the history of the MRF runs as follows: from early 1972 through 1974 it was a small covert under cover unit of three eight- or nine-man sections, operating from a secret compound location near Belfast. There was only one officer, already mentioned, and almost all the operational members of the MRF held ranks ranging from lance corporal to WO2. It was, however, a 'flat' not a hierarchical structure. No ranks were referred to among members (except for the OC, who was 'Boss'), and the milieu was democratic and open, with everyone contributing their opinion and ideas. Each section had a leader, but it was as unmilitary as you could imagine. There was no saluting or anything like that. It was not, an SAS operation, although some of the members were indeed former SAS members. Some also came from the SBS, others were from the Parachute Regiment or the Royal Marines, the Military Police, or were specialists from numerous other regiments, as Simon was.

More important than their background, was their personality and aptitude, their sang-froid, their ability to act alone and blend in under pressure, to kill up-close when required and not from half a mile away. One of the most fascinating things for me about Simon's account is his description of the selection process, which was indeed a gruelling, lengthy and highly selective one. Simon says that from over 50,000 soldiers, only around 120 were considered for the 30-man unit, and even allowing for turnover during the two or three years of its existence as he knew it, 45 soldiers at most could have made the grade.

In the early years the MRF undertook all the tasks that later came to be split between two different entities. The MRF was both an intelligence gathering organisation and a counter terrorist force.

Alongside the MRF in the early 1970s there was an extra very small section which specialised in running informers and surveillance projects but resided in another location, and which seemingly evolved years later, slightly separately into the Force Research Unit (or FRU) but this cannot be fully corroborated, although certain of its members stayed with 14 Intelligence Company.

I use the word 'evolution' because the transformation appeared to have been ongoing, and the end-point had neither been decided nor planned completely at the time. As Simon himself says, there was a period in early 1974 when much was changing in the MRF, its name and many of its operations. That it was masterminded from very high up, however, was never in doubt.

MRF: Shadow Troop takes us back to the time of the inception of the MRF. Simon joined in early 1972, a few months after it began to be fully operational. His document deals with the heyday of the unit in its most aggressive and formative stages, when Belfast was a war zone of burned-out houses and rubble-strewn streets, of aggressive vigilante groups and rifles being carried openly by IRA active service units. It was a time when the regular Army was acknowledged to be not fully in control of the situation on the ground. That was not the Army's fault: they were bound to abide by a system of formal conduct that allowed lawless terrorists to often run rings around them and which left them as sitting ducks. The regular Army had the wrong equipment – bulky overpowered weapons, outsized and sluggish vehicles, high-profile uniforms – that rendered them vulnerable and occasionally ineffective in what we have now learned to call 'asymmetric warfare'.

Somebody influential realised this, and the MRF was the first, tentative result. Simon argues that the MRF was a prototype among counter-terrorist units, probably one of the first to exist and one which honed and refined ways in which terrorists could be confronted and beaten – beaten in the sense of being deprived of their best advantages: fighting a 'courteous' enemy that could not break the law; and at the same time being able to disregard the law themselves while still enjoying its privileges and protection.

The MRF, stated bluntly, regularly put a stop to all that nonsense. It was designed, and its members were told, to take the battle to the enemy in its own front garden. 'To beat the terrorists, you have to think and act like a terrorist,' as Simon was informed. This meant living on the edge of the law in some respects, or at least very often stretching its boundaries. If the IRA believed they could get away with indiscriminate murder and mayhem, it was the MRF's job to curtail their activities and put a stop to all that. And it worked.

Just when the IRA felt it was in total control of the streets, and had begun to strut around Ulster as if it was a law unto itself, suddenly it had to start looking over its shoulder; suddenly it became scared and nervous; suddenly it began to watch what it was doing. That was because of the MRF, just 30 men, applying pressure and turning the screw. They turned it so tight that the IRA never again enjoyed the ascendance it thought it had won by 1972. Civil war was averted. Years later, 14 Intelligence Company obviously knew more and more about the enemy. Eventually the IRA would sue for peace: it all started with the MRF in 1971, with the obvious support and input of the uniformed forces.

I regard Simon's book as an historical document. There have been other books – many other books – making bold claims and telling tall tales about the period and even the MRF itself. Some of these are, as stated above, simply mendacious; some are erroneous and others are self-glorifying. Many have been ghost-written, second-guessing what the book-market demands: unlikely bravado and an almost *Carry On-*style cast of characters and repartée. This is intensely annoying to Simon, especially on those occasions when it comes from those who should know better. Simon did not want a ghost-writer to make his book more 'commercial': he couldn't care less about that. He is a serious, modest man blessed with a clear-sightedness that comes from not having an outsize ego. All he wanted to do was to tell the truth as accurately as he could recall it, and to honour the memory of his dead comrades.

As an editor, I have done very little beyond copy-editing and very slightly shaping the structure of the book. I was impressed by the honesty and the total lack of false sensationalism in what Simon wrote (he says he wanted to make dealing with terrorists sound like going shopping, 'as it was and should be'), and I think the result, nothing to do with me, is a unique and uniquely valuable document in which you can hear Simon's voice and Yorkshire accent clearly. He was above all concerned to get the facts right – especially the little ones.

As an example, here is a detail which somebody (who will remain nameless but should know better) wrote in a recent book about a button in the footwell of an MRF car that would operate the radio transmitter. The button was there so that nobody could see you were switching on the radio and talking over the air into a microphone, which was itself concealed in the sun visor. This person claimed that the button was on the passenger's side foot well. Think about it. What if you were driving alone in the car, as was often the case? How could you reach across and press it with your foot without swerving into a lamp-post? Of course, the button was – and had to be – located on the central 70s style dashboard. Simon was angry about that for quite some time, and it impressed on me the seriousness and the importance of getting tiny things correct.

'I am not a naturally aggressive person,' Simon told me, and I believe him. He is a professional, and he learned his trade on the hard, unforgiving streets of Belfast in the grim early 1970s, fighting hand to hand with some of the most psychotic murderers the British Isles have ever produced. *MRF: Shadow Troop* testifies not just to what the MRF achieved, but also to what has to be done in extreme circumstances to preserve civil society. Condemn it if you wish, but then don't complain when the 'baby-killers', as Simon calls the terrorists, come for your children.

Foreword by Simon Cursey

I would just like to say here that I know for certain the true story of the MRF has never been accurately or comprehensively told. I have read everything that has been written on the unit in which I served, and to be honest it is a classic example of the proverbial roomful of blind men trying to describe an elephant. We weren't the Military Reconnaissance Force or Mobile Reconnaissance Force or anything else. I am dealing in facts, and not ghost-written romances of heroic derring-do. I didn't win any wars on my own and I am not a superhero. But everything you read in this document, bearing in mind that names have had to be changed with other alterations, to protect the safety and security of surviving former MRF members, is unvarnished and accurate. I want *MRF Shadow Troop* to withstand historical scrutiny and act as a reference source so that people can stop getting things wrong all the time. I want that, and one other thing: to honour my dead comrades, who were some of the finest and bravest soldiers I have ever served with.

You will have heard no doubt, that we were a bunch of cowboys running wild and that the Army quickly closed us down to save scandal and embarrassment. In fact the opposite was the case, as this book will show you, but the official disinformation worked well. It seemed clear, at that time and later mentioned, the MRF appeared to be the seedbed of 14 Intelligence Company, ('the Det' or '14 Int'), which years later grew in different directions and size.

We were a counter terrorist combat squad as well as a reconnaissance force, and it's well known that the business end of MRF operations was later taken over by other specialist units. Today it can

be seen that the Det has perhaps a new name: the Special Reconnaissance Regiment (SRR).

That's all I want to say at this point. I'll begin my story now, after
leaving you with a few interesting quotes from news stories of the time
that show that our later reputation for recklessness did not come from
anything that happened back then:

*'They are not in business even to make arrests, but they are spe-
cialists operating in areas of greater risk than is experienced by
ordinary soldiers in Ulster.'*

'They are 300 times more effective than an ordinary patrol.'

*'If we are going to have murderers and terrorists roaming about
the towns, then we have to have somebody who is able to go out
to find them.'*

Finally, another report from when one of our members was killed:

*'Now that particular trick can't be used again. But there will be
other methods and other brave men to carry them out with no public
recognition for their courage ... Not while they are alive.'*

'Not while they are alive' has it in a nutshell...

Prologue

In late 1993 I was running an architectural services company with an office on the outskirts of Bradford. I had a couple of staff and had been doing OK despite a housing slump that was finally nearing its end.

Early one afternoon my telephone rang.

'Are you Simon Cursey, and were you on active service in Northern Ireland in 1972, based at Palace barracks, Belfast?'

'Who is it wants to know?'

The speaker was an Army MP staff sergeant from nearby Catterick barracks. I told him I was busy and to call me back in one hour, and hung up. I immediately rang a mate in the Intelligence Corp at York.

He checked and got back to me, saying that three men, an SIB (a military Special Branch detective), and two Royal Ulster Constabulary officers had arrived at Catterick and were messing there for a few days.

It seemed to be on the level. The sergeant rang me back as requested and I asked him how they had got my name.

'We talked to an uncle of yours, and he told us you were still in the area.'

So they'd gone through the phone book and checked off every Cursey until they found a link to me. That was very interesting: there was no other way they could have found me, and they clearly wanted to find me very badly. The sergeant asked if they could come to the office and take a statement, and I said sure. I sent the girls home a bit early that day, and after it was dark, at just past 6 PM, they turned up.

I wasn't taking any chances. The industrial estate was quiet and isolated, and three men – two of them Irish – were turning up to meet me on my own. As they came in and latched the outer door behind them I stayed sitting out of sight at my inner office desk, where I had a special surprise waiting. If this was an IRA assassination team about to walk around the corner, I was determined it wasn't going to go all their way.

Three hours later, after they left, I sat wondering how something that had happened 21 years earlier, something I'd almost forgotten about, could still be so interesting, sensitive and highly secret that the British State was determined nobody would ever know what me and a few other blokes had achieved in Ulster back in the early 1970s.

They had wanted to talk about a shooting incident in Belfast in1972. The main claim was that our patrols were claimed to have been driving around drunk and shooting at random – two accusations that could not have been further from the truth. So I told the RUC officers and the SIB man exactly how it was ...

1974: 'Actions on'

The 'V' check I requested earlier came back crackling over the air as a positive stolen car. I looked at John and we both knew that we probably had an ASU (Active Service Unit) of the IRA in front of us – two men in an old Cortina, as it happened. Kev, in the backseat, cocked his SMG, 9mm Sterling submachine gun, while my hand was under my thigh gripping my 9mm Browning pistol, or '9 millie' as we called it. We were alone with no backup vehicles available in the immediate area, which meant we had to stay behind the suspect car until some colleagues arrived. They could then take over the surveillance and we would revert to backup for them. Normally we'd follow for as long as we could and await instructions, either to tail the target to its eventual destination or to apprehend the occupants after we had some backup in the area.

Our weapons were standard British forces issue and were kept loaded and cocked ready to fire, but with the safety catch on, apart from the SMG. Usually, the guy in back only cocked the SMG if we caught sight of some other, hostile, weapons. However, on this occasion Kev had already cocked it and snicked on the safety as he also felt we might have a problem on our hands. Kev, who had come from the Royal Marines, was a tough guy, highly experienced and very professional and knew exactly what he was doing back there in the rear seat. I knew it and our driver, John, also knew it. We only ever drew our pistols from under our laps and took our safety catches off when we saw some weapons on the streets.

It's not good practice to stay with a suspect vehicle for long periods of time because you can be noticed and this can compromise your position. Under normal circumstances, numerous vehicles carry out a mobile surveillance on another car to prevent being spotted, constantly changing lead position so the target occupants don't see one single vehicle in their rear-view mirror for any length of time. Right now we didn't have that luxury. All we could do was to stay well back and try to blend in with the rest of the traffic scurrying around the centre of Belfast on a damp Saturday afternoon. We hoped our target would stay away from areas like Divis, Falls Road, Ardoyne and the Markets. If we had to stop them, check them out and hold them till some uniforms arrived, it would be much easier and safer outside those hard-core Republican areas.

In-between sending a running commentary back to base on the radio for the other teams listening in, we constantly talked through our 'Actions On' procedures in the event of a variety of shifting scenarios, which might involve the target vehicle speeding up or slowing down, stopping to pick someone up or stopping and leaving the vehicle parked. We also stayed keenly alert to any possible escape routes available to us, left and right, as we moved through the busy streets. This was in case we were suddenly blocked in and a hijack on us was attempted. Following a target vehicle is a very hectic and dangerous job with many procedures and actions needing to be considered, assessed and re-assessed again and again. As the Driver calmly drives, the Commander (beside him) will be checking the route maps and staying in regular contact with base HQ, while at the same time going over the changing conditions and options with his team. It's a role that demands ferocious concentration.

Over the radio we were quickly assured by Mike, our section commander in another vehicle, that we would have some backup in ten to 15 minutes' time. Mike was probably one of the finest soldiers I had ever had the privilege to meet and work with, which I could also say for all the others in my section. If Mike said he would be there, then he would be. If he wasn't, it would probably be because he was dead.

We had been following the target around the central part of the city for almost half an hour and as far as we could make out, the occupants of the car didn't suspect anything. But that didn't make us feel any easier, because as time goes on you begin to feel that everyone and his dog is looking at you; that everybody must have clocked you and put the word out by now. Moments later, the target vehicle turned onto Divis Street, and then up onto the Falls Road.

From the back came Kev's voice. 'I think they may have twigged us,' he said, as the target accelerated past Northumberland Street, heading further west along the Falls Road into the area commonly known among British troops as 'Indian Country'.

Immediately we had to speed up and get closer, to stay with them as they made their way in the direction of Andersonstown. By now both vehicles were flying along at approximately 50 mph down the busy Falls Road and through one of the most dangerous, aggressive areas in Northern Ireland – to my mind it looked like an obvious chase by now. What's more, it had become a very dodgy situation in a very dodgy area, as just about every person we passed was sure to be a Republican and they would all have some beef or other with the British. We were certainly drawing unwanted attention to ourselves.

'I really don't like this,' said John the Driver, and I agreed. 'I just hope Mike or one of the other cars turns up soon.' But I couldn't see or hear any sign of them.

Moments later, still speeding deeper into enemy territory, the radio crackled into life as Mike in car 'Delta' came over the air. 'I'm in heavy traffic down around the Markets,' he announced. 'Dave and Ben are in car "Charlie" but they're further away, at the top of Shore Road. Simon, stay with the vehicle and I'll be with you as soon as possible – just a few more minutes.'

Suddenly, the 'players' (as we called them) pulled in and stopped by some shops on the left. We did the same and parked between two cars about 50 metres behind them. Two men immediately climbed out, glanced around and down the road in our direction, then set off smartly together up a side street, each carrying a rifle. I still wasn't sure if they had spotted us, as the main streets were thronged with cars and Saturday shoppers.

I spoke quickly to John and Kev: 'I'll follow on after them. John, can you send back a Sit Rep then catch me up?'

'No problem, Sy. You go, we'll just be a minute or so behind you.... But you be careful, alright?'

As the gunmen disappeared into the side streets I jumped out of my car and began to follow, knowing that Kev and John would shortly be following. They still had to 'call it in', conceal any documents we were carrying and lock up the motor – we were driving an early 1970s Ford Cortina 1600E and there was no central-locking in those days. I knew Kev would bring along the SMG, especially with the two players seen to be armed. He'd fold down the butt and tuck it under his big jacket, out of sight until it was needed.

As I turned the corner left down Nansen Street, I saw the two men take a right into a back street which ran parallel to the Falls Road. As I went to follow, I registered the view along the back street as quite a familiar one – an alley curtained with brown brick and back-to-backs beyond with low, pitch-roofed sculleries – so like the old opening scene to *Coronation Street* that I almost looked for the cat sprawled on top of the back-yard wall.

There was no-one else around and I followed on along the alley. With my hands in my pockets, walking with purpose but trying to look natural, I turned another corner and immediately spotted the 'players' in the middle of the street, half walking and half running. They were holding their rifles tightly across their chests in both hands. They glanced back towards me, then began to run away faster. They knew for sure I was following them but they didn't know for certain who I was, so I gave chase until I was 50 metres from them, when I drew my 9-millie and flipped off the safety catch with my right thumb. The two men stopped for a moment, turned and opened fire at me – about five or six rounds between them. I saw clearly that they each had an M2 Carbine (the standard issue World War Two US assault rifle) – thanks, Noraid – and I ducked to one side trying to find some cover. I returned fire with my 9-millie, shooting two or three 'double taps' (two-round bursts). They ran on a little further and I jinked closer, staying near the wall on my right and bobbing around telephone poles, bins and other obstacles, wishing for some form of cover where there was none.

Fifty metres is a long way for a 9-millie and I needed to get a little closer to be more effective with my pistol – ideally within 25 to 30 metres of them for accuracy. The players turned again near the end of the alley, moved apart a little and opened up on me with a few more rounds. I dropped down onto my right knee, trying to cram my torso into a four-inch recess of a garden wall and gate, and fired back fast with what sounded and felt like an automatic burst of five or six rounds. I just needed to get some suppressive fire down on them. I clearly saw and heard rounds cracking and chipping the ground and wall all around me. The smell of cordite was strong, and I felt it in my eyes. I changed the magazine on my pistol; I knew I was close to my last round. I remember noticing that the working parts were forward, so I knew I still had one in the chamber: if the working parts are locked back, then the magazine and chamber will be empty. I carried on, squeezing off four or five more rounds, and was almost certain I had hit one of them.

Although this 'contact' had lasted only a few seconds, perhaps a minute, it seemed like ages. It's like that in combat: the alert brain, high on adrenalin, scrutinises every instant of time for danger and it has the effect of slowing down reality, a bit like 'over-cranking' an old-fashioned movie camera to achieve slow-motion. Your heart's pounding, your breathing's rapid, you're trying like hell to concentrate and keep your aim steady. Everything feels sluggish but crystal clear and you're trying to speed things along to get as many accurate rounds down as you can. It really is the kind of situation that nightmares are made of, like when you're trying to run away from a dream monster but your feet are too heavy to lift. In the back of my mind I just hoped Kev and John were close by and getting closer: surely they must have heard the shots being fired. Our car could only have been about 150 metres away, around the corner parked on the Falls Road.

The two players must have put down about 20 to 25 rounds between them, and the last thing I remembered before my nice day came to an abrupt end was that one was crouched in a corner, probably hurt, and that his pal was attempting to climb over somebody's backyard wall.

Then WHACK! A terrifying blinding flash in front of my eyes – I was thrown tumbling and rolling into the street from the shock of an explosion in my face and being hit by a supersonic lump of metal. Really, it was as if I'd been struck by a seven-pound lump hammer wielded by a West Indies test batsman. Initially, all I felt was a strong force and the white flash knock me off my feet. Then within seconds a deep, agonising burning pain followed, exactly like having a white-hot steel rod driven through your leg, which was pretty near what had happened. The bullet was in my knee but the pain stretched the entire length of my leg. The brain is quick in situations like that and began pumping out its endorphins – the body's home-made heroin – into my bloodstream, so that I quickly felt like I was in a hazy dream, lying there flat on my back looking up at the peaceful clouds blooming over me and being caressed by a gentle cool breeze trickling over my face. I didn't feel cold even though the ground was still damp from the rain earlier in the day.

Simultaneously, just as I fell still in the road, Kev and John were there. They were kneeling beside me like brothers, covering and shielding me while they 'eliminated the threat ... destroyed the enemy', as the good book says, unloading some awesome firepower down the alley that immediately neutralised the two terrorists. At the time I had a strange feeling of comfort and contentment and only felt relief that they had caught up with me in time. Within a few moments I had a field dressing on my left knee, but I couldn't stand very well and so big Kev hefted me over his shoulder in a fireman's lift and carried me back to the car, with his SMG in his left hand and John covering us as we went. By the Cortina, while Kev was bundling and shuffling me into the back seat, I noticed Colin and Tug from our Section waving their arms and holding the traffic back. Mike was in our commander's seat, talking into the radio and 'calling in' the contact we had just had. He looked over his shoulder at me and winked.

'Hey, you're in my seat,' I said. He smiled back as he opened the car door to get out. 'Sit back and relax, it's your day off today.'

Before we were leaving the area, the uniformed troops that had been called in were arriving to take over the situation, take control and collect any weapons. Kev jumped in the front with John and we set off for the hospital, with Mike and his team following after they had quickly handed over control of the situation to the Army.

My next stop was Musgrave Park Hospital where I was given the good news by the surgeon that I still had my leg where it was supposed to be. I was lying in a curtained casualty cubicle surrounded by a clutter of trolleys, white sheets and life-saving equipment. The others, Kev, John, Mike, Tug and Colin looked on, taking the mickey and cracking jokes about how small the hole in my knee was. 'It's quite a neat little hole' said Tug, trying to prod his finger in it to see how deep it went, until I told him to sod off.

I explained to the surgeon that I was hit by a ricochet off the wall in front of my face. He told me the bullet had broken in two, losing much of its power, then 'my' half had bounced downwards and entered my left leg sideways just above the kneecap. It had mashed up the cartilage on its journey to finally lodge in the centre of my knee. Looking at the X-rays I remember thinking that a fragment from a ricochet was quite powerful enough thanks very much, and I dreaded to imagine what a direct hit would have felt like.

His parting comment, as he looked up from his chart, was that if the whole bullet had struck me directly, in the same place, it would have probably taken off the lower half of my leg. I absorbed this good news and settled down with a cup of tea for a chin-wag with some of the lads while Kev and Colin chatted to the nurses. The guys set off back to base an hour or so later and I was alone.

The Boss, our only officer, turned up the next day to see how I was. He brought some magazines with him and spent a couple of hours with me, chit-chatting about how things were going. But before he left, he mentioned that I'd be out of action for quite some time and that he didn't know how things would go in the unit over the next year or so. He said that I could come back when I was fit again if I liked. But I'd already thought things over and said, 'I'm not sure at the moment. I'll see how things go with the leg.'

'Okay,' he replied, 'See how it goes but stay in touch. And don't forget, if you want to move on to some other specialist unit later, just let me know first.' This sort of informality characterised the outfit, and at the time I took it for granted, not realising that our set-up was unique in the British armed forces.

After he went I settled down to enjoy a few days' rest and some more visits from the lads. Kev and John were the final two who popped in, the night before I was transferred to the mainland. And the last thing that Kev said to me before they left was, typically, 'Take care of yourself, you little Yorkshire twat.'

I felt at the time I'd probably never see Kev and John or any of the other lads again, and it was a sad moment after they'd gone. And I'm sure they were also thinking the same as they left my room. We had spent a long time continually in each other's company, trying to stay alive and sometimes failing, tight together but strangely cut off from the rest of the world in our officially non-existent unit. Leaving it would prove to be a very strange and isolating experience.

The next day, I got myself packed up and was transferred to an English hospital to spend a few weeks learning how to walk again. Full recovery took over twelve months including lots of physiotherapy and light duties. I found it very boring and frustrating to be hobbling around on crutches unable to do anything I really wanted.

From the point when I left Musgrave Park Hospital, I knew my days as an Army Intelligence under-cover operator, hunting terrorists, were over. I didn't realise it at the time but it also marked the beginning of the end of my Army career.

This book isn't a chronology of general military activities in Northern Ireland, or an in-depth thrashing-out of the historical or political background leading up to The Troubles. There are many excellent books which have done this in great detail.

I have, instead, attempted from my own experiences and memory to unveil a little-known side of the British Army in Ulster. It is a story known only to a very few privileged people, many now dead, who regarded it as an ultra top-secret operation – and even those few people, in fact, knew very little of our unit's activities and what our Operating Procedures were.

Ours was a special department born out of the conflict early on in Northern Ireland at a time, just prior to Bloody Sunday, when the IRA seemed to be running beyond our control; a time when the regular Army looked as if it could not arrest the slide of the Five Counties into anarchy and even all-out civil war. We are now familiar, through heartbreaking experiences in Iraq and Afghanistan, with the difficulties of conventional forces engaging terrorists and insurgents on the ground, especially in an urban environment – one where the enemy can melt at will into the civilian population, and use them as human shields on a permanent basis. We know it now as 'asymmetric warfare', but back in the early 1970s it was quite a new experience. The regular army didn't have the right weapons (too large and high powered for street fighting), they didn't have the right vehicles (too big, too unwieldy, too damn visible), and they didn't have the right training for the down-and-dirty fighting needed to successfully tackle hardened terrorist murderers. The regular forces were regulated by the rules. They couldn't adopt the tactics employed by the IRA to get at the IRA because they were against the rules of this war, and the IRA well knew it.

The fact that our operation was established at this time is testament to the seriousness of the situation in Ulster. Somebody, somewhere very high up in the Army and in government, decided that an organisation of under-cover intelligence operators was badly needed as the eyes and ears – and the trigger finger – of an Army that was hampered by its disposition and rules of engagement. The British military was in need of a specialist under cover, covert group who were able, willing and capable to crawl down into the drains and sewers, seek out the enemy and confront the murders head on. However, what was most important of all; when it's all over, they had the ability and mind set to step back up onto the curb.

This is the previously untold story of the MRF, which stood for 'Military Reaction Force', a unit of approximately 30 men and a few women, specially chosen from elite Army units beginning sometime in late 1971. They were specially sifted, selected and trained to spy on and hunt down 'hard-core' terrorist killers, which Belfast was crawling with at the time. The aim was to beat them at their own game, striking fear deep into their hearts with expert and clinical brutality. We were a deadly ghost squad, a nightmare rumour in the guts of the baby-killers … a Shadow Troop.

1

The Wall

It was at the tender age of 14 that I decided Army life was the one I
wanted to lead. At that time I was far more interested in the glossy
recruitment posters and leaflets, which showed people enjoying life in
sunny foreign places of lush white beaches and clear high mountains,
than I was in guns, bombs and bullets. Lots of sport and lots of travel
was what appealed to me the most. Initially, I never really considered
the thought of military training, weapons and the possibility of being
involved in wars – in little known places like Yemen, Northern Ireland
and the Falkland Islands. I decided to join-up with the infantry, probably influenced by nothing more than the recruiting officer being an
infantry man himself.

He was a big guy wearing a dark blue peaked cap with a red trim
around the edge. It was pulled low down over his eyes, which made
him hold his chin up. He stood proudly with a variety of medals spread
over his chest. I felt like a little mouse looking up at him, thinking he
must be some kind of hero and as hard as nails.

Looking down his crooked nose at me he said, in his harsh and
gravelly voice, 'The best way to get involved in sports with lots of
travel, my lad, is to be in the infantry. The infantry travels to different parts of the world for long-term postings like a big family group.
In other units,' he added, 'you'll probably travel as well, but more as
an individual, and it may be more difficult to get into the sports scene
unless you have some specific talents.' My main sporting interests at

that time included swimming, high board diving and athletics. I realise now they were all individual sports rather than team ones. I'd never been one for games like football or cricket and always preferred the more technical activities where you pitched yourself against machinery, the elements, and most of all yourself. The list ran to cars, bikes and boats, together with world championship boxing and ski racing. I was especially mad about boxing – it carried a terrific freight of glamour at the time and I was quite good at it.

Henry Cooper had been beaten just a few weeks earlier in May 1966 by a black US fighter called Cassius Clay. The ref stopped the fight in the sixth after a deep gash opened over Cooper's left eye, and afterwards Clay visited Cooper in his dressing room and apologised for drawing blood. 'It's against my religion,' he said, which was an interesting remark from somebody who had decided to become a professional boxer.

Anyway, it was boxing all the way for me and that was my sport for the first two years of my Army career. Clay – soon to change his name to Mohammed Ali – went the opposite way, refusing to join the US Army and having his boxing licence revoked for his pains.

Coming across me, wanting to join the infantry without needing any prompting or persuasion, the recruiting officer was lost for words, probably for the first time in his life. This was the sixties and the hippy counter-culture was starting to boil up a good head of steam. Who wanted to join the Army when you could turn on, tune in and drop out? In those days, many of the young lads in the infantry were sent there by the probation service or magistrates offering them a simple choice: Army or prison. Remember that bitter memories of conscription from World War Two were still fresh among the recruits' parents' generation; and National Service – widely resented – had only ended in 1960. I'm sure some of the kids chose prison!

I originally signed up for the forces at York recruiting office in June 1966 after the medical check, but I couldn't actually join my Army unit until I finished school, in fact in August, because I'd missed the

April intake. So I had to sit it out, whiling away the time going for long walks in the Dales and swimming at the local pool during the summer holidays.

'I'll be a soldier, come September,' I boasted to my friends as I worked at getting my fitness levels up and earned some money as a waiter and dishwasher at a local hotel. They were already beginning to grow their hair long; I can't recall what they thought of me.

On 30 July 1966 we had a big party at the hotel, with everyone crowded into the main restaurant. England had just won the World Cup against West Germany and we watched the match huddled around the TV in the restaurant with most of the guests. It was a time of sunny optimism – we were world champions and I was about to start a new life.

By the end of that summer, with a bit of cash from the hotel job in my pocket, my bags packed and a travel warrant in my hand, I was off at the age of fifteen and a half on an adventure of fun, travel and sport courtesy of H.M. Armed Forces. Or so I thought.

My parents were none too keen on the idea of me leaving home at that age. I was and remain the baby in the family, and I fought to make my decision prevail (at that age my parents possessed a legal veto over my career decision). Eventually, after many heated discussions, they accepted it, but my older brother best voiced their main objection when he said, 'You must be stupid joining the Army. You'll get nowhere and just end up as cannon fodder. If you go, you should at least learn a trade.' I was so innocent back then that I wasn't even sure what 'cannon fodder' was. I imagined it was some type of special food only served in the Army.

In early September, my father and brother took me to the local railway station. We sat and had a farewell coffee in the station café while we waited for the train. We didn't have much of a conversation while we sat there, more of a companionable silence to be honest, although my brother said to make sure to stay in touch and let Mum know how things were going.

After a two-hour train journey I was collected at the end station by an Army green bus with a group of about 30 other boys my age. Half an hour later we arrived at the Army camp, home of a Junior Leader Battalion in the north of England. Junior Leader Battalions, which were cut in 1985, were very much like military college, with mornings of education and afternoons of military training.

On arrival, the first thing we had to do after dropping our bags on our beds and checking around our accommodation, was to line up outside our barrack room. A big ugly sergeant was there, like the recruiting sergeant looking down his nose at us from under his hat, with a face like the dark side of the moon that looked like he'd lost a lot of fights.

It was my very first experience of having orders such as, 'Get into line!' and 'Stand bloody still!' screamed into my face.

After shuffling ourselves into some kind of snake-like queue, he began growling his orders at us while we tried unsuccessfully to keep in step, tripping over each other's heels. We were then marched down to the camp barber to receive our shapeless Army haircuts. Sitting, waiting, in the little saloon by the NAAFI, we had no choice but to gaze in silent horror. Other hapless recruits still lined up outside peered through the windows behind us, over our shoulders, transfixed as if by some gruesome surgery. The butcher/barber happily whistled while he carved up our wonderful 'mods and rockers' hair styles, which many of us had all spent months or even years cultivating. Some of the guys were actually crying real tears as their amputated locks tumbled to the floor.

Afterwards, we were again marched off, stumbling over each other in our twisted line, to be issued with our baggy over-sized uniforms at the quartermaster's dungeon. There, we had to throw our flared trousers and brightly coloured shirts into a jumbled pile in the corner of the room, to be wrapped up and returned to us much later. After getting fitted out with our uniforms, boots, equipment and oddments, we had to fill in a stack of documentation which needed to be completed before dinner that evening. We were told that if we moved independently around the camp area, we must 'march' in groups (squads) of four to six, and that when carrying KFS (your knife, fork and spoon – or diggers) we had to hold them behind our back in our left hand. The right hand had always to be free so we could salute any officers when we met them.

That first evening, after dinner – which I thought was actually quite nice, being roast beef, Yorkshire pudding, chips and peas, followed by a big rum and raisin sponge pudding – we all had to get together for our introductory briefing. It was given at the education centre in the middle of the camp, a pleasant building with large glass cabinets lining the interior walls, displaying Army uniforms from different periods in military history. There were many wooden plaques commemorating battles dating far back to the days of empire in India. In fact it was more like a museum than an education centre, come to think of it. As we all tumbled and piled in through the doorway, we were confronted by another big man, this time in officer's uniform.

'Come on in, you lads. Take a seat, take your hats off, keep quiet and no smoking.'

He must have thought we were older 'Training Company' recruits and perhaps didn't realise we were all under 16 and that none of us smoked anyway. The Training Company recruits were usually aged between 18 and 20, and received only 12 weeks' training before going off to their units. We, on the other hand, were there for two years until we were seventeen-and-a-half, before moving on to our chosen units.

After we had shuffled ourselves about and settled down, he introduced himself. 'I'm Captain Blyth of the Training Wing and I will be your OC [Officer Commanding] until further notice. Also, the three corporals with the sergeant standing behind you are all called "Staff" … Don't look now, look later.'

He continued, giving us details of our training programme for the next six months and which included barrack discipline, fitness training, foot drill, weapon training and shooting, and of course education in the mornings. Barrack discipline was code for endless cleaning and polishing tasks. The biggest shock for me was when he explained that we were basically prisoners.

'OK, you boys get your barracks in order, get them cleaned and tidied, because tonight at 22:30 hrs I'm holding your first inspection. Also, for the next six months none of you are allowed out of camp.' Perhaps he saw the look on our faces. 'If you work hard, maybe we'll give you a weekend pass at the end of February.'

I leaned over and whispered to a new pal, 'Jesus, six months stuck in this camp. I don't know if I'll be able to get through all this.'

'Yes, but it'll be OK, the time will fly by after we get busy.'

Just then I thought to myself perhaps I'd made a mistake and that it was going to be too tough. Not physically – that was all right by me – but mentally or something, in a way that didn't gel with who I was, and that I had taken a very wrong turning. I was used to doing what I wanted, and at that moment I thought maybe the whole Army regime was something that might not suit me.

We all arrived in a group of about 30 lads that day and we stayed together as one platoon for the whole time we were there. However, quite a few other boys had arrived the day before and altogether we made up three platoons, making one company of about 80 or 90 boys. That's when I learned the Army is all about threes: three companies make a battalion, three battalions a regiment, three regiments a brigade, three brigades a division, three of them a corps, and so on.

The following six months were quite tough but the time did indeed fly past, filled with school classes in the mornings – covering the usual subjects of English, Maths, Geography and History – and military training in the afternoons. As promised by Captain Blyth, it involved lots of foot drill, weapons training, field-craft and shooting on the ranges. Almost every evening, for that first six months we had a room inspection, which meant continuous cleaning and polishing of everything that stood still. The ugly sergeant would always arrive before the OC and give us all a real tough time, shouting and throwing things about in anger when he decided they weren't clean and sparkling. The OC would turn up in a bad mood half an hour later and again everything was thrown up in the air. He would even tip over our beds. Sometimes we'd be sitting up until 03:00 hrs cleaning the toilets and showers, so to be ready for another punishment inspection in the morning.

As time went by and we began to understand the required standard, the inspections became less aggressive. I preferred the military training to the education and found myself longing for lunch time, so we could grab some food before drawing the weapons. We also had to spend lots of time in the gym, mixed with scampering about on the elevated confidence course. There were also regular cross-country runs around the range area behind camp, alternated with tiring 15-mile route marches a couple of times a week that weaved around the local villages and gave us the chance to wave to the girls as we passed by them.

Saturday morning was 'Assault Course Day', when we all had to thrash around the camp's obstacle course for a couple of hours, getting totally wet through and scratched to pieces as we tried to master a variety of traps and challenges. These included the rope water jump, tunnels, monkey rails and the notorious '12-foot wall' which dominated the end of the course – and us, when we stood next to it. I was five feet five inches tall when I was 15 and 'That Wall' seemed overpowering and quite menacing to most of us. It even gave us nightmares, as if it was some impregnable barrier to our future lives. We all spent many evenings gathered around with pens and paper, planning possible ways of getting over it as a team. During those early months we also had regular inter-platoon assault course competitions, although we never won, as many in my platoon were frankly quite short, weak and spindly. However, having said that, we did quite well and better than the other platoons at shooting on the ranges, which proves brawn doesn't count for everything. Also, we were much better at the field-craft activities – patrolling, radio communications, camouflage and concealment, and advance-to-contact-section battle drills/formations.

In time, we did eventually manage to master the techniques to get over that damn wall, which we did by formulating and building a specially-designed human pyramid. It began with the tallest five or six lads at the bottom and the smallest going up first, most of whom stayed on top and pulled the others up after. After we cracked it we enjoyed the assault course days so much that a bunch of us often spent our 'free Sunday' practicing there, until we were marinated in filth, scared and exhausted, but having a great time. Later, we all piled into the cook-house canteen for evening dinner, looking (and smelling) like shit and attracting some strange comments from all the others, which at that age we all thought was really good fun. We were just kids, really. But we were getting good.

By the time October came around we realised we had all slowly grown fitter and fitter. We were beginning to feel pleased and even proud, but on the twenty-first came news that genuinely affected us all as no other had done. At about 09:15 hrs that morning, just as the pupils were beginning their day's lessons, a vast spoil heap from the local colliery slid down into the village of Aberfan in Wales and totally smothered the local school, Pantglas Junior. More than 130 people were buried, most of them children, 116 of whom died. The last body was recovered almost a week after the disaster, and in one classroom 14 bodies were found. The body of Mr Beynon, the deputy headteacher, was discovered clutching five children in his arms as if he was protecting them. It took the wind out of our sails, the kids not being much younger than us, really; that and the idea of the vulnerability of the innocent, and that they should be protected. That's something that stayed with me.

February soon arrived: I had grown four inches and put on six pounds in weight. I had muscles. I had big lungs. At last it was announced that we were to be issued with 'weekend passes' so we could enjoy a couple of days off. But the problem was, we were given the passes at about 20:00 hrs on the Friday evening. I immediately checked the bus times and train connections to get me home that night. I'm from Leyburn in North Yorkshire, and to my dismay I discovered that I had missed the last connection that night and there was no chance to be home before lunch time on Saturday. So much for the weekend pass.

However (this is where the training kicks in), desperate to get out of camp and go home for the whole weekend, I decided to walk and hitch-hike even though it was more than 20 miles across country, overnight, and in freezing February rain. It really was bitterly cold that evening and the other lads thought I was nuts, but I said, 'Come on you pussies, it's nothing. We can all do 20 miles any day, whatever the weather.' And it was true, except that it was night not day, of course. It had got to the stage, without me even noticing, that I could take a 20-mile yomp in my stride, so to speak.

I wrapped myself up in some warm woollies, jeans and combat jacket, packed my rucksack with all my dirty washing for mum (naturally), laced on my army boots and was away. I must have looked like a short-haired toy version of John Rambo as I signed out in the Guard Room at about 21:30 hrs.

With it being late at night, wet, and almost deserted on the roads, I had no choice but to walk and run the entire way to my parents' home. Sometimes I'd take refuge, huddling in the corner of a bus shelter to warm up and eating a bar of chocolate, before moving on again. It was still dark and miserable when I arrived at approximately 04:00 hrs and everywhere was completely, ringingly silent in a way you just do not hear any longer. I didn't want to wake my parents that early, so I forced my way through one of the windows in our caravan, which was parked down the side of the house. Inside I found a couple of blankets, so I pulled off my boots and curled up to try and get a little sleep before first light broke. By 08:30 hrs, to everyone's amazement and surprise, I clambered out of the caravan window and walked in the front door to enjoy a nice hot bath, while mum made me a wonderful sausage, egg and bacon breakfast. They really couldn't understand how I had managed to walk and run such a distance through the weather in the middle of the night, and me still only 15 years old. It was the Army, Mum – but I began to realise it was also what I was becoming. I had developed the ability, and the competence, to do what I decided on.

'It was only 20-odd miles, and a good bit of exercise,' I said with a grin as I got stuck into breakfast. 'Just doing what I've been doing for the last six months.'

Back at camp time seemed to fly by. Before we knew it we'd done over a year, and the passage of time in the outside world seemed to be marked, at least in my memory, by news of deaths. In April 1968 Jim Clark – who had won the Formula One World Championship for the second time not long before I'd joined up – was killed during a Formula 2 race at the Hockenheim track in Germany, just 32 years old. He hit a tree and broke his neck, and I recall it so well because, as I said, I was crazy about motor racing. Graham Hill, his surviving team-mate at Lotus, won the F1 title that season.

Over the last 12 to 18 months we were at the camp, my fitness level just moved higher and higher. It was amazing, although being young I almost took it for granted. During this period of our intense training programme we went on expeditions in the wilds of Scotland and Wales, in both winter and summer. We trekked around the mountains and bivouacked in improvised camps in all kinds of weather conditions, which I thought was interesting and all good fun. But it was no holiday, and while we lived in the hills and forests we had to operate in a military way, with guard duties, night patrols and field training every day.

During my junior service I managed somehow to get myself selected for the company swimming and boxing teams. Our swimming team had to be at the pool for an hour's training every morning at 06.00 hrs, eat breakfast at 07.00, then be ready for normal training with the other lads by 08.00 hrs. That was all right. On the other hand, I really don't know how I managed to get into the boxing team – I must have just been lucky in my earlier bouts. I wasn't very big or exceptionally strong at that age, but if you happen to keep winning the fights you're given, the Army attitude is that you keep going until someone bigger and stronger beats the hell out of you. I was OK at boxing but I didn't think I was good enough to be in the team and I didn't really like the few beatings I had to endure for the benefit and enjoyment of the training staff. Truth be told, I much preferred to watch it on TV. Fighters with names like Ali, Frazier and Foreman were all big names in the late 1960s – a golden age of boxing as far as I'm concerned – and we all used to pile into the TV room when they were fighting, stocked up with cans of Coke and bags of crisps.

Earlier that year, in January of 1968, I took part in an Outward Bound mountain school in the North Yorkshire Dales for five weeks. They were civilian courses but the Army, usually Junior Leaders Units, had places available for boys to take part. But to my great surprise, upon our arrival we were told that the whole course was being immediately relocated to Luxembourg. This was due to the outbreak of foot-and-mouth disease we had going around the country at the time. It was detected in October 1967 and wasn't brought under control until June the next year after the destruction of 400,000 animals. Bad for the cows, but exciting for us: I had never been abroad. I recall that before we departed for our four weeks in Europe we had to have our shoes and boots thoroughly dipped in disinfectant at the airport.

I had a great time there even though it was bitterly cold, with two feet of snow lying on the ground. The place was just like a picture postcard, with a kind of landscape I had never seen before. Most days we were out and about navigating and trekking around the snowy hills, building camp fires and crossing rivers. One interesting wrinkle I learned is that when out in the hills and forests of Luxembourg, you should head uphill to find an inhabited area, whereas normally in mountains and jungles, the idea is to head downhill, following streams and rivers to reach civilisation. In Luxembourg, just about all towns and villages are located on plateaus on top of the hills. I don't know if that's a defensive decision on the part of its past rulers, but it is a fact that the principality has managed to retain its independence from the surrounding nation states, which have spent the past good few centuries fighting each other almost non-stop, and bulldozing everything in their way.

While out of our base on expeditions, we had to wash and bathe each morning in the freezing rivers after breaking away all the ice. I made some very good friends there and achieved top merits for the skills I learned. I also received an excellent final report, which on return to my unit produced my first promotion – to Junior Lance Corporal.

By July 1968 I had completed my junior service, and now that we were pretty well qualified in all things military, my platoon got itself ready to move. After the passing-out parade on a wonderfully sunny weekend, with my parents and brother looking on, I was 'badged' to my chosen Regular Army unit as a junior corporal, which I lost before moving forward into 'Man Service', as they call it.

The parade was quite interesting. Our platoon had developed a 'silent drill' sequence for the passing out while the other platoons gave assault-course and weapon-handling demos. All 30 of us in our platoon were lined up in three ranks, in the middle of the square, and our sergeant just gave out one initial order of command to start us off. We then went through a 15-minute sequence of numerous drill movements, with intervals of only three seconds, without another word. All this included marching away in various directions for 20 or so paces, turning around, marching back, halting, saluting, doing another about-turn and marching off in review order. It was all rather complicated but turned out well and my parents seemed impressed.

There was a buffet party afterwards and then the well-deserved prospect of a whole four weeks of 'leave', which in prospect seemed like a lifetime of holiday after the years we had spent in the camp. After that we were to join our regular units, wherever they were. The list was exotic and exciting, with destinations such as Hong Kong, Cyprus, Germany as well as the UK. As it happened, my unit was based in UK at that time, the short straw, but I wasn't too disappointed. I was just happy to be moving on to pastures new. I had made some really good friends during my time as a junior soldier and it was a little sad to be saying goodbye to most of them, before we set off on our month-long furlough

My first posting as a 'man soldier', in August 1968, was to Colchester in Essex, attached to an Infantry battalion based there, across the road from the infamous MCTC – the Military Corrective Training Centre. It was and probably still is known as the hardest prison in Britain (military or civilian) and I heard many horrendous stories from some of its survivors. The first thing they did to you when you arrived there was to shave your head, and you had to always run not walk when moving throughout the centre. The soldiers (in some cases ex-soldiers) I saw come out of there were as thin as a broom handle and fit as a butcher's dog. Still, rather them than me.

On my arrival at the barracks in Colchester I was put into a section called 'new intake', just brushing up on military skills with some other new recruits, while we waited to be placed in a department. After my introductory interview a couple of weeks later, to my great surprise and delight, I was offered a place in Support Company in the support weapons section of the battalion.

Ex-junior soldiers were not very popular in the battalions in those days and we were commonly known as 'junior brats', sort of the teacher's pets of the service, as we'd started so early – we were seen as altogether a bit too keen. Luckily for me, the officer at my interview was someone I knew, a captain from my junior days. He remembered me because I had volunteered to take part in a couple of expeditions in Scotland that he had organised a year or so earlier. He had always given me a good report from the expeditions and I think he saw me as a reliable, determined type. So he did me a big favour and assigned me to Support Company. In those days, Support Company, Signals platoon and the Reconnaissance section of the infantry battalions were normally where the best and most talented soldiers were sent. I felt privileged to be offered the opportunity of a place there, especially as I was to be one of the youngest of its members at the time.

During that autumn and winter of 1968, the battalion members were gradually arriving back from a six- month active tour of duty in Aden, which then (as now – it's a seaport in Yemen) was a trouble spot in southern Arabia. By then I was busy training with and getting used to the heavy weapons, vehicles and characters in Support Company. Being only 17 years old I was unfortunately much too young to join them out there in Aden. I didn't realise that there had been lots of trouble and I found out later that some of our guys over there had been injured and killed. All I thought, as I waited for the main body of the battalion to return, was that it sounded like a nice sunny place with perhaps some long sandy beaches.

One friend told me, many months later after he wearied of me pestering him for information about the scar on his knee, that when he was in Aden he was doing a driving job for some officer and that his own personal weapon at the time was a Browning 9mm pistol. One evening while sat on his bed cleaning it and watching TV, the gun accidentally discharged and he shot himself right through the knee. Luckily the bullet passed through the flesh, only skimming his knee cap (which I can testify is still unbelievably painful) and embedded itself in the floor. He was later 'charged' for the 'offence' and was awarded a £200 fine to go with his few weeks in hospital. He showed me the scar it left, which was quite long and jagged, running down about nine inches along the inside of his right knee. He never used to talk about it much because I'm sure he was very embarrassed about shooting himself, but these things do occasionally happen around weapons, no matter how well-trained and knowledgeable you are.

Some of the older guys I met in the Battalion were ex-National Service men who had stayed on after compulsory time had ended. Most of them were OK and quite helpful and friendly, but we did have some strange characters.

One chap I got to know in another section was a desperate alcoholic, I was told later, and was almost always well-oiled, day and night. When he had no money, he used to sip Brasso metal polish on a regular basis to get his fix. I often saw him making sandwiches, melting and spreading boot polish on the bread, then eating it. At the time I was baffled. Then, one evening, he caught me by surprise.

He walked into our section-room, where I was busy ironing my uniform by the window, and came over to me. 'Do you have any after-shave young'un?' he asked out of the side of his mouth. I thought he must have got a date for the evening in town.

'Yes, no problem Reggie, it's in my locker over there, take what you need.' It was always good tactics in those days to stay on the good side of the older soldiers. Reggie crossed the room, leaned into my locker and took out the full bottle of *Blue Stratos* aftershave my mum had given me for Christmas, even though I didn't really shave that much. Then, I'll never forget, he unscrewed the cap and lifted the bottle to his lips. He drank the lot, said 'Thanks young'un, see ya,' and walked out again. I couldn't believe what I'd just seen.

'It's normal with Reggie,' one of the other lads in the room told me. 'He's OK, but you should always keep your aftershave out of sight when he's around.' All I can think was that back then they can't have been using ethanol in scents like they do now, or Reggie would have been RIP.

Another couple of strange characters from one of the rifle companies down the road came up with a crazy plan to get themselves discharged out of the Army. They decided to cut off each other's trigger fingers with a bayonet. But the plan went for a 'ball of chalk' after one of them laid the blade across his friend's finger and hit it smartly with a floor bumper, chopping the digit clean off, according to plan.

However, on seeing what he had done and the mess it made, he quickly changed his mind about his own finger and ran off, screaming, with his fingerless friend chasing after him around the parade square, waving the bayonet and shouting, 'It's your turn now, pal!'

They were quickly caught and thrown into prison by the local MPs. Later, after the Court Martial, they ended up in MCTC for an extended visit. I never did see them again, so I suppose they eventually got the discharge they were hoping for.

On weekends, some of the lads from my section usually arranged to go out on the town on pub crawls which lasted two full days. Weekends were actually boring and there wasn't much to do except to get dressed up and go out on the town, or perhaps hitch-hike home to Yorkshire for a couple of days, travelling back on the Sunday overnight train via London. It was funny, every Monday morning at about 04:30 hrs you could see gangs of troops in civvies, dashing around Liverpool Street station for their connections to get them back to camp before 08:30.

However, there were one or two worthwhile pubs we often used around Colchester. One of which was 'The Grapes', over the back of the ranges and just a short walk from camp. Another, 'The Fountain', was further down the road, more towards the town centre. We often spent our free time in these places, drinking ourselves stupid. I wasn't used to alcohol like the others, and after about two pints of the local brew I was finished. Some of the guys would amuse themselves by getting me drunk and then telling the barman I was under age. The barman would throw me out and I'd have to sit on the car park wall waiting for them all to emerge after closing time. I soon got fed up with this form of entertainment and made my feelings very clear indeed to those involved, which seemed to elevate my status within the section.

One evening there seemed to be a little trouble fermenting in 'The Grapes' between a few of our guys and some squaddies from another regiment. One of my older pals, seeing this, quickly sent me off to get a load of fish and chips, mainly to get me out of the way till the trouble was sorted out. It was very thoughtful of them, because I was by far the youngest and least experienced in ultra-violent brawling. By the time I got back, everything had settled down after a couple of skirmishes in the car park, and we all got stuck into the food, laughing and joking as we strolled back to camp.

On another evening I was in 'The Grapes' with a few of my friends when we noticed Reggie clinging onto the bar at the far end of the room. A couple of my pals went over to ask him if he was all right because as usual he'd had plenty to drink (although he must have smelled fabulous). 'I'm going back to camp soon,' Reggie spluttered. 'Can some of you lads see me back OK?'

A few minutes later, we all started making our way home, singing merrily and holding Reggie up between us. Over the back fence to our camp there were a few 30 metre firing ranges with a footpath weaving between them to our building. Reggie couldn't seem to manage the winding path very well and decided to walk, or stumble, directly across the ranges, wading through the muddy ponds in the centre of each one. We occasionally hallooed to him in the darkness to check that he was OK, but by the time he arrived at the far end where we were waiting he was a terrible mess. He emerged from the swampy gloom, climbing up the banking on hands and knees, covered from head to foot in mud. All we could do was curl up laughing while we helped him to his feet and walked him over to his building and into the shower fully clothed, where of course we left him. The next morning, Reggie couldn't remember a thing about the night before. This was all normal.

Some training days we gathered the section Land Rovers together, six or eight of them outside our barrack block. We spent an hour or so fiddling around and fitting C42 radios from the stores in the back of them, before setting off out of camp in different directions. The idea was to spend the day out of camp and out of sight on a radio communications exercise of our own. They were great days out, spending an hour directing each other to different map reference locations. Then eventually we would meet up and all bunk off to some roadside café, miles away, for a relaxing lunch break, some of us filling our faces with sausage and bacon 'banjos' (sandwiches), while others just lazed about or slept in the back of the vehicles. This sojourn would last two or three hours, while we periodically did radio checks with our old mobile A41 radios, pretending to send our colleagues to various fictitious locations, because we knew that people back at camp will be listening into us on the radio net. Eventually, we arrived back at camp at around 16:30 hrs explaining to our superiors that we had had a busy day dashing around the countryside.

I was sitting on my bed reading a book one Saturday afternoon when a sergeant from the Combat Engineers section downstairs came up. He looked around for a moment and on seeing me asked if I was free the next day, as he needed a little help with something he was involved in. I told him I was around and at a loose end. 'It's a little demolition work, for a film crew making a film,' he informed me. 'It's about two hours' drive away but we'll be back by about 18.00 hrs.'

A nice Sunday drive, the glamour of the movie industry: it sounded great to me. 'What time do you want me ready?' I asked him

'By about 07.00 hrs outside will be fine, just put on your combat suit and beret. I'll arrange food for the day, before we go.'

Early the next day, while all the other lads were still drunk and snoring in bed, I was outside waiting as a Land Rover pulled up with the sergeant at the wheel. 'Get in,' he said. 'I've got everything we need. By the way, can you drive?

'I'm afraid I don't have a license yet, but I can drive,' I replied enthusiastically.

He just smiled at me. 'No problem, I'll drive,' he said.

I jumped in and off we went. I'd seen this sergeant before as he worked out of the same building as me, but I didn't really know him.

As we drove out of camp he turned to me and asked, 'What's your name then young'un?'

'Private Cursey, Sergeant.' I replied, while I was attempting to peer in the back to see what we had with us.

'I'm Richard, but my friends call me Richey', he said, still smiling. 'So what's your name again?'

'I'm Simon,' I replied, catching on. 'But my friends call me Sy.'

'That's better,' he said; 'But back in camp, don't forget, I'm Sergeant Bennett. Now let's go and have some fun with these explosives.'

Explosives? I thought. 'No problem,' I answered, and off we went.

We should have had an armed escort, of course, but Richey just said we'd be OK as no one knew we were carrying the stuff. Naturally, that made it safe as houses.

That day was absolutely fantastic. We met up with the film crew a couple of hours away at some disused Army training camp. They were unloading their trucks and getting everything ready to make some kind of commercial and wanted us to provide some big bangs. I drank a coffee with some of the crew, while Richey had a meeting with the Director to find out exactly what and how they wanted things to go. I then spent most of the morning helping Richey, after he had explained everything to me about how to mould and where to place the 808 plastic explosive charges, which we commonly used in those days. It was like blocks of Plasticine and I happily moulded the stuff in my hands, except that after a couple of hours it gets into your skin and gives you a bit of a headache. The charges had to be placed in a special sequence of positions with a cap of gun cotton impressed in the mould, so that Richey could later insert the detonators, such that the explosions appeared to move closer to the camera while they were filming. Richey, meanwhile, was busy checking the safety angles and laying out the det-cord and firing wire, but made the connections just before it was time to blow them.... The idea was that the film people wanted us to set off the explosions in belts of two or three at a time, moving closer. We started about 200 metres away then slowly closed up with about six or seven belts to a distance of about 30 metres from the camera.

By 15.30 hrs the whole thing had gone off like clock-work and the film crew were overjoyed with the material they had. We set off back to Colchester and on our return, when Richey dropped me off, he said, 'OK, many thanks for your help young'un, we did a good job today. I'll no doubt see you around.

I said, 'No problem, any time ... Sergeant Bennett.' Then, with another smile, he drove off. The Army never knew a thing.

By the early part of 1969, the battalion was selected for what was known as 'Spearhead'. At any one time, in Britain, there is a Spearhead battalion on almost immediate standby to be called-out and deployed anywhere in the world on an emergency tour. This standby duty lasts only for a month then another battalion takes over.

During the Spearhead standby, the entire battalion, its equipment and vehicles are serviced, checked and made ready to go anywhere at officially two-hours' notice to move. All the vehicles are packed with equipment and parked on the main parade square in the centre of camp. All personnel have a full documents check, are dressed in combat suits with personal weapons issued them, and are confined to barracks for the whole period – except for the married lads, who are allowed to go home at night. As for us, we couldn't even get undressed to go to bed, except to take off our boots. If we wanted a shower, only two at a time from each section of eight were allowed to go ... quite a boring period, really, when all we could do was sit around and wait.

Sometimes we had call-out drills, usually late at night, just to test how quickly we could all get our boots on, get ourselves together and be outside standing by our vehicles ready to go. It was on one of these call-out nights at about 20:30 hrs the real thing happened.

It was February 1969 and we had been the Spearhead battalion for about ten days. We were just sitting around the barrack room, watching TV or reading. Lulu had just got married to Maurice Gibb of the Bee Gees at a church at Gerrards Cross, Buckinghamshire, if you can believe that.

We all heard the call-out signal and started to rouse ourselves for what we assumed was just another 'waste of time' call-out practice.

Within about forty-five minutes, we were sorted and everything had been checked and made ready. We didn't normally board the vehicles and just went through a head count before standing down and going back to the TV or bed. It was a miserable misty night, very cold and damp, and everyone was wearing thick parka jackets with the hoods up, huddled around the motors, some chatting and others smoking. The parade square was full of vehicles parked in long lines in Company order – 'Battalion Orbat' (Order of Battle) – and there must have been almost 1,000 men there, trying to keep warm.

This time, after the head count, we were instead told to board the vehicles and await instructions. Some of the older lads were joking around, saying it was just part of the drill and that we'd be finished soon. So we sat around, and sat around and nothing happened for about an hour. Then, suddenly, the word went around: When we set off, keep in line and keep your convoy distances. We had no idea what was going on and the feeling among the older lads was still that this was nothing particularly out of the normal run of things. 'We're just going for a spin around town as part of the loading drill,' they said, but they were wrong.

After what seemed like another age of waiting around, vainly trying to stay warm in the back of our Land Rover – no heaters for passengers in those days – we began to move out at about 23:30hrs. We left camp and drove and drove for hours until we arrived at Brize Norton RAF base. On arrival the drivers were told to stay with their vehicles and the rest of us were ordered to disembark and line up in the troop movements reception centre.

'No problem,' came the knowledgeable voices again. 'We're just going through a documents check and we'll be back in Colchester for breakfast.'

There was indeed a documents check, after which we were given boarding cards and told to climb aboard the aeroplanes looming darkly on the apron. Meanwhile, the drivers started to load their vehicles, crawling up the 'planes' rear ramps. And there we sat for another hour.

'We're not really going anywhere,' said the experts. 'It's just part of the drill.'

At 05:00 hrs, we took off with the first glimmers of pre-dawn gloom behind us and the tone of the wise men changed slightly: 'Where the hell are we going? I've got things to do tomorrow back in camp.' 'OK, the joke's over. Let's go home.'

Within a couple of hours we landed at some wet and windy airport, which most of us assumed was Brize Norton again, until we looked out, and in disbelief saw a sign: 'Welcome to Aldergrove Airport, Belfast.' A panicking friend turned to me, looked me straight in the eyes and said, 'My wife will go crazy when she finds out where I am. She expects me to take the kids to school in an hour.'

Within ten minutes we had taxied to the terminal and pulled up. A couple of people boarded the plane. One of them wore civilian clothing and another was an Army sergeant in uniform, but I couldn't recognise his cap badge and didn't know which unit he was from. They came to deliver a briefing and let us know why we were all there.

They concluded by saying, 'OK, can we have all the drivers out first, and when you others leave the aircraft, make your way to your vehicles and you'll be given instructions for your transfer to the base camp you'll be housed in.' That was it, and we were off.

We were told in the briefing that we had been sent to Northern Ireland as a precautionary measure, because of recent unrest between small groups of the Catholic and Protestant populations. We had all watched TV news over the last few weeks which had reported minor incidents of disorder in Ulster. But it never occurred to us that we would be called out to end up there. Neither had anyone mentioned anything to us about an Irish Republican Army – the 'IRA' as we would come to know it. It was not until later in August, that a little old lady, late one night on a street in Londonderry, surprised me with these words: 'The IRA's commin tae get yous lot.'

We got ourselves together with our vehicles and set off from Aldergrove in convoy at about 13:30 hrs, after we had eaten some lunch and checked over our equipment and weapons. Our destination turned out to be a small transit camp called Ballykinlar, between Downpatrick and Newcastle, County Down. And our route took us right through the centre of Belfast.

Passing through the city in February 1969 was nothing like passing through in 1972. Everything seemed quite normal, just like any other busy city anywhere, and the scene actually reminded me very much of the city centre of Leeds. Traffic bustled about and people were busy going about their daily business. Most people noticed us, but just smiled and waved as our long convoy passed by. Sometimes groups of girls and other individuals came up to us when we halted at the lights and patted us on the arm. It felt almost as if we were part of some liberating force in a war that had just been won. I had little idea then of what the problems in Ulster actually were and couldn't see what all the fuss was about.

Ballykinlar transit camp was just outside the coastal village of Ballykinlar, with a large Army base, Abercorn Barracks, nearby, and a beautiful long sandy beach leading to the town of Newcastle a few miles away to the west. During our stay, to break the monotony of more waiting around, we often popped over the road to visit Sandes Home coffee house. It was a nice little place with good food and friendly staff, but unfortunately it was bombed in October 1974 with a substantial loss of life.

We spent about seven or eight weeks just hanging around at the camp and most of our training went on inside the camp grounds. We were allowed to go out during our free time in the evenings and at week-ends – but not in uniform or alone. Sometimes a few of us would pop into the village for a couple of beers and listen to recent hits belting out of the Juke Box, from bands like The Beach Boys, The Beatles and The Kinks.

It was in the village pub that we heard how the Kray twins had been found guilty for the murder of Jack McVitie. On March 12, sitting there with our beers, we heard that Paul McCartney had married Linda Eastman in Marylebone register office in London. So it appeared that it wasn't just the Northern Ireland troubles that were providing the newspaper headlines. In fact everything was pretty quiet. We heard the odd reports of some small gang fights in the main city streets, together with some minor bombing incidents carried out at power stations and other installations, usually around the countryside. These bombings appeared fairly harmless at the time, being quite small improvised explosive devices, and they did little more than scratch paintwork or chip the walls. But clearly a trade was being learned.

In military intelligence parlance there is a situation known as 'Transition to War,' or TTW. This involves early warning signs such as subversive activity, civil unrest and sabotage. The theory is that if such problems are not addressed, rectified and controlled at an early stage, the situation will inevitably grow worse and worse, until it is totally out of control.

The local police, along with the B-Specials (a voluntary, reserve police force), were being targeted more and more by the Catholic-minority gangs in the cities of Ulster, suffering many injuries. Along with this, we could see that the bombings and incidents of civil unrest were growing more and more frequent during the spring and summer months of 1969.

We were occasionally required to drive out from Ballykinlar and visit some of the vulnerable installations around the country that had been or were likely to be targets, and to carry out guarding duties for a few days to a week at a time. These included power stations, dams, exposed pipe lines and water plants. We felt we acted as a deterrent more than anything, because nobody ever showed up when we were guarding these places. One night, at about 02:30 hrs, we were on 'stag' – guard duty – at a small power station out in the country. I was having a bit of fun, trying to frighten a friend with stories of banshees, telling him they were female ghosts shrouded in white that wandered around in the darkness. But all I managed to do was scare myself to death thinking we were surrounded by ghosts. I recall that because it tells me we could still be scared by ghosts at that point: such innocence, never again.

Behind our camp at Ballykinlar, about 300 metres down a dirt track, stretched our wonderful sandy beach, miles long. A few of us used to go down there for a walk on the strand or for a game of football. Quite often some of the guys brought their muddy Land Rovers down to the beach to give them a wash down, and later they would rinse off the salt water back at camp.

A friend of mine from another section, 'Noddy' Wheelan, decided one sunny day to take his Land Rover down to the beach for a wash. Afterwards, on trying to back away from the water's edge, he found he was bogged down in wet sand. He decided that his best option – the tide was coming in – was to get a friend from camp to help pull him out. Twenty minutes later he returned in another Land Rover with his friend only to find his vehicle was up to its axles in the briny. After a few vain attempts to free it up, the friend made a suggestion.

'I think it's best to go back to camp and bring a larger recovery truck to pull it out,' he told a doubtful Noddy. 'You stay here and I'll be back as soon as I can.'

About 45 minutes later the friend returned with the big truck and was amazed to find that all he could see was Noddy, sitting on the top of his vehicle's roof, about 300 metres out to sea already. Somehow, eventually, they recovered the Land Rover and managed to tow it back, where Noddy had a lot of explaining to do as his vehicle was almost written off. I say 'almost': the Series II was a great truck, although in this case I don't think the electrics survived.

Another friend, 'Sligo' Evans – now as then I am sure nicknames are extremely common in the Army – had been down at the beach washing his Land Rover and was back in camp drying it off. Once he had done that, he lifted the bonnet and began cleaning the engine with rags and a solution of 'av-gas' helicopter fuel, an interesting concept. After he had finished, he dropped the bonnet down, jumped into the driver's seat and pushed the starter button. To his surprise, the whole front of his Land Rover exploded in flames, destroying the bonnet in front of his face. Fortunately, he was unhurt but his vehicle was in a bad way, with all the wiring and hoses totally burned out.

I didn't go out too often in the evenings during my time at Ballykinlar. I used to stay in to read, watch TV or go to another hut which some of the guys had turned into a bar. It was a nice little set-up and used to get quite busy. We had a good music system pumping out songs from behind the long bar while we drank ourselves stupid on most nights. One rainy evening, at about 23:00 hrs, there must have been about 30 of us in there, all having a good time. I was sitting at a big round table with about ten friends from my platoon, laughing and telling jokes. We had been there for about four hours and we were all pretty well-oiled. Some guys were staggering around and others falling off their chairs. Through a drunken haze, I noticed one of the lads called 'Punchy' Newton get up and go to the toilet. He had less than half his beer left in a pint glass, and one the other guys sitting next to him took it, put it under the table and urinated in it.

On Punchy's return, he started to drink his beer and tried to catch up with the conversation going around. After a couple of sips, however, the beer had his whole attention. He peered at the glass and held it up to the light. 'Something is definitely wrong with this beer,' he said. 'I don't like this.'

Everyone else knew what had been done but didn't take much notice and carried on chatting amongst themselves. A few moments later, Punchy lurched out of his chair, stumbled over to the bar and complained to the barman. 'This beer isn't right mate, something's definitely wrong with it.'

The barman who was stone-cold sober, took the beer, held it to the light, then took a large drink himself. 'You're right, mate, it must be off. Here, have another on me.'

Punchy wove his way back to our table, quite happy with a fresh beer in his hand. None of us said a word as he sat down, which wasn't surprising, considering how Punchy got his nick-name. To this day, I'm sure he has no idea what was wrong with his beer that night in Ballykinlar.

At the end of April, we were told by the Company Sergeant Major (CSM) that we were pulling out.

'We'll soon be moving to a new location,' he barked. 'It's a nice place near Londonderry in northern Ulster. There have been more and more riots taking place in the larger cities and we are required to move forward in case we are needed. The police are handling things at this time and we're intending to move as a precautionary measure. There are no plans for us to go onto the streets with the police at this time.'

Our new home turned out to be an RAF base by the village of Bal-lykelly, about 20 miles east of Londonderry, near Limavady. On arrival we were allocated accommodation which was compared most favour-ably to Ballykinlar – and the RAF cookhouse-canteen was absolute luxury, offering a wonderful choice of menu and a coffee lounge to relax in near the entrance. Things were getting better and better, and the facilities at Ballykelly were of a much higher standard over all, as well as being placed in a much nicer setting. Best of all there was a great gym which we used almost every day. Most of our time there was in fact spent fitness training and riot control training, just in case we were called out onto the streets to help the police. The riot control training we received was the old system of the box formation, with a big banner and a loud speaker to give instructions to any rioters we might come across. Needless to say, all that changed within months of the troops being deployed on the streets, and the Army devised much more up-to-date methods over the next year or so.

The RAF lads that we mixed with at the base were very friendly and helpful. We all got along very well together and they always made us welcome at their bar in the evenings. For our part, we were always on our best behaviour while we were there. They never asked us why we were there and didn't have much to say about the growing troubles in the urban areas. All we knew ourselves was what we saw on TV like everyone else. We enjoyed our time there and the only regret was that we stayed a mere five weeks.

Mostly we were training, as I said, but on some days we were invited to go for a flight with some of the air crews. One time I went up in an old Shackleton bomber for a few hours, enjoying the wonderful views over Northern Ireland. It felt great climbing aboard, like something out of an old war movie. We had a great day up in the clouds, soaring about like a big silver bird, following the coastline then swooping inland for a look around. I spent most of my time up there forward, strapped into the co-pilot's seat, at times actually taking the controls while the skipper slipped away to grabbed a bite to eat, after he had explained a few vital points, such as that I had to keep the power on, watch the altitude metre and keep an eye on the horizon dial – keeping it horizontal, preferably. I took the controls before he got up and flew this enormous fighting machine, a little up, then a little down, banking left a little and then a little right. It was fantastic and looked very much like a smaller version of the old Lancaster bomber. Most of the time we were up in the air, my other two mates made themselves comfortable in the gunner's turrets and slept most of the time. On our way back to base, I asked the pilot if I could have a go at landing it.

'Let me land it sir, I know I can do it if you talk me through it.'

'I'm afraid not son, it's more than my job's worth,' he said, smiling across at me. 'But you can stay here with me as we land.'

After we were safely back on the ground I felt glad that the pilot had refused my request and brought us down himself. It was frightening watching the ground rearing towards you at about 150 mph while sat up front in the nose of an elderly aeroplane.

By early June the rioting in Londonderry seemed to be worsening on an almost daily basis and it was becoming apparent that the police and B-Specials were having problems trying to control it. One morning, later in June, we were informed we were to be moving again, this time a few miles nearer to Londonderry. Our new location was a shore naval base just outside the city, HMS Sea Eagle.

Again, after cleaning everything and repacking all our equipment in the middle of the night, we were loaded up in our vehicles and ready to move by 06:30 hrs. Soon after that, at about 07:15 hrs, we set off in our Support Company convoy of about 25 vehicles and made it to HMS Sea Eagle for 08:00 hrs, just in time for breakfast.

HMS Sea Eagle, a 'stone frigate' on the outskirts of Londonderry, is quite a small base but in a pleasant setting, overlooking the river Foyle, with Londonderry a few miles off in the distance to the west. Our accommodation turned out to be very much like that at Ballykelly, very tidy and comfortable, except that here there were not so many people around and the place seemed quite deserted at times.

We spent about six weeks at Sea Eagle, again just keeping fit and covering the ever more frequent commitments to guard installations around the countryside. We also kept up regular practice of the soon-to-be obsolete riot drills.

Most evenings we spent glued to the TV, watching reports of the rioting that had gone on around parts of the city during that day. To us, Belfast appeared to be relatively quiet at that time and most of the problems seemed to be in the area of Londonderry. If we got fed up with watching TV, we sat on our balconies with a few cans of beer. We spent many hours during the night just looking across the river Foyle to the northern part of Londonderry, watching it burn, with the sky glowing eerily red in the distance. It transpired we were actually witnessing the destruction of Bogside in Derry. But we were all thinking the same thing: we could be in the middle of that mess any day now.

The street rioting over those next few weeks of July and early August 1969 gradually became more and more intense, and we saw on TV some terrifying scenes of the police and B-Specials taking horrendous beatings. And every evening the city street fires spread wider until the entire city looked like a glowing inferno. Night after night, clutching our beers, we nervously watched those ferocious Derry skies from the safety of our balconies.

By late July we all knew perfectly well we'd have to go in sooner or later. The TV and press was full of it: vicious rioting, houses burned out street by street, the police and B-Specials suffering terrible injuries. I hauntingly remember on the news seeing one member of the B-Specials totally engulfed in flames, rolling desperately in the street after some youth had thrown a petrol bomb at the Land Rover he was standing next to.

It was surreal to switch from that image to Neil Armstrong steeping down onto the Moon's surface in the Sea of Tranquillity, which happened exactly then, on July 21, 1969. 'We came in peace for all mankind,' read a plaque that Armstrong laid on the lunar surface. I turned to gaze at the flames on the Derry horizon. Yes, peace.

■ ■ ■

After lunch, one day at the beginning of August 1969, we were told to strip down our Land Rovers, remove the canopies, fold all the windows down, get rid of any loose items which were normally tied or clipped on the sides or backs of our vehicles, such as tow chains and shovels. The windscreens on those 1960s Series IIs unclipped and lay down forward on the bonnet, resting on top of the spare tyre. The side windows we took off completely or just wound down, but later decided it would be best to totally get rid of the doors, which allowed much quicker access in and out of the vehicles, if required. For some reason in those early days we didn't think about protection, but then we'd never been in a riot. We were more focused on quick access in and out of the vehicles; our personal protection at that time was an afterthought. Less than a year later, Land Rovers were being heavily armoured and kitted out with Makrolon sheeting.

Our personal equipment included the old Second World War-style British steel helmet we had at that time and also our old pattern full grey combat suits. Our weapon was the 1960s self-loading rifle, the FN SLR 7.62mm. We were told to unclip the sling from the barrel end and clip it onto our wrists in case someone tried to snatch away our weapon on the streets.

Then the inevitable happened. After lunch on August 13, Support Company was called to a briefing in the gym by the Officer Commanding. We all piled in there at around 15:30 hrs wondering what the OC had to say. Some of the guys were standing around the walls but most of us had to sit down so everyone could see. The OC turned up and sat at the front, with a couple of his HQ staff and his dog.

'As you all know,' he intoned, 'the police in the city have been having quite a difficult time over the last few weeks.' He looked around at our attentive faces. 'Therefore, arrangements have been made for us to enter the city tomorrow and we need to be ready to move by 10:00 hrs in support of the local police. We are to support the police and support is what we will be there for. We will be armed with weapons and five rounds of ammunition each, kept in your pouches, but on no account is anyone to load-up and open fire in any circumstances. I mean *any* circumstances.'

That night was a very tense and nervous one for us all, as we pondered what we could expect in the morning. We had all seen the fighting from across the river but tomorrow we'd be right in the middle of it all. That night, at the age of just 18, I began to understand what it was like to sit around and wait before entering a combat zone, and I learned that fear of the unknown is a very powerful one.

After a quiet and sombre dinner, we spent most of that evening packing our kit and cleaning our weapons. Some guys were cracking jokes and throwing things at each other, trying to relieve the tension that was thick in the air. I don't think many of us slept very well that night.

Over breakfast at 07:00 hrs the next day, August 14, the tension levels were a little lower and the atmosphere seemed more relaxed. Most guys were more cheerful and chatty. The older guys on my table seemed confident.

'Don't worry young'un, we'll have some big guns with us. Maybe we can't use them but the Paddies don't know that,' said one veteran of Aden. 'When you're on the street just hold your weapon up, stand your ground, look as if you mean business and you won't have any problems.'

Another older friend leaned over and whispered to me, 'Just stick close to me when we go in, 'Sy, you'll be OK.'

I looked at him. 'Thanks, yes. We'll be OK.'

By 08:30 hrs we were all loaded up, weapons, equipment and radios checked and ready to go. It was a calm sunny day and I could see on the western horizon beyond Derry a few blooming white clouds. At 10:00 hrs I climbed in and settled down in the back of our stripped-down Land Rover with another lad called Dave Brunswick. We held our SLRs vertically in our hands with the butts resting on the floor. Our driver was Punchy Newton and our section commander was Sergeant Pip Rowland.

'OK you lot,' he said as he pored over the maps. 'Turn your gas plugs around the other way and load-up those five rounds into your magazine. But keep it in your pouch until I say different.'

I was surprised. 'But the OC said we shouldn't load-up the rounds in our magazine and we had to keep them separate.'

'Hey, just do what you're told. The OC is only covering his own arse. If some son-of-a-bitch pulls a gun on us out there today, I want you lot ready to take the bastard's head off at a moment's notice, and I don't care who it is – man, woman or child, OK?' I felt stunned for half a moment but we all said, 'OK, no problem,' at the same time.

'Also, when we set off, hold your weapons in the "ready" position' – that was, butt in the shoulder with barrel pointing down – 'and keep your eyes open. If we're going in, let's look the business and maybe those Paddies will leave us alone,' Pip muttered.

Pip Rowland had been in the Army for many years and had spent plenty of time in quite a few conflict zones around the world. Every-one in the company respected him and we always jumped at his command. Back at Colchester some months earlier, at the end of a company dinner party, slightly inebriated, I slipped away to try to find a taxi to take a group of us back to camp. I had no luck, but I did notice an old GPO van parked up with the keys still in the ignition. Not long after, I turned up in it to take everyone home. But Pip persuaded me to take it back where I got it from before the cops nicked me for (a) theft of the van, (b) drunk driving (this strange new law had come in about 18 months back) and (c) driving without a licence and insurance. After a few moments of reflection I saw his point and returned the van just where I'd found it.

The reason for turning our gas plugs round the opposite way was that if any of us did get in a situation where we opened fire, we could only discharge a single round. Then we would have to re-cock the weapon manually. Normally the 7.62 SLR reloads itself after each round. The weapon is gas operated and cocks the working parts back by means of a gas rod and spring in a cylinder on top of the barrel. When a round is fired, some of the exploding gases pass up through a gas vent in the barrel into the gas chamber. This in turn drives the gas rod back like a car piston, forcing back the breech block (working parts) to feed a fresh round into the breech ready to fire. It all happens in a split-second. If the gas plug is turned round the opposite way from the normal position, the gas chamber is closed and all the exploding gases pass directly out of the barrel and the weapon will not re-cock itself.

It was 13:00 hrs and we'd all been sitting there for three hours just waiting, when the CSM appeared. 'OK you lads,' he told us. 'Get away and grab some lunch, we're leaving at 14:00 hrs … and don't be late back. I want you all here and ready to go by 13:45 hrs.'

At 14.00 hrs we started up our vehicles, which burst deafeningly into life with clouds of exhaust fumes all around. As we set off from Sea Eagle there were quite a few of the Navy lads watching and looking concerned, giving us the thumbs up as we drove out through the gates. I remember thinking that we must have looked really fearsome that day with our vehicles all stripped down like some gladiatorial fighting patrol from the Long Range Desert Group – precursor of the SAS – setting off on a top secret mission behind enemy lines.

The drive into the city centre only took about half an hour and then we turned onto and across the Foyle Bridge towards the northern side of the river. The entire population on the streets was looking at us, neither smiling nor waving, just staring, perhaps a little surprised to see us driving along in convoy looking aggressive, with everyone carrying weapons at 'The Ready'. I was feeling some apprehension, as I'm sure my friends also were, especially going over that Foyle Bridge. While we were on the south side of the river I didn't feel too bad, but after crossing the water we seemed to be totally alone, totally exposed, heading into the 'Badlands', probing deep into unknown enemy territory. It was really scary for everyone, not just me.

As it happened, this day, August 14th turned out to be quite a significant one, as it was the first time in perhaps hundreds of years that British forces had been deployed on the streets of Britain on internal security operations. I didn't know it at the time but I was taking part in an historical event that people would be talking about for many years to come.

After we reached the far side of the bridge we slowly weaved our way through the streets, passing quite a few burned-out houses and more people simply standing and staring. We made our way along the Embankment to Foyle Street and then onto Bishop Street, en route to the 'area of responsibility' that had been allocated to us earlier. There were still plenty of people around outside, but none of them appeared threatening to us as we made our way up to Bishops Gate, an ancient gateway in the old city wall which overlooks Bogside.

While we parked and started to unload our equipment in a backstreet near the gate, a friend came over and said, 'One of the guys in the other Land Rover lost his gas plug when he was turning it round as we passed over the bridge. The gas rod, spring and plug flew out of his hand and the plug went bouncing across the road.'

'He'll have to just leave the gas rod and spring out and use the SLR as it is,' I said. 'It'll be OK. He'll just lose a fraction of its power if he fires it.'

Soon after, we settled in and the CSM walked over.

'Make yourselves comfortable, lads, this is your new home for the next five weeks.'

I looked at Pip Rowland and said, 'Where do we sleep?'

'You sleep over there by the corner of that wall. I hope you don't snore because I'll be sleeping next to you.'

The area around Bishops Gate was in an elevated position of the city with a low 'battlement' type of wall. In places you can look over the battlements into the streets some 20 feet below. This walkway section of the wall was now to be our home for the fore-seeable. We had our sleeping-bags and we erected our waterproof capes to use as lean-to bivouacs to give us some cover at night. Luckily it was August and the weather wasn't too bad during our stay. It was months later that old warehouses and mills were taken over, to be used as troops' living accommodation for the many years to follow.

Later that afternoon, the CSM got the platoon together and gave us a briefing:

'Until further notice you'll all be based here and what I need you to do is this: During day and night hours, cover the Bishops Gate arch-way entrance' – he pointed at his map – 'with a guard of four men. Also, I want a two-man OP [observation post] set up in the old library building opposite with an A41 radio, checking in every half hour. And at night, I want you to send out five-man listening patrols to this area, through the other side of the gateway.'

He slowly looked around at each of us. 'If you come across any suspicious characters, you're allowed to search them and confiscate anything you feel can be used as a weapon. You can also send any suspicious people back to their own side if they are trying to cross through the gateway.'

During the next week or so we did see some gangs of youths chasing individuals through the streets but none of them came near us except once, after about 10 days. Four of us saw a group of around 200 youths running up the street directly towards us.

As they drew closer our patrol commander, Corporal Geoff Napinski, shouted 'Fix bayonets!' and without hesitation the four of us did exactly that. We just stood there side by side, facing the approach of the angry mob. But suddenly they turned left into a side street, chasing a lone man running in front of the group, and within moments they were gone. We stood there for a while, bayonets fitted, looking at each other in amazement. Again, this must have been another first: British troops, fixing bayonets on British soil in an aggressive stance.

Many things were going through my mind during that incident. Later, I asked myself, 'Would I have used my bayonet if we were attacked?' The answer was yes, for sure I would have and without any hesitation. I was scared to my wits end standing there, watching that crowd getting closer and no way would I have run for it, or just stood there to be mowed down by some crazed mob. My job was to protect myself and my three friends, together with the rest of my platoon, and I know they would have protected me just the same.

On another occasion, again on guard duty, with three others at the Bishops Gate entrance, a couple of youths about my age approached us and demanded to go through the Gate. Punchy Newton was doing the talking and trying to reason with them.

'Sorry lads, you'll have to go back, we can't let you through.' I was covering his back, just a metre or so behind and to his right.

The Irish lads became agitated; they were arguing and demanding to go over to the Catholic side. After more discussion I could clearly see Punchy wasn't impressed. I think the youths also noticed this when Punchy moved closer to the leader of the two and tilted his head down a little, preparing to stick the 'nut' on the bridge of the kid's nose. Both of them quickly backed off, fully aware that being nutted by somebody wearing a steel helmet isn't healthy. They were lucky and wise to back off. I'd once seen Punchy drop three guys in Colchester with his head, the last two before the first one had even hit the floor. Punchy was a great guy, but he wasn't the type to mess or argue with, not even when he was sober.

We carried out searches on suspicious youths on quite a few occasions, and confiscated knives and steel bars. Many times we had to send back lads, usually Protestant, who were trying to pass through Bishops Gate over to the Catholic areas of Bogside, obviously looking for trouble.

I wasn't very keen on the occasional night patrols. It always seemed very dark, leery and a little spooky over the 'other' side. We typically set off at about 22:30 hrs, making our way through the dismal Catholic streets towards Bogside. There were usually quite a few people hanging around in the streets, just watching us. Many people, mainly the older folk, seemed quite friendly and offered us tea and cakes as we passed them by. But others just stood, watching us like we were zombies or some kind of freaks. Every half an hour or so we stopped, took up fire positions in all-round defence and spent 15 to 20 minutes just hanging around in the shadows silently watching and listening. It all seemed a bit of a show, taking up fire positions: we had bullets but couldn't use them if we were attacked, or we weren't supposed to. But the locals didn't know that, and looking the business probably helped keep us safe.

I got quite a bit of a scare on one of these patrols. We had been out for about four hours around the Bogside area, walking and occasionally stopping to listen. On our way back, Geoff Napinski suggested we stop in the old derelict prison for a while, which was a few hundred metres along the road from Bishops Gate. We set ourselves up in all-round-defence to just observe and listen for a couple of hours. We arrived there at around 03:00 hrs and at that dead hour it was really spooky and I did not like it one little bit.

As we moved in, passing by him kneeling, Geoff quietly indicated to us where he wanted us to position ourselves. He came around ten minutes later, to check our positions and brief us all on our arcs of fire and the escape routes he wanted us to use if we had to make a quick exit. He was just going through the standard operating procedures (SOPs) and we all had five rounds (bullets). But as the OC had said: in no event could we use them.

'If we are attacked from this side, jump over that low wall behind you and make your way around to the front to our pre-arranged RV position,' Geoff told me. 'Keep your eyes and ears open and we'll set off back at first light, about 05:30 hrs – and don't fall asleep.'

He needn't have worried. For the next couple of hours I sat there silently, squatting up against that wall, eyes wide open staring into the ghostly darkness, ears straining to listen for any out-of-the-ordinary sounds. I spent the entire night imagining all kinds of things happening around me. There was no way I was going to fall asleep. I was far too scared to do that. To help pass the time and relieve the tension, I silently sang to myself a couple of my old favourite Roy Orbison songs, 'Blue Bayou' and 'Penny Arcade'.

The night passed slowly and by the time we were ready to leave, with the dawn breaking, I took a look over the low wall, my 'avenue of escape'. To my horror, on the other side was a 30-foot drop to the street below. If I had jumped over there in the dark, it would have surely been the end for me.

It became clear to me during my stay in Londonderry during the summer of 1969 that much of the rioting and aggression in the early days of The Troubles was instigated by groups of Protestant youths directing their anger at the Catholic minority. It was later that it turned the other way. One factor which helped to fuel this reversal was that the police and B-Specials were seen to be on the side of the Protestants during the early rioting and fighting. Later, when the Army took control of the streets, the situation calmed for a short period. Both sides were watching us closely, monitoring our intentions and actions. The Catholic minority was genuinely happy when the Army took over control in Londonderry that August. They felt we were there to protect them against the Protestants, as many of them told me. In fact, we were there to protect everyone against aggression, wherever it came from. Religion didn't come into it as far as we were concerned.

It was only later that the tables turned, when the Army was instructed to and was commonly seen to be standing on the Protestant side of the fences and barricades. Even though I was only 18 at the time, I had been in the Army for three years and I had a reasonable idea of what I was doing. I smelled the changes in the air and the tide turning before we finished our first tour in Ulster, by the end of September 1969. I had never heard of the IRA before, until the night that little old lady delivered her witch-like prophecy:

'The IRA's commin tae get yous lot.'

By the early part of October we were all back in Colchester after handing over our part of Londonderry to another unit. It was fine to be back on familiar home ground, but I had found my Northern Ireland experience to be very interesting and it was a good learning curve. But within days of being back to our normal duties – together with evenings holding up the bar in The Grapes – the OC had news for us.

'For our next posting, we will all be spending two years in north Germany as part of BAOR [British Army of the Rhine], with opportunities of training visits to Africa and Canada while we are there. But first we have to fulfil a commitment of a short tour of Northern Ireland again, in January. Sorry but I couldn't get us out of it.' He paused and smiled vaguely. 'We obviously did a good job in Derry over the summer.'

We were due over in Belfast in the New Year and after a few weeks' leave most of December was filled with Northern Ireland training, which included the new riot-control techniques we had to learn, together with the issue of some new equipment. This included new helmets, new-style DPM (Disrupted Pattern Material) combat suits and improved respirators. We didn't have the Kevlar armoured flak jackets at that time as they were issued a year or so later. The trouble in January 1970 wasn't as bad as it got by January the following year, but the rioting and bombing incidents had worsened since we left in September.

By the first week of January 1970 we were on our way to Ulster for our second tour within six months. This was due to us being based in the UK: there weren't many other units to choose from. We were informed that we would be taking the ferry with our vehicles this time, from Liverpool direct to Belfast. After disembarkation, we would move to a location not far from the terminal on Donegal Quay, on the north-west side of the river.

After we arrived and settled in to our accommodation, which was quite basic, we were heavily occupied with many briefing sessions for the first day or so, before taking to the streets on familiarity patrols with members of the outgoing unit.

We had a pretty uneventful three months at our new location, an old warehouse near the Grove Playing Fields to the east of the M2, along from Donegal Quay. We spent most of our time on regular patrols around the local streets and carrying out VCPs (Vehicle Control/Check Points) on the country roads north of the city. This wasn't a particularly hard area compared to other parts of Belfast. There were some minor incidents, but nothing that caused any gossip or anything worth writing home about. One good thing that happened for me was that I was put on a driving cadre (driving course) which took two weeks of driver training a couple of hours a day around the local streets, and at the end of it I took and fortunately passed my test. I don't think there are many people that can say they took their driving test with a loaded submachine gun lying across their knees.

At the end of March we had handed over to another unit and then were all back on the ferry to Liverpool, looking forward to another couple of weeks' leave before preparing for our posting to Germany.

When the time came we flew to Germany with only our personal equipment because we simply took over all the vehicles and heavy weapons from the outgoing unit there.

I enjoyed Germany. Our duties mainly involved patrolling along the East-West German border area, together with regular battalion exercises, some of which lasted between ten days and two weeks. We'd all move off in our tracked armoured APC-432s, and spend the next fortnight driving around north Germany and living out of the back of these vehicles. Usually the summers were OK, but in winter it was extremely hard going. We broke down in our APC one time, miles from anywhere, and had to sit there on the edge of a remote forest waiting for recovery. All we could do was play cards and sunbathe for three days while we waited. Our food quickly ran short, so we lived for two days off corn-on-the-cobs which we stole from the nearby fields – quite tasty when grilled over an open fire. Our biggest problem was that we had to survive on one tea bag for the three days, six of us living off a five-second 'dip' twice a day.

On the border guard-and-patrol duties, we often waved to the Soviet-Bloc troops as we patrolled past their watchtowers, which were dotted along the frontier, and the communists always smiled and vigorously waved back to us. To most people's surprise, I generally enjoyed these patrols. It was interesting rolling along the frontier and being able to see our so-called enemy. Sometimes we were so close we could see the whites of their eyes.

The best part of my time there, however, was leaving for our scheduled training visits to Canada and Africa. We spent about six weeks at Suffield training base, Canada, on advance-to-contact 'live-firing' exercises. We flew from Germany to Edmonton airbase via St John, Newfoundland, where we stopped off for a few hours' break.

Suffield training camp was a few miles from the small cowboy town of Medicine Hat in Alberta. It was a fairly comfortable place on the edge of an enormous training area. On our arrival, we took over all the vehicles and weapons, cleaning and checking them, before setting off on our first exercise. We'd return to base camp every five or six days to clean up and re-check all our equipment.

We moved through the countryside as a tactical company of 100 troops in vehicles, taking on a variety of targets along the way. At night, we harboured in an LUP (laying up position) and planned our next day's direction of advance, to carry on the war games. This lasted on-and-off for about five weeks. Then later, at the end of the exercise, after cleaning and packing away our equipment and weapons for the last time, we had another three weeks' leave before flying back to Germany.

Taking advantage of this, a few of us hired a big, gleaming Ford and set off touring around places like Calgary, Banff in the Rockies and a lovely place called Radium Hot Springs. The Banff Springs Hotel there was eccentric and wonderful hotel, made up in a Scottish theme: even the doormen were Scots dressed in kilts. Another hostelry we stopped at for a while on our way to Radium was a hotel on a cliff, overlooking a swimming complex with thermal pools everywhere. We had a great day there, swimming, eating and drinking. Most nights we crashed out in the car, two in the front, two in the back and one in the boot. In the morning we all washed in the river before setting off again. Being in the Army we were used to roughing it and didn't think twice about the discomfort.

On our return to Germany, everyone was talking about the death of the Rock Legend Jimi Hendrix, who had apparently collapsed at a party in London on September 18. A number of sleeping pills were found at the house in Notting Hill but the police felt there was no reason to suggest any foul play had taken place. Whatever the case, it was another of many signs that the 1960s were truly over. Altamont had been less than a year earlier, and Janis Joplin would be dead in a few weeks' time. The atmosphere seemed to be somehow changing to something darker.

The following year, on a visit to Kenya, with me promoted to lance corporal, we were involved in field training exercises for about five weeks, initially located near the village of Nanuki. But most of the time we were up in the hills, living in make-shift base camps in an area called Don Doll, practicing field-craft and patrolling in the bush and forests.

The African trip was great, especially living out in the bush. Soon after our arrival at Don Doll, we had a task to repair and re-build an old road/track in the hills above our camp. A kind of 'hearts and minds' initiative for the local villagers. But we didn't find it easy while the baboons on the cliff-tops above entertained themselves for most of the time by throwing rocks down on us.

After racing around finding and putting on our steel helmets, we managed to finish the road in a couple of days, which pleased the locals. The Baboons must have thought it was great fun, screeching and jumping around, until we started throwing stones back at them. The villagers probably thought we were all crazy, involved in stone-age skirmishing with a pack of baboons.

A day or so later, one of the cooks was told to set alight the cesspit where all the waste food was put. This needed to be done a few times a week, to stop animals creeping around the camp area at night. Then later, when it was burnt out, the pit would be covered with earth.

It was his first time, and the young cook-house lad apparently overdid it with the petrol, emptying about two gallons over the slops. A moment later, he threw a lit match into the pit while he stood by the edge. After the enormous explosion, which bowled him over, the young lad emerged from the bellowing black smoke on his hands and knees, covered from head to foot in all sorts of smelly crap, and his hair had vanished. He was OK but far too embarrassed to discuss the incident with anyone.

The combat engineer platoon designed our relaxation and bar area, cutting trees down by wrapping det-cord around the trunks and blowing them. They cleared away any unwanted tree stumps using explosives – great fun. Then the engineers redesigned all the convenient stumps with a chain saw to make chairs and bar stools for us to sit on while we got drunk most nights on 'Tusker' beer.

Also, the combat engineer lads must have built the deepest toilet in Africa. By using a 'Camaflay' set, they drilled a neat 12 inch diameter hole approximately one hundred feet deep. Needless to say, we kept that young cook-house lad away from this pit with his can of petrol.

At the end of this month-long training period living in the bush, the CSM announced that all junior ranks below Corporal had to be on parade in five minutes. He got us all strung out in one long line and told us to sit down and take off our left boot.

'Today gentlemen,' he began, 'we're having a mucky foot competition, and the one with the muckiest foot will be the winner.' To our mutual surprise, most of our feet were quite clean.

Your two feet are an important asset in the Infantry and we are always reminded to take care of them. However, when the CSM reached an older member, an ex-national service chap in our company who was known as a bit of a scruff, he went nuts. The guy's feet were black with thick jungle dirt and on closer inspection we all noticed that his boots were full of holes, worn out with age and split along the sides. His boots were effectively full of mud and his feet stank like swamp water and had been like that for weeks. The CSM announced him as the winner and his prize was to buy us all (50 of us) a beer in the bar that night.

We did manage a few days off at the end of our stay and some of us went off in a couple of our land rovers, visiting Lake Navasha, and later the game reserve at Samburu National Park – all great fun and just the kind of life I had been hoping for.

On the day of our return to Germany we had a bit of fun at the airport in Nairobi. One of the guys in our platoon decided to take back loads of extra cigarettes. You could buy cigarettes quite cheaply in Germany but they were half the price in Kenya.

This guy had hidden away in his kit and equipment very many extra cigarettes. He even decided to pull the springs out of his weapon magazines, filling them with about 30 cigarettes in each magazine, of which we all carried about eight, and then sealing them up. He also went as far as slotting cigarettes down the barrel of his rifle, which took about 15 end to end.

Another nutty chap caught a little monkey about the size of a small cat wandering around our camp one day. He kept it as a pet for a while, feeding it, playing with it and taking it out on patrols with him. But when it came time to leave he decided to hide it in his kit bag, to smuggle it back to Germany so he could give it to his wife as a birthday present.

Needless to say, they both got caught passing through the customs at Nairobi and had the cigarettes and monkey confiscated with just a slap on the wrist from the authorities. Back in Germany they were both charged for attempted smuggling, but received only a small fine for their stupidity. The officer-magistrate was probably struggling not to laugh.

Back in Germany, nearing the end of the tour in November 1971, with us noticing miserably how much colder the northern European weather was than the African, word started going around that we were up for another tour of Northern Ireland, probably starting in March or April 1972. This was to be immediately followed in August by six months in Dover before perhaps a two-year posting to Hong Kong. My thoughts at that time were simple: 'Great!' Europe, Africa, Asia – I was becoming a real globe-trotter already. Ireland would be a doddle and only be for four months. What more could a young lad of 20 want?

By Christmas, Belfast was confirmed for early March together with a few months in Dover later, but nothing so far was fixed for Hong Kong.

Most of January and February 1972 was again spent on Northern Ireland riot-control training, together with familiarisation with some of the IEDs (improvised explosive devices) we might expect to come across. While Don McLean's epic new song, 'American Pie' was racing up the charts, we were busy being issued with some new-style helmets and respirators together with our new, armoured, flak jackets.

We hadn't seen these jackets before and found them bulky and heavy, being made of a kind of woven fibreglass type of material. But we were told to carry them around most of the time, especially while training, to help us get used to the extra weight. The kind of training we had to undergo for Northern Ireland was based on riot-control techniques, prisoner handling and patrolling formations and techniques, together with familiarisation of the area we'd be responsible for during our forthcoming tour.

By early to the middle of March, we were all packed and ready. Before we departed, we were told to make out a will and pack away all the equipment we planned to leave behind, just in case we didn't come back, so no-one else had to pack it for us. This time we flew from Germany direct to Aldergrove International Airport, just outside Belfast.

On our arrival the first thing we noticed, as we climbed off the plane, was that the security level was much higher than the last time. The whole place was heaving with armed police and troops all over the airport. And the car park outside was full of armoured vehicles known as 'Pigs' because that's what they looked like from the front. Also, parked alongside, were some other larger vehicles which we learned were Saracen AFVs (Armoured Fighting Vehicles). It was as if we had arrived in a war zone.

The CSM told us, 'OK lads, these vehicles are ours. Get yourselves into your sections, check your equipment – then the vehicles for UIEDs [under-vehicle improvised explosive devices], and get on board. We'll be setting off for our base location in 15 minutes.'

We left the airport spread out in platoon convoys and as we passed through it, Belfast looked totally different to how it appeared in 1969. The whole central area of the city was fenced off with high metal-railing fences. All the entrances were heavily guarded by armed troops, who were checking cars and pedestrians wishing to enter the restricted areas. We also all noticed the heavy presence of police and troops patrolling the streets, some on foot and others in armoured vehicles, which included 'Pigs' and armoured Land Rovers. Something clearly was not going too well here.

Our location turned out to be a ship on the quayside near Sydenham on the outskirts of Belfast, and was to be our home for the next four months. We offloaded the vehicles and spent the next day or so settling in and unpacking our gear. This was followed with many briefings on our 'area of responsibility' and the characters we would be looking out for.

Within a couple of days we were out and about, regularly patrolling the streets and checking the areas where we'd be setting up regular VCPs. We did have some other guard duties to cover but they were only at a few locations near to our base and didn't involve me.

2

The Call to Special Duties

The year was 1972 and the Army found itself committed to a long, hard military slog. Terrorist activity was growing rapidly throughout the Province and the politicians and military commanders were beginning to face some of the greatest challenges of their careers. We had just experienced 'Bloody Sunday' in Londonderry, involving the Parachute Regiment, from which horrendous political and legal consequences would follow for decades. Escalating hatred had taken a grip of the Protestant and Catholic communities and they were isolating themselves behind barricades. Intimidation and tension were rife, while armed terrorists were moving freely around the city streets indiscriminately killing and maiming. The fight for control was between the IRA and the British government. The British Army was under no illusion that it couldn't afford to lose the struggle.

Apart from the daily coverage of the troubles in Northern Ireland, the news on the mainland was full of the miners' strike. With the power cuts that ensued, these were quite literally dark days (or nights). The strike began that January and seemed in harmony with the other grim economic news of unemployment levels topping a million, the highest since the 1930s. British Steel made closures at Newport and Gwent, shedding 1300 jobs, while the Port of London announced the loss of 2000 dockworkers, and there was the loss of 1600 jobs at GEC. The country was in a mess and Northern Ireland was the kind of thorn in its side that Britain could have done without. That's not to forget the petrol shortage we were suffering, to such an extent that UK speed limits had been reduced in an attempt to save energy. Gangs were actually stealing – siphoning – gasoline from the tanks of parked cars.

I had only recently arrived in Ulster from a two-year tour abroad and my parent unit had just taken over from another in Belfast. It was March but there was still an early morning winter chill in the air and I had felt it, having been out on the streets on uniformed patrols quite a few times already. These covered the general areas around Sydenham, and in towards the city centre.

Like my other Ulster visits, first in Londonderry when it all started in 1969 and then later in Belfast in 1970, this one was just another usual run-of-the-mill regular four-month tour, securing one of the areas of Belfast. Little did I know at the time, but this one was going to turn out to be far different than I had expected. It was also going to change my life and my personality and was to last, all told, for a hell of a lot longer than two years.

Within only a few weeks of being in Northern Ireland I was, unusually, called in from one the patrols, which is known as a 'brick' due to the usual four-man formation. Together with a handful of other guys from my Battalion, I was required to turn up for interview at our company HQ. None of us knew why: we were simply notified that we had to be there. Like everyone else, I automatically worried that I had done something wrong, or that the OC wanted some lads for a dirty job. I reassured myself that everything must be OK, because my slate was quite clean and I was never normally in any trouble. I generally kept in the background and stayed out of the usual sort of squaddie nonsense, but nonetheless I was wondering what might be up. I dropped off my cleaned and checked weapon at the armoury, dumped my helmet and webbing on my bed and made my way with a couple of others to Company HQ. We adjusted our berets as we walked there, slightly nervously.

On arrival, lined up outside the CSM's office, we all looked at each other, still wondering what on earth was going on. I knew two of the guys in the line, who were in my company, but the three others were from another section. We had to stand and wait there for about half an hour before the CSM turned up, and I spent most of that time listening to someone's radio in the accommodation area across the way belting out recent hits like John Lennon's 'Imagine' and 'Power to the People', which had been floating around the charts for the last few months. Just before the CSM arrived The Doors were singing a great song, 'Riders on the Storm', which I felt suited the occasion, standing there in apprehension and having no idea what was going on.

Some passing friends were making the usual sarcastic comments. 'You're in the shit now,' said one, with an evil grin. 'What have you lot been up to, then?' asked another chap, and I honestly would have loved to be able to tell him.

One by one, we were 'wheeled in', as they say.

Straight away the CSM surprised me. 'Close the door and sit down,' he said mildly. You what? 'Nobody sits in the Company Sergeant Major's office except myself and Prince Phillip,' he often used to take great joy in announcing; so to say his comment took me by surprise would be the understatement of the century. But more was to come. He looked me up and down in CSM fashion: 'You, corporal, have been singled out from the rest of the battalion. An opportunity has arisen to join a specialist unit which has recently been formed. They're looking for suitable recruits and we thought of you.' I must have looked puzzled. 'Don't ask me why. I don't know very much about it, but it's a plain clothes unit operating in Ulster and if you are selected, the tour will be for around two or three years.' It was quite a short interview, hardly an interview at all, really. At the end of his little speech he just asked, 'Are you interested?'

I was intrigued and my head was buzzing with the phrase, 'plain clothes'. That would mean no more freezing-cold patrols, I thought. I was intrigued but I acted a little cagey. 'Yes, I'm interested, but I would like to know a little more about it, sir,' I told him. That there might be a range of dangers involved in being out of uniform didn't register with me at all at this point; and the reasons I might be considered suitable never entered my head. I was just instantly excited by the prospect of getting involved in something different to the usual routine.

'OK,' said the CSM, 'the OC will see you tomorrow and fill you in with a few more details.' On that note, he jutted his chin in the direction of the door. 'Send in the next man, will you,' which I did.

Outside, with Land Rovers across the way roaring around, and over the sounds of Rod Stewart grinding out 'Maggie May', the others asked me, 'What's it all about, Sy?'

I wasn't so sure myself, but already I knew it was good enough that I didn't want to give them any advantage over me, so I said, 'Oh, you'll find out soon enough,' and left them to think on their feet when they went in. All's fair in love and war.

The next day we all turned up, slightly less nervously, for interview with the OC-CC (Officer Commanding-Company Commander) and again were sent in one by one. Again I was politely asked to remove my beret and sit, while the OC prepared to give out a few more details. Self-consciously, I pulled up a chair and shuffled into position in front of him. I felt a little apprehensive as he spent a few moments looking over some papers; and with the tiniest squint and inclination of my head I saw that they were my Army records and reports. I felt myself craning forward, so I made an effort to sit back and stop fidgeting and concentrated on looking relaxed – which I was not – while he flipped over the pages.

'If you are selected for this new unit, you will be operating undercover in Belfast,' he paused thoughtfully. 'Mainly.'

'The unit will be only 35 to 40 strong and you'll be involved in photography and surveillance operations.' I must have looked a bit baffled. Photography was not one of my specialisms. I was a weapons instructor.

'It's a special unit,' he explained, 'looking for … special people, volunteers to be put forward for selection.' There was another pause. 'And I have earmarked you to go forward for the job.'

'Thank you, Sir.' It all sounded great but still very sketchy and vague to me.

All the time I had a strange feeling from both the CSM and the OC that they were softening us up for something, and memories of my brother saying 'cannon fodder' drifted through my mind. I didn't care too much about that, though, because the more I thought about it, the more it sounded like a great shot at something new and exciting: as long as I kept my head clear, my eyes open and everything in perspective, I should be OK. It was, in the end, a voluntary job and I could get dumped or dump it myself if I didn't want to go on with the selection process.

'This unit,' he fixed me with his eye, 'has been formed to literally take the fight to the IRA, right in his own back yard.'

Little did I know how true those words would turn out to be and I often thought of them during the following two or three years.

The OC elaborated: 'The unit requires people with certain attributes. A spotless military record. At least three years' Army infantry service. Two to three tours of Ulster and excellent military skills background.' Military skills meant shooting, weapon handling, field-craft, first aid, signals and communications – I was an instructor for most of them, and fitted all the other requirements, which had certainly narrowed down the field a good bit.

The list of qualifications seemed endless and I just sat there silently taking it all in. The most bewildering part was when the OC began to mention personal qualities, ('... you must be quiet, methodical, and have the ability to work alone and under pressure ...'). I was told that the successful volunteer would need to be self-motivated, have no visible marks or tattoos, be of average height and weight and have brown hair. Considering all that, I thought it would be a miracle if they found even 30 of us. It occurred to me that they should maybe give Clark Kent a call.

The more he talked on, the more complex it seemed and the less I understood this 'thing-organisation-unit' or whatever it was. But I stayed keen and wanted to know more. I felt it was something important, highly secret, and I wanted to be a part of it.

The OC ended his interview saying that he felt I was one of the few people that fitted the required profile. 'What are your feelings about it?'

'I would like to know a few more details of what the unit is actually involved in, Sir,' I replied simply. 'But I am very interested.'

The OC appeared pleased. 'I'll be in touch, but in the meantime you must not discuss this interview with anyone that's uninvolved, understood?'

Later, the six of us all got together in the cook-house over a brew of tea and a large portion of steak, chips and peas, to air our thoughts about this 'new unit'. Forty years on I still remember finishing off the meal with treacle pudding and custard. (I've always had a sweet tooth and love my sticky puddings. My older brother still gives me a big tin of Quality Street every Christmas – strange what the memory retains.)

Some friends came around our table, trying to join us and asking questions. 'What's going on, then? What are you up to?' As ordered, we said nothing – but then we didn't know very much about it ourselves. There were mixed feelings within our group of selectees; some were very keen, some not sure and some, like me, who were keen but wanted to know more about exactly what we were being drawn into.

My father had been in the Army, in fact a despatch rider in North Africa during World War Two, and he ended up in Austria by the end of the war. He was a small guy, very quiet, but adored his cars and bikes, and I always had a lot of time for him. I often helped him tinker with his motor whenever I was home on leave. He always used to say, when I first joined up, that I should *never volunteer for anything*: it was life-preserving, combat-troop wisdom from an all-engulfing conflict in which the price of a life fell almost to zero. I must admit, I thought about what Dad had said and was a little sceptical to start with, but later I began to feel more and more that my selection was a great opportunity to do something special and more interesting than just basic soldiering. There was a fork in the road and I took it.

I had spent just over two years as a junior leader in an Infantry Junior Leader Battalion and then another three years plus with my regular battalion. Altogether, I had served more than five years, mostly being attached to a Support Weapons Company (which is an infantry heavy weapons company). With youth comes ambition, and I think I was probably ready for a change.

I spent more than a week, thinking intensely about my possible future before I heard anything more.

Abruptly, the CSM called us all in to his office again. 'You all have to go to the adjutant's office at Battalion Head Quarters tomorrow for more interviews,' he announced. 'So,' I thought, 'Things are happening and starting to move forward.' I began to grow excited. The next day we were again lined up, expecting to be interviewed by the adjutant or someone of a similar rank. The adjutant was a nice chap, always friendly and very helpful. He duly emerged from his office, checked we were all present, then walked across the hall to another office.

On this occasion we were all split up and put in different rooms. Mine was bare except for a table and a single empty chair for me. I sat before two strangers who didn't seem like Army types. They were both slim, unimposing men in dark suits and collar-length hair. They began without ceremony by asking lots of questions, really digging deep into my background, often in quite an aggressive and forceful way. Although physically unthreatening to me, I distinctly felt their authority, and it was a bit intimidating.

The adjutant was there with me for a while, standing at the back of the room, out of the way and acting as an observer. This interview lasted for almost two hours of question after question; questions about my father, my mother, my brother and my personal background; demands for my views on a variety of subjects, such as politics; what interested me, what didn't; what I liked, what I didn't. On and on it went, relentlessly. They even asked me which newspapers and books I read. Why this? Why not that? I didn't know it at the time but we were all interviewed simultaneously in different offices with different people and they'd gone through all six of us in a couple of hours. It appeared they wanted to get the interviews over with as soon as possible, for some reason or other.

At this stage, very little was given away of what we would be doing in this new unit. They made it very clear that they were the guys who were asking the questions.

All they really said was, 'Its name is the MRF.' That is, Military Reaction Force, to those who know anything about it. But people outside the loop, (most of the Army, press and police) have given it different names over the years since then: Military Reconnaissance Force or Mobile Reconnaissance Force; but it doesn't really matter. Creating confusion and misinformation suited them just fine.

All this didn't really mean much to me. The men who interviewed us simply reiterated much of what we had already been told by our OC a week or so earlier. They even refused to show me any ID at the beginning of the interview, which I asked to see before I would speak to them.

When I asked them to prove who they were I noticed out of the corner of my eye that the adjutant was smiling. I think he was amused by my request and gave me an approving nod. 'It's OK to speak to these people, Corporal Cursey, they're on our side,' he told me. If it was OK with him then it was OK with me.

The overall selection process continued to take the form of many interviews – or interrogations – over a further couple of weeks. These started at my parent unit level and then progressed to daily interviews and aptitude tests with people I later realised were selection staff from Military Intelligence. These later interviews appeared to be an in-depth psychological assessment and profiling. The kind of things I had to do included puzzle solving, similar to the sort of thing you see on ITV's *The Krypton Factor*, but not quite so sophisticated. Initially the puzzles were quite simple but became more difficult as we went on, with time limits added. Gradually the time limits grew tighter and tighter until it was impossible to complete the tasks.

In other tests picture books were presented to me that contained strange shapes and shadowed objects. I had to tell them what I could see, a bit like the Rorschach test, while the interrogators flipped the pages over every couple of seconds: not so simple, when you are being pushed to answer as quickly as possible. I was also made to sit for extended periods on a one-legged stool with my feet together – a task that would have been much easier if I was allowed to plant them apart to maintain balance. Meanwhile my friends in the dark suits continually fired words at me, and I had to reply quickly with the first word association that came into my head. I was being constantly stressed both physically and mentally, which was of course the whole point. At other times, I was made to sit for what seemed like hours on that stool, bag on head and hands tied, alone in the room while the Int. guys went off to lunch. On other occasions I would also just have to sit still and quiet for sometimes a couple of hours, without moving, speaking or getting up. I was sure we were being watched so I sat there thinking, focusing on pleasant things like holidays I'd recently had or roast chicken meals with roast potatoes and veg, finishing off with a rum-and-raisin sponge pudding ... wonderful! It made the time fly by.

Other methods used in the initial selection/training involved observation exercises, such as going into a windowless or blacked-out room for a few minutes and then afterwards having to write down as many items as I could remember seeing in there. After practicing this many times, I then had to do the same except in pitch darkness, feeling around on hands and knees for objects and later describing exactly what they were.

I was made to write down the descriptions of my fellow colleagues and friends, estimating their height, weight and ages. To pass I needed to be accurate to within two inches for height, five pounds for weight and five years for age. Age wasn't really a problem in the beginning as we all knew how old most of our friends were. But later, I had to go through all this again, describing relative strangers wondering around our base camp. There are in fact some methods and tricks which can help, such as comparing someone's height relative to the top of an average car, or comparing someone's figure with a standard-sized doorway or window frame.

These kinds of test carried on for another two weeks, and for most days and a couple of nights a week, for eight to ten hours every day. At the end of each session, as we all finished for the day, we were reminded not to talk to anyone not involved.

We were all effectively in quarantine during this period and weren't allowed out on the streets of Belfast in uniformed patrols. The Intelligence guys told us that we couldn't even mix too much with our friends or make any reference to what was going on if we contacted our families back home. That didn't bother me too much as I rarely called home anyway. We were told that we had to keep a low profile, keep in uniform, but generally stay out of sight for security reasons. Therefore we stuck together, watching TV or playing cards and generally keeping fit, for most of the little free time we had.

Physical fitness training wasn't, or didn't appear to be, much of a priority during this initial selection phase. We were anyway all extremely fit, with most of us having strong sporting backgrounds at regimental and Army level. However, we did have to spend many afternoon sessions training on the 'confidence course', building up our agility and strength, climbing around and swinging like monkeys on the elevated obstacle frames.

In later years, when the unit shook out a little, was more settled into its main roles and had departmentalised its responsibilities, the selection process was obviously modified, especially because it was recruiting from all arms of the British Armed Forces. But during this chaotic period in the early 1970s, when the British Government and the Army were under extreme stress in Ulster, and with anarchy and civil war threatening, we felt that our selection and training was being focused more on an individual's determination and ability to keep going, to function and calmly work alone under pressure. The training was designed to enable us to operate in the kind of harsh deadly environment we would soon be experiencing, rather than spending valuable time building our fitness to the level of supermen. Most 'contacts' are over in less than a minute, so you don't have to be a marathon runner; but you do have to master your adrenaline and shoot straight if you want to live.

So we were told that keeping our fitness levels up was our own affair. As it was, we spent most of our free time in the gym and took regular night-time runs for enjoyment. Later, of course, the penny dropped and we realised that leaving all this up to us was another test, to see whether we would swing the lead if given the chance. They wanted to observe us and discover if we had the motivation, determination and self-discipline to go out at night, in all weather conditions, and in our own free time.... In fact, we actually were being constantly observed, 24 hours a day, by someone or something.

Overall, it was a strange kind of selection process. In the past when I had been on training courses in the Army or in civilian life, the training staff would generally help and give encouragement. However, on this course-selection, as they called it, the staff never gave any encouragement or assistance whatsoever. They were always very quiet and withdrawn, only making whispered comments to each other. If we had the determination, focus and drive, we could complete the tasks to an acceptable standard; if not, we couldn't and that was that. Sometimes the staff actually suggested to one or another of us that we should give up and pack it in, subtly encouraging us to fail. If we got fed up with it all, we could simply leave – and the staff trainers were happy to see that happen. No one got us out of bed in the morning and we never had a break till the end of the day's training, except half an hour for a grabbed lunch.

We were simply told to be ready at a set time and if we were late, we were out; there were no other punishments as there would normally be in the Army. They were constantly trying to drive the emotionally weaker volunteers away and making no attempt to train or teach us anything. They just continued to test our drive, determination, maturity, stability and initiative. Either we had what it took, or we didn't.

The only other process I am familiar with that adopts a similar approach is SAS selection. Perhaps that's why they call it 'selection'. On a course, you learn things but on selection, you should already know! And they select only the people they want, the people that make the grade.

It wasn't until some weeks later, after these sessions had finished, that I learned about the type of work I could expect to be involved in.

Late one afternoon, after we had finished for the day and we were all watching the TV, our OC sent a message and called us in to see him – or rather, three of us. 'Take a seat and sit down,' he said as we entered, wondering if this was goodbye or congratulations.

But he confirmed that we had passed the initial selection process for the MRF and that we would be leaving to start full training within the next 48 hours. He actually seemed a little emotional and began telling us that he was very proud that three of his men out of a battalion of 1,000 had been chosen for Special Duties. He wished us all well and said for us to work hard and not to let the battalion down.

'Thanks, we'll do our best,' we all said, almost in unison, and then as we were about to leave his office, the OC revealed something more to us.

'By the way,' he said. 'Part of the testing you've been going through over the last few weeks was to see if any of you talked to your friends about what you have been doing.' We glanced at each other: had anybody said anything? 'Your Section Commanders had been briefed earlier, to find out as much as they could from you about the MRF and the tests you've been undergoing.' Then with a smile he said, 'Well done, you three kept your mouths shut.'

I remember thinking that it was a sneaky thing to do, getting our friends to spy on us and to try and get us to spill the beans for them. However, this appears to be standard procedure as you move forward into the world of espionage, sabotage and a little subversion thrown in for good measure.

On the way out of the office, the CSM grabbed us and growled, 'Well done you lads, you made it and I know it wasn't easy. Now pack all your uniforms and equipment, then bring them to the company stores in the morning for safe-keeping. You'll not need any of it for a long while.' Then he underlined the instruction: 'Make sure it's *all* your kit, even things like photographs which have anything military in them. And you want to take absolutely nothing military with you at all. That also includes your ID cards and dog tags. You three are finished with the military system, for a while anyway.' He wished us lots of luck.

I thanked him and thought, as I walked back to my room, that I might need some of that luck in the near future. I was still a little unsure of what was going to happen over the next couple of days and didn't fully understanding what I was getting into. But take nothing military? Not even any ID? My brother's line about cannon fodder drifted through my mind again.

All we knew was what we'd been told up to then, which would easily fit on the back of a postage stamp, but I had a feeling we would know a lot more quite soon. We were assured by the OC that we could RTU (return to unit) at any time during the next few weeks, if we wished, after learning more of what the MRF was all about. If any of us were unhappy about it, we could jump off and come back to the battalion with no hard feelings on any side. If however, we decided to stay after initial training, we'd be there for up to three years, no arguments. After getting this far, I didn't think for a moment that I'd pack it all in and I was looking forward to the training process we were about to embark on.

After a big sausage, eggs and bacon breakfast the following morning, we presented all our kit as instructed, and it was sorted and packed away in the company stores. Almost everything we possessed had to be given up; nothing was left out except our washing gear, civilian clothes and things like personal radios or hi-fis. At about 10:30 hrs, the CSM sent a message that we had to be outside his office and ready to leave at 15:00 hrs, and that a vehicle would be waiting to pick us up. We kept ourselves to ourselves during the intervening period, hanging around on our beds, listening to a friend's John Denver LP and singing along to songs like 'Take me Home - Country Roads'. It was an atmosphere of excitement and slight nervousness; the time went fast and yet dragged for us as we waited around for our transport. We went to the NAAFI at 11.00 hrs for a coffee and at 13.00 hrs we ate lunch. The rest of the company was away on some job that afternoon, leaving just the three of us and a few other guys from HQ hanging around the accommodation area.

We weren't even allowed to tell anyone we were leaving or say good-by to our mates. Our departure was planned in such a way so it looked like we simply disappeared. It occurred to me that the company's disappearance that day might also have been arranged.

At 15:00 hrs, outside the company office, the CSM strode up and asked us if we were sure we had everything packed away. Then a few moments later a dark-blue, civilian Hillman Hunter car pulled up with a lone driver. He stopped but made no move to get out. He didn't even look at us but just stared ahead. I didn't know what was happening – didn't realise he was waiting for us until the CSM piped up.

'There you are lads, there's your transport.' He smiled at us with what almost looked like real affection. 'Take care of yourselves, then,' he barked, 'keep your wits about you and keep switched on at all times.'

I had never known him to be so friendly: he helped us load our bags in the boot and even shook our hands – the CSM! – as we climbed in with the driver.

The driver, dressed like a workman with a haircut far from military standard, was super-relaxed: 'Hi, how are you all doing?' he said casually in greeting. 'Sit back and relax, it's not far and you'll be at your new home in no time.'

This unbuttoned manner seemed oddly out of place as the CSM waved us off, but just moments into the journey the driver pressed a button and said with crisp professionalism: 'Hello Zero, this is Delta ... I have my package and leaving now. Over.' I couldn't see a microphone and it probably looked as if he was simply talking to us. From the outside, it would look like he was perhaps just singing along to himself or chatting to us with him. Seconds later, though, we heard a different voice from some speakers: 'Zero, OK, Out.'

Ben, who was in the front seat, turned to us in the back and simply said, 'Nice.' This was certainly interesting stuff.

After about 30 minutes of cruising along a motorway and dual carriageway we turned into a large Army camp. We neither stopped nor had an ID check, which struck me as very odd given the level of security in Ulster by this point. Further up the road we pulled left towards a strange-looking compound area and up to a wide gate which mysteriously opened as just we reached it. This was the MRF base location: an inner compound invisible from the outside and fenced around completely with very high, corrugated-metal panels and looked very much like a builder's storage yard. We were greeted by a couple of characters resembling dock workers from Hull, really rough-looking with long hair and unshaven, who closed the gates behind us. They turned out to be very friendly and took us to a portacabin at the far end, down a pathway along both sides of which stood more green and corrugated metal portacabins, to show us where we would be living. Our cabin had two main rooms each containing three beds draped with blankets and sheets, together with some metal lockers which we could use. One side was clearly occupied by three other people but they weren't there when we arrived, so we took the bunks on the vacant side and dumped our bags on the mattresses. The shower block and toilets were located in another cabin just along the path outside. We later found out that three other members of our future section were housed in another cabin across the path, sharing with another section in the unit.

Before they left us, the two guys told us we needed to be in the operations room for an introductory briefing with the OC in an hour. One pointed to another corrugated metal portacabin on the right, up the path. 'You may as well make yourselves comfy and unpack your bags for now.'

We all agreed that it was a strange kind of place, very private and deliberately hidden by its twelve-foot tall metal perimeter and covered gate by the area where some cars were lined up, side-by-side in a row. It reminded me very much in some ways of a builder's yard or the POW camp in *The Great Escape*, except that it was smaller and here the purpose was to keep people out rather than imprison them.

After a few minutes a chap popped his head around the door of our room. 'Hi, I'm Mike, your section commander, 83 Section. What are your names?'

Dave and Ben introduced themselves and I said, 'My name's Simon but most people call me Sy.'

'Just feel free to have a look around the place before the briefing later,' said Mike. We followed him outside and he pointed to a few installations, such as the operations (ops) room and the stores, then he said, 'I'll see you all later tonight for a chat.'

The atmosphere seemed very relaxed and non-military in the compound area. Nobody was shouting orders at each other and people just seemed to be getting on with what they were doing. Some were cleaning weapons, some testing radios and others wandering in and out of the ops room, which housed a large radio console and map-covered walls of Belfast and the surrounding area, showing the usual segmented areas of the city.

Adjacent to the ops room, in the same cabin, was the briefing room. The walls in here were papered in little photos of nasty-looking people. Examining the rows of sullen faces, the only ones I recognised were those of 'players' like Gerry Adams, Martin McGuiness, Martin Meehan, 'Darkie' Brendan Hughes, the Price sisters and James Bryson, who were some of the most wanted people at that time. There were many, many others, literally a couple of hundred of them.

About 15 chairs in neat rows filled the central area of the room, with a table and blackboard at the front. Sandwiched between the ops room and briefing room was the OC's office, just an anonymous plain door with no plaques or stencilling. Behind the ops room console and the radio operator was the weapons armoury and ammunition store, shielded by heavily-bolted wooden doors.

It didn't occur to me at the time, but in the world of military intelligence and security it was and still is a big no-no to have weapons and ammunition stored and locked in the same room. They should be stored not only in separate rooms but ideally in separate buildings. The same thing goes for transporting weapons and ammo: separate vehicles. Clearly the rules, for some reason, had been suspended here. But we were in Northern Ireland and I suppose it was probably the most secure place in our compound, especially when a duty radio operator sat there 24 hours a day with a loaded Browning 9mm pistol beside him on the desk.

While we were looking around, we saw nobody say much to anyone else except the odd 'Hi', and no-one said much to us either. One chap, though, was tinkering in some box and I asked him what he was doing.

'I'm fitting an optical device,' he replied enthusiastically. 'It's a good way of hanging around in the street, covertly observing.'

The people we saw seemed to accept us being there as if we already were part of their gang, as if they knew who we were and what we were doing. It all seemed a bit strange and alien to me but the guys who did speak to us appeared very friendly. I surveyed the compound again, now that it was becoming familiar to me. In total there were six portacabins, three on each side facing each other, with a long narrow flagstone pathway in the centre, leading to the tall, covered main gate. Half of the cabins were occupied with beds and of the others one was the ops/briefing room/OC's office cabin, and two more were basically empty and looked like classrooms or training rooms. By the main gate the cars were parked up, but they didn't look like anything special, just normal family saloons reversed in, obviously ready to move out fast at a moment's notice.

On our way to the introduction briefing, we met the OC of the unit, who we learned later was an Army captain, walking down the path. He appeared tall, hard-bitten and tough: the classic dark and quiet type. As he turned to go into the cabin containing the ops room, he stopped and called us all together in his office. We entered and he explained that we should just call him Boss, not 'Sir' or 'Captain'. 'Boss', of course, would sound non-military if overheard in the street, say. He asked us to take a seat while he shuffled through some papers and we made ourselves comfortable. My first impression of Tim, our internal name for the Boss, was that he was quite formal and that formality was his natural demeanour. But he surprised me when he very quickly began to relax, taking in the sight of our three fresh faces staring wide-eyed at him.

After the formalities and introductions were out of the way, the Boss started to explain things to us, and at last we began to get a proper picture of what we were becoming involved in.

'Officially we, the MRF, don't exist – on paper, that is – and very few people actually know anything about us. We're directly responsible to the GOCNI [General Officer Commanding Northern Ireland] and no-one else.' It was an incredibly simple chain of command, cutting out almost the entirety of the Army structure.

'We operate totally outside the bounds of the uniformed forces,' he confirmed, 'and we normally train to work alone or at the best in small groups of two to four, forming part of a very small, top secret specialist counter terrorist unit [CTU], a totally new concept.' He carried on, 'If we are ever caught on the streets by a terrorist group, the authorities will emphatically deny all knowledge of our existence, and a cover story will be put out that you were probably just an off-duty soldier.'

This was serious stuff: we would be totally on our own without any safety-net. I thought of us swinging around in the air like monkeys on the confidence course.

'It doesn't really matter, you realise,' said the Boss. 'If you were ever caught, the IRA wouldn't hesitate to kill you straight away. As the Americans would say, we are a classic black ops unit or "spooks".... So welcome aboard, gentlemen. Do you have any questions so far?'

Needless to say, I was lost for words after an introduction like that, and I'm sure my two pals were also a little shocked.

I replied, 'No questions, Sir – Boss, that's fine. It all sounds very interesting.' My two friends agreed.

He continued. 'The unit consists of me as OC, together with three Intelligence Corps fellows. They work closely with me in co-ordinating operations, collating information and generally taking care of the ops room and manning the radios. The overall unit strength should be approximately 35 members who are specially chosen from numerous selected Army units, including the Royal Marines, Parachute Regiment, Military Police, former Special Air Service members and Special Boat Service. We are divided into three sections of eight to ten men,' he added. 'The sections' radio call signs are 81, 82 and 83.'

Pointing to his right with a tilt of his head, the Boss indicated the armoury behind the radio console in the next room. 'We also hold quite a variety of weapons in our armoury: 9mm Browning pistols, Walther PP and PPK pistols, Sterling submachine guns – two or three of them fitted with silencers. We have at least one Thompson machine gun, plus some other weapons together with some Pye hand-held radios and a large amount of camera and photographic equipment.'

It was an Aladdin's cave of boys' toys, and I also noticed later that in our store room we kept an impressive variety of equipment which enabled us to keep up a close target reconnaissance (CTR). This included the box I saw earlier and some other items like wheel barrows and cleaning equipment. I could just see myself dressed in overalls walking around the city pushing one of those around – which, as it turned out, actually happened quite regularly.

'The unit vehicles,' the Boss went on, 'are a Hillman Hunter, two Ford Cortinas, two Morris Marinas and two Hillman Avengers, but don't be misled by their appearance. They are all tuned up, with larger engines than normal. Plus, there are one or two other unofficial vehicles that will mysteriously appear for a while then disappear.'

I learned later that these unofficial vehicles were actually stolen or 'confiscated' from the IRA during some of our operations. We held onto these vehicles after Special Branch had finished going over them and sometimes we used them for a while before dumping them.

I remember that once we had this lovely big white car. John, a chap in our section, told us the IRA had previously used it for transporting weapons and the odd shooting. It was a great motor, ran like a dream. It looked like a big Maxi, but I think it was one of the old Austin 18-22 series. We played with it for a few weeks, taking it out for a spin along the coast road while 'off duty'. Then one morning, sadly, it was gone.

Our vehicle radio call signs were Alpha, Bravo, Charlie, Delta, Echo, Foxtrot and Golf. Therefore, with my section being 83, if I used vehicle Bravo my call sign would become 83 Bravo. If I was on foot, I would use my personal call sign of 'Sierra Charlie' (my initials). Occasionally we would drop these phonetic call signs altogether and just use our first names, depending on what we were doing or where we were.

The unit operated on the basis of a three 12-hour-shift system. One section would be on duty, one off duty and the other on standby, usually hanging around the ops room area so they could be called out at a moment's notice. Even the off-duty section was always on one-hour standby to be called out if required to help any of the other sections.

After our little briefing, the Boss took us into the operations room where we were introduced to a number of characters milling around who looked like plumbers, builders and decorators. They happened to be the standby section and were just waiting around, fiddling with items of equipment or checking over their maps, preparing for their duty stint. While the OC was showing us around, he made it clear that we were in a training phase and if he felt we were unsuitable, he could RTU us – send us back to our parent units. He also added that if we were unhappy with the job, we could leave at any time during the next few weeks, with no hard feelings. Exactly what we'd been told by our OC back at camp.

'The training phase takes approximately five to six weeks and for most of this time the training will be on the job,' he explained. 'We are extremely busy, we have many commitments and I really can't afford to have people or trainers away or detached for long periods of time.'

Our training phase involved such subjects as mobile and static surveillance techniques, OP (observation post) work, long- and short-range covert photography, hijack techniques, anti-hijack techniques, lifting and snatching operations, house breaking and lock picking, prisoner interrogation, CPP – close personal protection or CP - body-guarding, advanced driving – offensive and defensive, resistance to interrogation (R to I) together – most interestingly – with an ongoing programme of 'demilitarization'.

It had been a month or so since our initial interview with our old OC and CSM, and along with my two friends, I had a distinct feeling that we had just been dropped into the middle of a dream world. The job certainly appeared to be different from anything I'd been used to for the last five years. Some of the weapons the Boss mentioned, I'd never even seen before, never mind actually having used them. And all this surveillance stuff, covert photography and CP work, just left my mind boggled, making me question whether I could manage to learn all this new covert stuff.

It was definitely a strange place to be, where everyone seemed to wander around dressed as they liked. And they were all so relaxed: it was more like a civilian world, where people didn't have to be constantly told or reminded what to do and when to do it. Everyone knew what had to be done and just got on with it. Planet MRF was very different from the regimented, saluting and marching-around kind of life we had recently left behind.

That evening Mike turned up in our room again. 'Hope the intro went well,' he said. 'The Boss is OK, a bit quiet, but he's a good guy.' Then he made an announcement: 'Tonight I'm going to take you all out into Belfast for a look around the city and some familiarisation with the area. We'll all be in one car together and each of you can take turns at driving while I sit in the front passenger's seat – the commander's position.' He unfolded a map and prodded it. 'I'll be talking you around town and showing you some areas of interest. You need not worry too much although you'll probably feel quite vulnerable at first, being on your own without 20 or 30 uniformed friends around you. It's OK, you'll find that being in plain clothes you'll blend in and feel quite secure … eventually.' He looked up at us. 'Have any of you used the 9-millie pistol before.'

We replied that we had but not very often and not for quite a while, so he pulled his pistol out of his waist band, then unloaded and cleared it to remind us how it worked.

'Make sure, if you fire it, that you take a two-handed grip. I don't want to see any of that one-handed shooting shit you see on TV. Only fire accurate, aimed shots and hold it with two hands.

'Sure, OK,' we said.

Mike smiled. 'Right, you guys go now and get something to eat and I'll see you at 10:30 pm in the operations room. Don't be late.'

I noticed the way Mike said '10:30 pm' and not '22:30 hrs' in military style. Dropping the use of the 24-hour clock I discovered was one of our first lessons in demilitarization.

We trundled off to grab some food after picking up our cups and diggers, while Mike went back over to the ops room to collect some extra maps and have a chat with the Boss. As we ambled along the path, we were all thinking and saying, 'This all sounds really great and exciting. I can't wait to get started, down in the city.'

We were back in the Ops room early, by 10:00 pm. We didn't want to miss this trip for the world. Mike arrived soon after and took us behind the console into the armoury. There, he gave us each a 9-millie pistol with two magazines and a full box of 9mm rounds. We checked and cleared the weapons as he gave them to us, then we had a couple of minutes to get the feel of these new and unfamiliar weapons while Mike tinkered with some radio equipment.

Mike picked up a submachine gun and began clearing it. 'We don't need any hand radios as we're not walking around. For tonight, and until we get you three lads trained up on the 9 millie, just fill both magazines with 12 rounds each, then pop one on the weapon but don't cock it. We normally carry two magazines of 12 rounds each, plus one round placed into the breech ready to fire, and a handful of loose rounds kept in a pocket.'

Back in the Briefing room, Mike laid out some large scale maps of Belfast across the table. 'Gather round you lads and look in,' he said, and began to give us a short briefing on where we would be going, pointing out some dodgy areas.

He watched us as we looked at the danger spots on the map. 'Don't worry, we won't be going into any of those hard areas tonight,' he reassured us, then flashed a cheeky smile. 'Maybe tomorrow.'

His comment didn't make us smile, and to be honest we were quite happy to be cruising around the quieter areas of the city, at least on our first night. I was thinking, 'We'll worry about tomorrow when it comes.'

I was feeling a little nervous, as I am sure my pals were, too. It was one thing going out onto the streets of Belfast in an armoured 'pig' with a big powerful rifle, loads of bullets and an armoured flak jacket to give you some protection. But it's totally another feeling altogether setting out in a flimsy little family saloon with a pistol stuffed in your belt and just 5mm of glass window between you and the enemy.

By 11 pm we had our weapons and car documents together and piled into the same car, the Hillman Hunter, that had picked us up earlier in the day. Mike jumped into the front passenger seat and said, 'By the way, this car is car "Delta" if you happen to hear us mentioned on the radio later.'

Dave got in the driver's seat while Ben and I climbed in the back. We headed down the road and out of the Army camp gates, again without stopping, and only switched on our lights as we turned left towards Belfast city.

'OK,' said Mike. 'Take your 9 millies and slip them under your lap – we usually carry them this way while we're in the cars. It's quicker and easier to get to in that position, under your leg.'

That evening was an interesting ride round the city and Mike was obviously very knowledgeable about the area. He was very witty and kept cracking jokes, which I felt was to help us to relax in our new environment. During the evening we called into a couple of Army locations around the city centre and one down by Musgrave Park Hospital on the fringes of some of those hard areas. We were introduced to the unit's intelligence staff over a coffee while Mike collected some documents we had to take back. He did most of the talking while we just kept quiet and stayed in the background, observing things and people while we sipped our coffees and chatted with each other.

We couldn't help wondering what the other people must think of us, sitting quietly in our civvies and observing them as Mike chatted away. They probably thought we were just three more of those 'master spies' observing and gathering information on them.

Little did they know, but on that first day we had almost no idea about anything that was going on. We were the blind men in the jungle. We sat there, quietly minding our own business, only pretending to be switched on. Needless to say, over the next few days of studying the maps and patrolling the city with the rest of the section, we became totally switched on.

If we hadn't, we would have probably been dead.

By the time we got back to our hidden base it was almost 3 am. We had been out for four hours but it only seemed like one. The Int. boys were there waiting for us in the ops room with some stewed tea and dried-up sandwiches, and they asked us if we had had a good run around.

The truth is, that first trip out had been an exhilarating experience for me. Patrolling around those dismal streets as a 'civvie' was a new and stimulating experience: we were all buzzing from the rush. After packing our weapons and equipment away, we drank our tea and ate our snacks, while enthusiastically chatting to the ops room lads. After a time, Mike spoke up.

'OK lads, get some sleep when you're finished. Breakfast starts at 8 am and I'll see you all at 10 am in the briefing room.' I'm sure he could see and feel that we were all fired up with enthusiasm for the job, even though we were fresh and didn't have much idea at that time. Mike must have known that it was his responsibility to keep us safe during these vital first few days, when we were infinitely more likely than later on to commit fatal errors of judgement.

Back in our room we sat on our beds, put on some easy music and looked at each other in amazement. We didn't need to say anything because we were all thinking the same thing: What a strange place this was compared to normal military life, where everything, absolutely everything was so different. It was as if we had stepped through the looking glass. As indeed we had.

After we settled down, Dave and Ben came over to my bed, sat down and asked me, 'What do you think about it all, Sy?'

'What do I think? Well, it all seems pretty good to me. We've got some learning and studying to do regarding these new procedures and weapons ... but I think it's great.' I didn't know what I thought until I said it, but I realised it was true: I thought it was great, and a challenge. A great challenge.

'Well, we feel the same,' they both replied, and then we all turned in for a good night's sleep – or a few hours', at any rate.

The next day, arriving in the briefing room across the pathway, we were introduced to the rest of our section, 83. At first glance as I walked in, I thought to myself, 'Jesus, what kind of a section is this?' It was a real mixture of characters waiting there for us to arrive. They all looked a bit odd to my Army mind, with their long hair, unshaven and scruffy clothes, like a bunch of reprobates waiting to audition for a part in *The Dirty Dozen*, although there were only six of them. But after a couple of minutes of 'hello' and 'how are you', they came across as a really friendly, switched-on bunch of lads and totally accepted us right away, gathering around us, offering coffee and chatting to us like we were long-lost friends. It wasn't scruffiness at all that I saw, it was savviness. I was learning about a different kind of camouflage.

I noticed that although they asked us many questions about our backgrounds and where we came from, and about our Army careers and parent units, there was not a single enquiry about our ranks. Nobody was interested, and here was another shock: whatever this unit was, rank did not matter. It was a strange way to run a railroad, or rather an army, but it felt somehow very good.

Soon after we sat down with our mugs of tea, Mike arrived and made his way to the front of the room by the table. As he passed me, I noticed that he had his 9 millie slipped neatly into his waist band. He pulled up a chair and sat down facing us all. 'Right then, let's introduce ourselves, shall we?'

First of all was Mike, our section commander, a sergeant and former member of the Special Air Service, about six feet tall, dark with quite an athletic build, very relaxed and with a jovial, faint Irish accent.

Next was Tug, Parachute Regiment, a music buff and a northeastern lad, fair, shorter and quite stocky, with an engineering background – he always had time for a joke even in the most stressful situations.

Kev was a Royal Marine, on detachment from the Special Boat Service. He hailed from west Yorkshire and was tall, well-built, rugged and looked like a big bear. He had long, wavy brown hair and a moustache. Kev was a very strong, jolly character and looked like he could really take care of himself – plus all the rest of us if need be. He had a strange habit of taking out the 8-inch flick knife he always carried around, and cleaning his fingernails with it. It didn't matter where he was at the time and it often attracted some disapproving looks if he wasn't doing it to intimidate someone. Kev was to become a very good friend of mine.

Colin was also with the Special Boat Service but from north Yorkshire. He was a little shorter and slim with it, with a blonde, wavy Donny Osmond hair style. He was much more softly spoken than Kev, more reserved and with smoother looks – but still as tough as they come.

John, a Royal Anglian who we sometimes called 'Titch', was a lance corporal from Lincolnshire, blonde and a little goofy. But he was very good at mechanics and an excellent driver who could do almost anything with a car, in forward or reverse gear. I'm sure he could have gone on to be a top rally driver, given the chance.

Last was Bob, a Royal Marines corporal; dark, quietly spoken and from the south of England, slim built and always very cheerful, constantly keeping us entertained.

Then there was us three, Dave, Ben and me, hoping to fit in, to fill the gaps and help create the 'Magnificent Nine' of section 83. We were all from the north of England, with varied military skills, coming from signals, reconnaissance and support weapons backgrounds.

I was introduced to the others last and after giving my five-minute stand-up chat on my background, I was put into a team to work with Kev, John and Bob; but as a sub-team I was to work directly with Kev. This decision made me feel quite chuffed, because if we got into any trouble I would have the big bear next to me – and believe me, I was glad that he was on our side.

I'm five feet ten and was 12 stone in those days, but Kev at six feet two, with arms like my legs, could pick me up with one hand, and he always made me feel like a dwarf when we stood together. Kev and I always got on really well and he made me laugh on countless occasions, especially when he took out his flick knife to clean his fingernails in a life-or-death situation.

Dave and Ben made up two more teams with Mike, Tug and Colin. More usually, however, Bob and Dave would switch and work directly with Mike, so effectively we operated as three teams of three much of the time. At this briefing, we officially found out that the three guys in our cabin were Kev, Colin and Tug; Mike and the other two of the team would share the cabin opposite with 81 Section.

Later that day, I walked along the path and into our cabin and saw Dave and Ben sitting chatting with John, the guy who told us about the lovely white car. They were asking what types of operations we could expect to get involved in, and what they might entail.

In reply, John went over much of what the Boss had told us the day before, but added more detail, telling Dave and Ben about a surveillance job a couple of months earlier, when a couple of the lads from another section had been mobbed in the Shankhill Road while out patrolling on general surveillance one afternoon. They noticed a suspicious car and followed it around the area for a time.

Shortly after, the target car stopped and our two lads pulled in and got out of theirs to keep the target under surveillance. Unfortunately they were noticed and attacked by a group of Protestants who assumed they were IRA terrorists. The group had attacked with sticks and crowbars, giving our two lads quite a beating and destroying their car. But fortunately, during this beating, someone in the Protestant group suddenly shouted at the others, 'Stop, stop! These guys are Army – I know this one from when I was in the forces.'

At the same moment, a uniformed patrol pitched up, dispersed the crowd and took our two lads away to the Musgrave Park Hospital. They had both suffered a lot of punishment and one of them sustained a broken arm in the scuffle. Within a few weeks, they had both recovered and were back on the streets patrolling with their section again.

During the attack, the target vehicle managed to escape from the scene and was never traced.

3

Fired-Up and Fine-Tuned

Over the following few weeks we were kept very busy. Often, while on standby section, we had to sit in on briefings and study sessions, learning about the Belfast streets and studying the photos of the characters we were interested in, and their areas of the city. Then later, while on duty section, we'd be on-the-job training while patrolling. This was quite dangerous, especially in a place like Belfast when a gunman or bomber could pop up at any moment. In 1972 gunmen were freely roaming the city streets, and could be waiting to launch an attack from around a corner at any time, a fact which undoubtedly fine-tunes your senses. As a result, you tended to learn things very, very quickly. You knew that just one simple mistake could easily cost you your life – or even worse, your friend's life.

In those early days we all clearly felt there was a great sense of urgency in the air, on the part of the Army, to select the best people available and get us trained up as quickly as possible. All sections of the MRF during this initial, chaotic period were made of corporals and sergeants, known as NCOs (non-commissioned officers), although almost all of us were qualified, top-grade small-arms weapons and firing-range instructors, and we generally came from a working class back-ground – with good reason. We didn't have any officers in the sections working with us, getting involved on operations with us at all. Sometimes the Boss would accompany a section for a couple of hours on general patrol, but only on rare occasions. Much of our time on duty was spent mixing closely with the local population that inhabited some of the most dangerous, unforgiving and fearful parts of Northern Ireland. We felt that the average British Army officer, in uniform or plain-clothes, stood out like an elephant on a ski slope … with their private school and silver service up-bringing, which was much more noticeable in the early 1970s than today.

On the streets of Belfast during this very dangerous and explosive period, when every stranger was meticulously scrutinised, it was absolutely essential for us all to blend in with our surroundings. We had to completely fit in, looking like and acting just like the locals. And we found that the average Army officer-type on plain-clothes operations simply defied this profile: you could easily have seen that they were Army from miles away.

It's common knowledge that later, in the 1980s and '90s and well known that the activities of 14 Intelligence Company – the Det – was restructured and took on more of a passive, surveillance role and the social profile was not so vitally important. Then, other plain-clothes departments were tasked to take on any aggressive confrontational operations with the terrorist groups.

However, in the early 1970s, we in the MRF took on all these offensive, defensive and surveillance roles ourselves. The fires were burning furiously and it appeared there was little time or any existing structure available to departmentalise our responsibilities and efforts. We had to just get on with the tasks and operations, whatever they were and be ready, when required, to confront and deal with the terrorists head on.

It was inevitable that our small unit of the MRF would become compromised sooner or later. This was partly due to the relentless, heavy commitments and the aggressive nature of some of the operations we were tasked with. But I feel it was mainly a handful of reckless press reports, released from some so-called 'Army spokesmen', which exposed our unit.

The Army, under quite some pressure from the press to 'come clean', appeared to openly give out details of some of our operations.

It seemed like they simply handed out press releases admitting to a couple of incidents we were involved in. It looked like they freely gave out the initials of the unit, which some then guessed at the time to stand for Military Reconnaissance Force or Mobile Reconnaissance Force. Information regarding the weapons we used, our general area of operation and the strength of the MRF unit was also leaked.

Instead of sticking to the original plan we were told – of denying all knowledge and toughing it out. There appeared to be some nervousness and backsliding, especially with regard to some earlier reported incidents.

No-one knew for sure anything of our existence or involvement in those few publicised incidents until the Army let it out to the press, generating provocative headlines such as 'Tommy Gun ... Plain-Clothes Killers', 'Troops Taken For IRA Men', 'Plain-Clothes Army Patrols - Whitelaw Challenged To Come Clean', 'Republicans On "Military Murder Squads In Mufti"', 'Army Secret "Civvy" Squads', 'Army Murder Gangs - The Faceless Ones ... Secret Squads Spy On The IRA Gunmen', 'Secret Agent Is Shot Dead By Terrorists' and 'Flare Line Spies ... Silently, They Risk Death To Save Ulster'. It sounds glamorous now, but at the time it was deadly dangerous for us, as our lives depended on being invisible.

We were involved in a wide variety of operations and the few publicised actions were just the tip of the iceberg. Nonetheless, someone behind a desk lost his nerve, got cold feet and compromised the entire unit's activities, risking each and every one of our lives all over again.

Contrary to popular belief, the MRF did not appear to be totally disbanded in 1974-75. There seemed to be little change in the unit at that time except that many operations were toned down. We also went through a variety of name changes over a period of a couple of months, from MRF to various other names but some time later, eventually settling on 14 Intelligence Company. This seemed to be purposely done to shake the enemy off our scent and sow confusion everywhere, and it worked quite well by making everyone assume we had been disbanded and rendered non-operational. It sowed confusion with us, too, mind: in fact, our name was changing so quickly and so often I wasn't sure from day to day what we were supposed to be called.

During those first few months after I arrived, much of our time was spent on surveillance techniques, both mobile and on foot, together with counter-surveillance – making sure you're not being followed while you follow the target. This was all very intensive and energy draining, mentally and physically. We worked in a group of five to eight men, all in radio contact with one another. The main objective was to follow the target, not necessarily the person himself, without being seen.

For example, on foot: we would be watching and following something distinctive such as a hat, a coat or an item the person was carrying. The reason for this was that we never wanted to make eye contact with the person or get so close as to see their face in detail. If eye contact was ever made, the lead position had to change immediately and the next man in line took over the surveillance. Radio contact within the team was essential and a running commentary of every move the person made was relayed back through the whole team. Useful aids in foot surveillance can be things like vehicle and shop windows because you can stand with your back to the target and still observe them in the reflection. But you must take care which windows you choose: you would look a little odd staring for ten minutes into a shop full of ladies' underwear or one that was empty and undergoing renovation.

We often practiced the various formations on foot and in vehicles. In the city, we would sometimes 'bracket' the target, with operators in parallel streets, ready to take over the lead if the target turned left or right. Or we would 'box' the target, with operators to the front, rear and sides, which usually depended on the amount of other people or traffic in and around our area of operation. Or perhaps the weather conditions at the time allowed us to move nearer and to close in all around the target, as was possible if it was foggy or raining heavily.

You also had to act in a natural way and with a purpose, pretending to do one thing while actually doing another. What if you followed a target into a shop but as you walked in the door, the target walked back out straight past you? This is one way a target tries to shake off a tail if he thinks he's being followed. As it is, you would have to carry on in, without flinching or hesitation, as if you really wanted to buy that neck-tie. Then as quickly as possible you informed the next man in line, by radio, who would be close by outside. You would tell him that the target had left the building, say where the target now was, and ask your colleague to carry on the surveillance. You would emerge a decent time later to join the rear of the counter-surveillance team.

The whole process is mentally very draining and takes plenty of practice for the team to co-ordinate its movements. You need your wits about you and must be totally focused forward on your target and everything else that's going on around him or her. You can't afford to miss anything: the passing of a note, the shaking of hands or a simple wave of a hand – you must see it all and relay every move back to the team while they are busy making notes and watching your back.

With mobile, vehicle surveillance, the process is very much the same but we would use four or five vehicles. However, in practice it's a little more difficult to carry out because co-ordinating movements is more complicated due to traffic and stop lights. Furthermore, it's not so easy to slip a tonne of metal out of sight, like it is for a man on foot to hide himself. I always felt less vulnerable and more confident carrying out foot surveillance as it's much, much easier to blend in with your surroundings.

The OP (observation post) and photography were next. I was actually re-learning how to set up an OP, as I had done it a few times before in my parent unit. The new element to it was setting up and operating in an urban area where the enemy might be only a few feet away, and then having to stay and virtually live in your position for days on end. Simple things like eating and shitting become a major undertaking. The most important things to remember when sighting and preparing your OP are your avenues of escape in case you have to make a quick exit. Also, you need to take the correct equipment with you for the type of OP you are operating. If you were in the countryside, you would need ground sheets and camouflage nets for protection from the damp earth and also from the weather above, together with chicken wire to hold up the bracken after you cut into it so it doesn't all collapse in on top of you. Small garden trimming cutters and string are handy to cut into the bracken and tie it back afterwards.

In a house OP, on the other hand, your kit would obviously be a little different. If you were located in an old broken-down attic or a room of a burned-out building, handy things would be tables and chairs, blankets and some face-veil type of material. You need to be elevated with the chair on the table, well back from the window, with the blankets and face veil over you as cover, and with just the camera lens or rifle barrel showing. In this position, anyone outside, down in the street, would have great difficulty in seeing you. Not only are you elevated (people rarely look up) but you are well back in the shadows or a corner of the room, and your shape is totally broken up.

Another type of OP is from a vehicle, casually parked for a short time watching someone's house or an area you're interested in. In this situation we'd periodically get out of the car, call into a shop and mingle with others in the street.

Or perhaps we might set up an OP in the hills overlooking a housing estate or an area of interest, looking out for movements of weapons or explosives around the area. We could even find ourselves standing for a while on a street corner observing a house or houses, and relaying back information on activities in and around the target area.

Sometimes we set-up OPs in large gardens in the grounds of a house, provided there was plenty of cover from trees and shrubbery and of course good avenues of escape. A couple of us would simply sit and live there for two or three days at a time, taking photographs and making notes, while we had other section members nearby, patrolling in cars as our backup if they were needed.

One time, John and I had been positioned, located in the bushes of a large garden on just such an OP on the fringes of Belfast. We sat there for two days living on tins of corned beef – 'corned dog' as we all called it. We were dressed in camouflage and had blacked-out, camouflaged faces and hands. The weather had been totally miserable with lots of fog interspersed with light and heavy rain showers and we were both pretty well fed-up with being cold and damp.

It was a never-ending task trying to keep the cameras and our weapons clean and dry. We had been taking lots of photos of a variety of people as they arrived and left the property. Then suddenly Kev turned up in the middle of the night, called us on the radio and threw a big bag of hot fish and chips over the wall into our OP. We quickly grabbed them and John and I got stuck in with wide smiles on our faces. We told Kev on the radio that we owed him for that. Kev just quietly replied, 'Enjoy lads ... catch you later.'

After an OP operation was concluded, we had to clean up all around and leave absolutely no trace that we had been there. The extraction was normally carried out in the very early hours of the morning. Our cars closed in on our position when we radioed them to say we were ready and we moved out with all our equipment packed and weapons at the 'ready', joining up with the nearby cars within moments. And then we were gone.

The photography instruction was enjoyable and usually part of the OP training. We learned developing, enlarging and the use of different films back at the minilab, a large broom cupboard at our base. Setting up and locating the different cameras and long lenses on tripods was interesting; we had to get to grips with things such as f-stops, focal lengths and depth-of-field, and learn about ASA, ISO and DIN settings as part of normal OP practice. It was a little complicated at times, but all very fascinating to me; in fact it turned out to be a life-long hobby.

Another enjoyable part of our training were the kidnap, hijack and anti-hijack drills we had to master. We always worked in small teams, and everyone was beginning to gel and work well together, spending our rest breaks talking over the drills and procedures, often with a pot of tea and a sandwich, while watching another team go at it and figuring out the best methods, until everyone knew exactly what to do and when to do it. We did have our occasional cock-ups, such as two of us running around the car, in opposite directions, weapon in hand, so that we'd crash into one another and end up sitting on the ground, looking and feeling a little embarrassed, with Mike standing over us, hands on hips and looking unimpressed. Fortunately, this type of training was done way out of town, usually in secluded countryside or some place in the middle of nowhere. Alternatively, we'd occasionally practice on the nearby firing ranges while awaiting our turn.

The house-entry techniques and instruction was a relatively small part of our training programme. We were informed that the unit don't have much hardware – meaning mini cameras and listening devices – for that type of operation. There was some, but nothing like they have now. 'It will be on very few occasions that you'll be fiddling around with locks and latches to enter a house,' we were told. 'Perhaps you'll only be doing it to place the odd listening device.' Ordinarily, if we entered a house, we would be simply bursting in 'fast and furious' to lift the occupants for questioning.

The MRF was a completely new concept in Ulster at this time, in 1971 and early 1972, and much of our training and the procedures we learned hadn't been fully tried and tested on operations. Most of the high-tech electronic equipment in use nowadays wasn't available or even invented in the 1970s: we had to work with what we had. We knew that we had to continually reassess our procedures and techniques as incidents occurred. At times we had a distinct feeling we were like trail blazing, Wild West barnstormers flying by the seat of our pants, or explorers foraging and skirmishing as we followed new paths ever deeper into the wilderness. It was stimulating but a little unnerving at times to be more reliant on our knowledge and senses than on electronic gadgetry. What bolstered us all, was that the job was very important and dangerous and we were not here to make arrests or take prisoners. Our objective was to gather information, spoil and interfere with IRA plans and operations, and when possible, to track down terrorists. If we caught any we were supposed to hand them over to the uniformed forces to arrest and deal with, which indeed we did.

Close personal protection (CPP or CP) training was interesting but again mentally quite draining, as we learned the different formations and procedures for 'Actions On', even though we didn't often operate extremely close to our subjects, shoulder to shoulder, as you might see on TV as a celebrity is guided through a scrum of paparazzi by a beefy bodyguard. The point of us was to remain invisible. For most of our CP work we operated with most of our section on foot around the subject with the others in vehicles acting as backup for the CP team. We hovered, a few metres away, placing a kind of cordon around our subject, and often blended in with crowds in the street or mingled with other people around the room in a restaurant or bar situation, all the while keeping our subject under observation. At the same time we'd be watching everyone else in the vicinity for any aggressive movements or indications.

Our aim was to intervene if someone made an approach, or tried to, or looked as if he was about to attack our subject. The subjects always knew we were close, but never saw or noticed us while we posed as photographers, onlookers or road sweepers. One thing we always insisted on was that the subject's regular Special Branch bodyguards were unarmed (if indeed they carried any weapons), while we were on the job. We didn't want them drawing and shooting at us by mistake if anything happened, and they were there to act solely as the last line of defence if a large scale attack went in. We made it very clear that we were to be the only people controlling the shooting if it started.

Advanced driving was normally combined with live firing, with teams changing over from the range to the vehicles. We learned hand-break turns and 'J' turns together with various procedures for use during 'lifts' and 'snatches'. These we combined with extraction techniques, for our own people, if ever they became caught up in an emergency situation or found themselves otherwise trapped.

Sometimes we used the vehicles to practice different firing positions: from inside, over and around the bonnet and boot. Often we practiced firing at targets while exiting and rolling out of the doors, shooting as we moved to a different position. I often wondered whether I would see someone put a bullet hole in one of the cars, as we used to get up to some crazy things; but it never happened – we had one or two close calls but none of us ever accidentally shot one of the cars while I was present.

We had to carry out quite a lot of live-firing practice, getting used to our new personal weapon the 9mm Browning pistol. I had used the 9 millie before, a couple of years earlier, on the ranges and on weapons-training courses, but not as often as I'd have liked. Now, instead of hefting a long rifle around, our plainclothes operations meant we had to carry something smaller. Previously, I used to carry around the standard SLR 7.62mm (Belgian FN self-loading rifle), very powerful and quite accurate with practice, and this was superseded many years later by the SA80 5.56mm with mixed feelings among the regular troops. The size of a round (bullet) was the mm measurement across the head of the round, so a 7.62mm is about 2mm thicker than the 5.56mm and was longer and much more powerful than the smaller round.

Initially, my knowledge of the Browning 9 millie was quite limited. As mentioned, I had last fired it a couple of years earlier, probably in 1970, but it's not normally the regular soldier's weapon. The officers, medics and some drivers used to carry them while all the rest of us had the FN-SLRs.

The 9 millie tends to be a little agricultural and fairly simple to strip down (take to pieces). There is a 'T'-shaped pin in the centre by the trigger guard and when it's taken out, everything simply slides apart from itself. This pin also acts as the 'locking back' mechanism which holds back the working parts when the magazine is empty. They have quite a solid feel about them and it's surprising how accurate you can become with plenty of practice.

We also had to get used to all the other weapons and ammunition that we held in our armoury, as we might need to change at a moment's notice, depending on the type of task we were given. Two of these were the Walther semi-automatic pistols (PP and PPK), which are smaller, more accurate and of a higher build quality than the Browning. Also, we had to get used to the Sterling submachine guns, some of them supplied to us with their long, bulky suppressors fitted. The SMGs tended to forfeit some hitting power when fitted with these silencers, as the propellant gases released and ignited by the bullet were slowed down so much before the (ideally subsonic) round was airborne. So we practiced on buckets of sand and old ammo boxes to test the difference and power loss, eventually calculating that three rounds from a silenced SMG would offer similar hitting power as would a single round from a non-silenced weapon – quite a loss of force and something to bear in mind.

Prisoner Interrogation and Resistance to Interrogation played quite a small part in the training programme because our trainers told us that normally, over here, we didn't take prisoners. However, if we come across a 'player' of some importance, we could lift him and bring him in for interrogation. But if we did lift someone, we were not to spend days asking polite questions and offering soft drinks. The people we were dealing with were brutal and aggressive killers and we had to waste no on them.

Innocent people's lives depended on how soon you acquired the information. However, we were simply told we would almost never bring in any prisoners for interrogation. It's all very well playing the 'good guy-bad guy' routine for hours on end or some psychological games if you are the police gathering information on other suspects in some crime, but we didn't have the luxury of time.

When you are dealing with psychopathic terrorist killers and bombers who don't even hesitate in killing their own people, speed is absolutely essential to protect innocent lives. We were not to be looking for confessions – we just wanted information on terrorist operations. We had a difficult, dangerous job to do and we would have had no time or interest for playing games with fanatical brutal killers. The objective was to get the information fast, to save innocent lives. We were told, we were only interested in the information and the speed we could acquire it, if in fact we did bring anyone in. However, we did have some requests to lift some terror suspects for the uniformed forces but we never brought any in for ourselves to interrogate.

Very few wild animals will actually kill their own kind but a terrorist will for his cause. Some prisoners who were brought in were eventually 'turned,' becoming informers, but very few of them were totally loyal or reliable and we all had to be very careful if dealing with these informers.

With regard to Resistance to Interrogation, it was made very clear that if we were ever caught by a terrorist group, our life expectancy would be no more than five or ten minutes. The IRA was far more interested in vengeful bloodletting than gathering information from us. Therefore, after a few lectures on R to I, we were simply told this:

'Don't get caught. But if you are trapped or cornered, empty your magazines on them first. Don't get caught with any ammunition left on you. They may get your weapon, but don't let them get hold of your ammo. If you're going down, go down with empty magazines and if possible try to destroy your weapon or dismantle and disperse it before they get their grubby hands on it.'

These were harsh, murderous times and we had to be as aggressive as they were – if not more so. We had to show them that we could be just as horrendous and vicious as they were, in order to give them second thoughts about their chosen course of action. The restricted regular Army didn't scare them so much but we did. It was survival of the toughest, mentally and physically, and the IRA had to see they were not the only ones that could be bad.

We made it very clear to the IRA on many occasions that when they crossed our path they weren't dealing with 'pussycats.' It became possible, because of the way we operated, to begin spoiling and compromising terrorist operations and attacks. That in the period I was with the MRF, during the early 1970s, the whole unit of approximately 35 volunteers combined – really only the size of the average platoon – may easily have saved hundreds, perhaps thousands of innocent lives. Exactly how many, who knows? We will never really be certain. But I do know that we saved many, many lives.

Our initial training took almost two months, going out on operations while on duty section, and then training hard while on standby section. Demilitarization wasn't as easy as it sounds, after spending many years being trained to stand, act and walk in a disciplined way. For me especially, as I joined the Army direct from school at the age of 15 and knew nothing else but military training and discipline, it was a struggle to become a 'civvie' in my deportment and language. But after a month or so, I managed to shake off that military stance and attitude that you can see regularly in most railway stations around the UK on a busy weekend. However, I was quite surprised how easy it is to slip up – for example, if someone in the street asked you the time. It's so automatic and second-nature for a military person to say something like '19:35' or '22:40 hours', which in some of the hard areas of Belfast was an open invitation to a one-way ticket home in a box.

Strange as it may sound, having an English accent was never really a problem, as we almost never spoke when mingling close with people in the city. And if someone did manage to hear our accent and say something, we had numerous sets of ID. These ranged in variety of identification cards proving us to be employees of numerous companies and organisations. I possessed a particularly nice piece of ID due to having applied for and acquired a part-time job in a local sports centre. That employee's identification card worked wonders for me on many occasions. Remember, also, that not only was Northern Ireland part of the UK, so that it was neither a crime nor a rarity to speak with an English, Welsh, or Scottish accent, but also that Belfast was a major port, and that the local population was well-used to hearing a variety of sailors' accents from all over the place. No, the essential thing was not to let anyone suspect you might be a soldier.

One thing we never attempted was try to put on an Irish accent, as the Irish would surely know immediately that it was faked: it was much safer not to try. Even if we did try, very few people would actually say anything to us then and there. All that would happen is that we would be found face down in the dirt, late one night in some back alley or roadside ditch with a bullet in the head. Or perhaps we would simply disappear from some pub or bar car park without trace, which is what happened to at least one Guards officer in plain clothes a few years later.

We would have had to live among these people for twenty years or more before we could master to any degree a good-enough Irish accent to pass ourselves off as locals. The regional Ulster accents are quite different and after spending many years there, mingling with the people, still now I can recognise the slight, and sometimes more distinct, variations.

Just to place what we were training for in some kind of context – namely the context that the world at the time was pretty much innocent about how to deal with the variety of homicidal terrorist groups that were starting to spring up around the world – I remember casually strolling with Tug past our ops room one clear, slightly chilly early evening in September 1972. The peacefulness was suddenly broken by Kev, who came sprinting out of our cabin shouting and waving.

'Sy, Sy, Tug, come quick, come and see what's on TV, it's unbelievable … Come on, come on quick.'

Tug and I dashed into our cabin to find Dave, Kev and Colin glued to the TV set. On the news, we could identify the Olympic village in Munich. The 1972 summer Olympics had started a few of days earlier, but now it looked as if the whole place was swarming with German police, buzzing around like angry bees whose nest had been kicked.

'There's been a terrorist attack at the Olympics,' Kev exclaimed. 'Some guys are holding hostages in that building. They've been wandering about and negotiating for most of the day. The reports at the moment are that some shots have been heard and they think someone's been killed.'

We soon learned that a squad of Palestinian terrorists, calling themselves 'Black September', had burst into the rooms of the Israeli Olympics team. As far as anyone knew, two Israeli athletes had already been shot. The siege had been going on since dawn, but we had been 'off duty' and asleep for most of the day so it was the first we had heard of it. As we were just starting as 'standby' section at the time, we spent most of the night watching as updated reports come through.

By 7 pm UK time a bus turned up, then a couple of hours later the terrorists came out of the building surrounded by the Israeli athletes, using them as shields from police snipers. They slowly boarded the vehicle and set off. Initially nobody knew what was happening and it wasn't until later the next day that the full story began to unfold.

As it turned out, the attempted rescue plan by the German police seemed to have been a total bag of nails. The bus that arrived the night before took the terrorists and nine athletes to a nearby makeshift landing area, where they were picked up by two helicopters at about 10.30 pm. They were flown a short distance to an air-strip, where a waiting plane was on standby to take them all away.

It was then, however, that a fierce gun battle broke out during which all nine hostages, together with five captors and a policeman, were killed. Three of the Arabs were captured. Two other hostages, as we knew, had been killed in the village accommodation block earlier the day before they all came out.

It soon became clear that the German police were totally unprepared for any kind of terrorist attack and the whole episode was indeed a shambles. Firstly, police snipers positioned around the siege building were untrained, dressed in track suits and many had little experience with weapons or tactics. Secondly, the same thing happened at the airstrip: the police snipers had precious little weapons or field-craft experience, had the wrong weapons and were badly positioned to take on the terrorists. Three or four of them were on top of the airport control tower and two or three others were positioned or lying prone in the grass by the landing strip ... in direct line of fire from their colleagues when the shooting started! Thirdly, the helicopter pilots landed in the wrong place, contrary to their instructions, which made the police snipers nervous and confused.

Days after the siege, Kev was still grumbling about it in frustration, saying things like, 'They should have called us over to Munich, we could have sorted those bastards out, no problem.' Or, 'We could have shown those Kraut cops how it should be done.'

I actually think it was probably true. We could have done a lot better, even just as consultants. But my thoughts at the time were, 'Yes Kev, I'm sure you could easily have sorted them all out ... all on your own.' Kev was great, a really tough, hard guy. Nothing was too much for him or stressed him out, and he didn't take any crap from anyone ... except me. I was the only one that could say anything to him where he would laugh it off. Martin Riggs (Mel Gibson in *Lethal Weapon*) was a pussy compared to Kev, who was nonetheless a very good friend and totally trustworthy in any situation. We were all very close and knew we could always rely on each other, out on the streets.

I recount this little piece of terrorist history to explain that governments and their security forces were just not geared-up for the kinds of situations that we have now sadly become familiar with. Kev's bravado was characteristic, but there was truth in it. We were not supermen, but we had the training and methods to deal with terrorists, honed in the perfect theatre of early 1970s Ulster. We were probably the first such counter-terrorist unit to exist anywhere in the world, except perhaps Israel.

Of the three captured terrorists, two were later released following their colleagues' demands after a Lufthansa plane was hijacked in

Beirut. Mossad eventually tracked them down and killed them both. The only good memories that I have of the Munich Olympics are of seeing Mark Spitz win seven gold medals in the swimming events.

It was a period when the Baader-Meinhof Group (or Red Army Faction as they called themselves) was highly active in Germany and initially we all thought it was them at the Olympics. Baader-Meinhof was formed soon after convicted arsonist Andreas Baader, helped by a friend, Ulrike Meinhof, escaped from prison while visiting its library in June 1970. Together with a group of followers, they were very active around German from 1970-77 after being trained by the PLO. Eventually the main players were captured, tried and imprisoned for a variety of crimes including murder and attempted murder. Ulrike Meinhof hung herself in prison in 1976 and Andreas Baader shot himself in his cell in 1977, using a smuggled pistol.

Terrorism seemed to us to be rife in the late 1960s and early '70s, but we all felt it would come to end sooner or later. How wrong could we have been? Today, the media is full of stories about the Taliban and Al Qaeda, and the western world is on the edge of its seat, just waiting for the next big, big attack.

Personally, I don't think we'll see many more major attacks on airplanes for quite a while, though we'll perhaps have some scares. Generally speaking, terrorists normally go for 'soft' targets, those that have maximum media impact and the best chance of success, and they strike when we least expect it. Airports and airplanes are not so much soft targets any more as the western security levels are quite high.

In my opinion, if I was a terrorist, I would be looking at railway stations, cruise ships and ports, which are much softer right now – actually, any place where there are large groups of people gathered together, like subways, nightclubs, sports stadiums or pop concerts … places I avoid whenever possible.

I was recently in the UK, and I noticed when boarding the ferry at Calais that the security was rubbish. Passport control were busy chatting amongst themselves as I drove past. Also, no one bothered to check my boarding ticket. At Dover, there was no one around checking vehicles as I drove through, except for a sign saying: 'Slow down and stop if requested'. I could quite easily have driven a bomb onto the ferry in Calais, parked it and simply walked off again.

4

Covert Whispers

One of my first major operations was to provide close personal protection (CPP or CP) to Willie Whitelaw, then Secretary of State for Northern Ireland, who was to visit Belfast. He had a couple of his own Special Branch people with him, but we planned to put up an outer protective ring and we insisted that the SB boys were not armed while we were on the ground with them. We didn't want them taking us for terrorists if something happened and ending up with a 'blue-on-blue' situation. Mike would not have been impressed and neither would the rest of us.

During our earlier briefing, we decided to have four of us in the protective ring while the other half of the section stayed mobile in cars, close by and acting as backup for us in case we found we had a big problem on our hands. With my press pass and cameras hanging around my neck I took on the role of a photographer. Two others, Dave and John, were acting as part of a TV camera crew: they had headphones and a mic. boom – the lot. John was carrying the recording unit but it was an empty case where he kept his 9 millie, just in case he needed it quickly. They looked quite impressively authentic from where I stood. One other, Kev, planned just to mingle with the crowd. He was a big guy but when he shrugged his shoulders, hands in his pockets, he usually blended in really well with the other people around him and didn't look at all out of place.

After we had finished our briefing and pots of tea, we piled into the ops room armoury to pick up our weapons and the equipment that we would need. Kev gave me my 9 millie and a box of rounds. I took the weapon from him, checked and cleared it and began to fill my magazines. Normally it takes about eight to ten seconds to fill a magazine with 12 rounds. The best and fastest way is to place the base of the magazine on your knee or the top of your thigh, in the cup of your left hand with the forward edge towards you. With your right hand full of rounds, you then feed them in by pressing them down and back one-by-one, guiding the bullets with your left and right thumb.

From there we made our way out to the cars, and as we walked along the narrow path Mike said, 'OK, today we're in cars Delta, Echo, Alpha and Golf.'

Dave, John, Kev and me – the four of us in the CP team – split up so we were one in each car, the idea being that when we arrived at the location we could easily and quietly filter out and move unnoticed into position, ready for the arrival of Mr Whitelaw.

Once in position and after carrying out our checks, we would all remain in radio contact with each other and the cars, and we also kept each other in visual contact at all times. Prior to and during Mr Whitelaw's visit I wasn't taking many photos and the other two weren't making a movie. We were all very busy covertly observing everyone else in the area for any tell-tale hints of aggressive behaviour. Often there are signs if someone is up to no good: the hands, the posture, the face and eyes will almost always give someone away if they are planning or even spontaneously thinking of launching an attack.

We were observing everyone around us, closing in on any suspects, visually checking them over, staying close for a while and then moving away again. Our plan was to home in on any suspect and to intervene the moment he (or she) tried anything. As it was, the operation only lasted a few hours and all went well, without any problems. Mr Whitelaw had his little walk-about, chatted to a few people and eventually left the area with his SB boys and a uniformed escort that was waiting in the background. The idea had been to allow him to freely mix with the crowds without any uniformed forces being near him.

Later we withdrew individually and moved off to link up with our other half of the team in the vehicles, then headed off back to base. Once there we all piled back into the briefing room, filled our mugs with tea and got stuck into the sandwiches as we made out our reports of the day's activities. I had taken a couple of photos of some suspicious characters I spotted in the crowd, so I handed my film to the Int. boys to develop.

Just as in training, you need to have your wits about you on a CP job. You need to be watching *everything* – the subject, your team members and any aggressive actions or movements in the crowd. It is not an easy job and the boys that do this kind of work commercially deserve every penny they make, for errors can easily cost lives.

We received a call from an Army unit in the city: it was to be another CP operation, this time involving an Army major meeting an IRA informer he had made contact with on a previous occasion through his own Int. section. The meeting was to be in a bar near his unit's location and he had requested some form of plain clothes protection for a couple of hours during the meeting where he was to be in plain clothes, too. We didn't really like the plan or the location, off Crumlin Road, but we decided to go along with it. It's always dodgy and can be quite dangerous covering meetings in confined places in hard Republican areas. You need to be very careful and keep your wits about you constantly, as situations can be very fluid and circumstances can change very quickly.

We had our briefing with the major at about 4:30 pm the same day and we were given precise details of the location of the operation. The plan was for the major to meet his contact in the lounge bar at 9:30 pm that night. The contact was a woman about 30 years old, with bottle-blonde hair, about five feet six inches tall. We had a photograph of her and the major, and four of us planned to make our way individually to the bar before 9 pm. We were carrying our own 9 millies and only one of us had a radio. On this occasion it was Kev, Tug, Mike and me in the bar with our other half of the section mobile in three cars just a few minutes away. Mike had the radio, which he would use to call in our backup if we needed them, or call them when we had finished so we could arrange our pick-up, rendezvous (RV) with them and make our way back to base.

Mike and Tug arrived individually at about 8:45 pm while Kev and I walked in together at 9:00 pm. Mike was seated at a table in a corner of the large lounge about five metres from the door, while Tug was at another table nearer the door but on the opposite side. Mike had a drink and a newspaper he was flicking through and Tug facing him had a drink and was making some roll-ups while flicking through a magazine. Kev and I made our way directly to the bar and stood there together, chatting.

Standing there side-by-side, we must have looked like Han Solo and Chewbacca, in the famous Mos Eisley bar-room scene of *Star Wars*. Yet we didn't look suspicious because we were dressed just like any of the locals. Quite often back at base, Mike and the others used to laugh and say that Kev looked like he was my minder and it did look authentically like that when we stood together.

From our positions, we all had a good view of the lounge area and of each other. There were about five or six other drinkers in the room and also a blonde woman sitting alone at a table, dressed in jeans and an off-white blouse. She had with her a coat which was draped over the back of her chair, by the far end of the bar. We all felt that she was the woman the major had arranged to meet. In addition, Kev and I both thought she looked a little nervous and fidgety, while all the other people seemed relaxed and casual.

When the major arrived at about 9:30 pm he stopped in the doorway for a moment, looked around, saw the woman and went over to join her straight away. He looked utterly out of place in his shirt and tie, brown sports jacket and slacks – an outfit that screamed British public school and military: the elephant on the ski slope. She just about managed a brief smile as he pulled out a chair and sat down near her. He didn't bother to order a drink, which I knew was a mistake. Kev clearly thought likewise and subtly raised his eyebrow as he turned to me. However, all seemed to be going OK for quite a while: nobody in the bar paid any attention to their little meeting. Then, at about 10:15 pm, two men entered the lounge, walked past Tug and approached the bar. They positioned themselves at the other end with Kev and me between them and the major. They ordered a couple of drinks and at first they too didn't take much notice of the meeting. After a while, though, Kev and me both began to grow a little suspicious of the covert whispers they were exchanging with each other.

Kev was standing square to the bar with one hand on the countertop, the other in his pocket, and his right foot on the bottom rail. From this position he could observe them occasionally in the mirror facing him on the rear wall of the bar. I was facing Kev with my back to the two new arrivals, my left elbow resting on the bar and my left foot on the rail. But I could see them quite clearly in another mirror at the far end of the bar. I also noticed that Tug and Mike had their eyes on them and as time went by we all grew in certainty that they were discussing something to do with the major. We couldn't see if they were 'carrying' (armed) but we suspected they were, possibly with pistols.

Between 10:15 and 10:30 pm two more couples arrived for a late drink but sat well away on tables near the windows. They seemed to be involved only with themselves, and took little notice of anyone else. We all knew the signal to make our escape with the major: if Mike stood up before the end, we would all draw our 9 millies. Mike would go for the major, Tug would get up and cover the lounge-bar door – our exit – while Kev and I turned to confront the threat.

Kev was observing both the two men and Mike in the mirror, and I could clearly hear him whispering to me, 'Here we go, here we go, here we go.' I could see that Kev was preparing himself to turn on these two 'players' by withdrawing his hand slowly from his pocket. He didn't appear nervous, but I surely was. I could feel my chest tightening and my pulse pounding in my neck, because I knew exactly what was coming next and what our procedure had to be. It was absolutely essential that when Mike stood up, we all went through our planned actions. If any one of us didn't do what we were supposed to do at the right time, we would have compromised the whole operation and put the lives of our colleagues at great risk. We were all totally committed to the operation the moment we entered the bar and we were all reliant on each other for our own survival.

In my position I had Kev covered. My 9 millie was jammed in my waistband on the left side, butt-forward beneath my jacket, and my left arm still rested on the bar. The seconds hammered by: we all knew it was going to happen and we were only waiting for Mike to stand up. At last he did. Simultaneously, Tug leaped into the doorway with his pistol in both hands, panning around the area and craning his neck to check the situation outside. He indicated with the barrel of his weapon for people to stay seated.

Kev and I 'pulled,' (drew our pistols) but kept them down by our sides and spun around to face the two men. 'Keep your hands on the bar and stand still!' Kev said to them. We both aimed our 9 millies directly down along our legs and they stood there stunned for a few moments. Tug was talking to the room, telling the innocent customers that if they remained seated, looked away and didn't move that they would be OK.

At the same time, Mike had drawn his 9 millie and in a single movement took hold of the major while indicating for the woman to stay seated. Then at once he was manhandling the major out of the door. Tug had his back to them and was covering them, sweeping his gun around the room as the two quickly made their way outside.

While this was happening, Kev and I stepped back a couple of paces from the two men at the bar, who still appeared bewildered. I looked them in the eyes and asked them for documents, effectively challenging them. They could see our weapons pointing down. We gave them a few moments to show us something or offer an explanation of who they were, but they made no attempt to show us any ID.

Suddenly, one of them moved fast, then the other. Their hands shot to their waistlines and beneath their jackets we glimpsed the handles of pistols as they drew them out. As soon as Kev and me saw that, we knew what our procedure had to be. They didn't know who we were and we didn't know who they were, but it was now simply them or us. They had their chance.

From a range of about a one-and-a-half metres, with what sounded like a couple of short bursts of firecrackers, we managed to fire first; two rounds each into the chests of the two men and they just dropped like stones, wide-eyed and guns in hand. After I checked them and picked up their two pistols, we immediately backed away to the door, covering each other left and right as we made our way there. After the loud, startling crack of the shots and the instant confusion of the action the customers remained seated, looking shocked and confused. None of them moved, fortunately. In a split second Kev and me were out of the door into the cold dark night

Our cars were waiting outside and we bundled in ourselves and the major, constantly covering each other with the aiming arc of our pistols as we did so, in case any other gunmen were outside waiting in ambush. Loaded up within seconds, we were ready to set off for our location, after the Army uniformed patrol that we had called, arrived to take over, clear up and take the witnesses away for interviews back at their base. In situations like this, after a close-quarter shooting, witnesses were always taken away to be interviewed. On specific operations such as this one the Army would normally arrive and we would hand over to them, but if we were caught in a random shooting incident, the Army would usually arrive a few minutes later.

On our return to base we had a short de-briefing, handed over the two pistols and made out our reports for the Special Investigation Branch. Then we took the major back to his HQ.

Under normal circumstances and military rules, we should have if possible, tried to detain the men and handed them over to a uniformed patrol to be arrested. But we had been confronted by two terrorist gunmen with weapons drawn and attempting to fire. We were utterly alone, with just some of our own section members nearby but leaving the building.

The two men who were shot had reached for their weapons, and drawn them with intent to kill. They could very easily have had backup themselves waiting outside for us to emerge, ready to hit us hard as soon as we stepped from the bar. We would be foolish not to plan for and expect such a situation. The two 'players' had made their own commitment. They came into that bar armed and with the full intent to kill. They also assumed that the worst that could perhaps happen to them was an arrest. Unfortunately for them they met the MRF instead and paid the ultimate price for their murderous activities. Arresting armed terrorists in the process to attack us or anyone around us, was almost never an option for us and when we came across them in situations as this, we hit them extremely hard.

This was how we had been trained to operate. If we came across armed terrorists actively in the process of launching an attack, we took the initiative straight away. We had to be overtly aggressive in our approach when we needed to be, simply to survive. We were far too small a group for any other options. In this instance, the other people in the bar that night were totally stunned, frozen in their seats and without a clue as to what was going on. They might have been wondering who kidnapped whom at gun point (which is how Mike's accosting of the major would have appeared to a bystander), or who was the man with the blonde woman, or who shot the two armed men at the bar. We ourselves could easily have been the IRA, the UVF, Israel's Mossad or even US Delta Force for all they knew. No-one had any idea who we really were and every one was completely confused about exactly what was going on. That was just the way we liked it. Only the IRA would know that they were suddenly missing two volunteers, and they would be scared. That was also the way we liked it.

On this occasion there had been tension in the air of the bar room and we knew there might have been some trouble. The situation had begun to show signs that it could quickly and easily turn nasty. For that reason we made the first move and, as it turned out, we really did have to rescue the major from the clutches of an IRA hit squad. He had walked into a trap and got our unit involved but we all got out of it in one piece. After that episode we made sure that all informers were vetted much more thoroughly prior to those sorts of contact.

There were other instances when one or two senior Army officers manipulated and arranged things so they could go out and get involved in some form of plain-clothes operation – in other words, play at being James Bond. This was how the nickname 'Secret Squirrel' evolved, and sometimes these officers got a little bit out of their depth. One time, we were called in for a briefing to an Army location over by the Turf Lodge district of West Belfast, which most troops used to call 'Indian Country', together with the rest of the Falls area. On this occasion an Army officer from the local unit wanted to meet a member of the press.

After the meeting Mike reasonably asked, 'Why not get this press person to come into the base? These people often call in to military locations for one reason or another.'

'The person concerned couldn't possibly call in to see me as she is well known around the area and it would cause suspicion if she was seen coming here,' the officer, who was another major, quickly insisted.

So, after a bit of discussion we agreed to cover his meeting for him, which was to be another bar off the Whiterock Road. This time, however, it was to be in her car, in the car park of the pub.

It was a little misty and chilly that evening but fortunately we didn't have any rain. It was 5:00 pm by the time we had finished our briefing, so we all drifted off to the canteen for a bite to eat and a pot of tea, and to discuss our plans for that night. There were a few other troops around in the canteen so we sat alone in the corner of the room away from everyone else.

'I just heard a couple of those guys over there talking about us,' Tug said with a smile, when he sat down. 'They were asking each other who we were, and one of them said we must be some of those "Kitson's Kids" or Squirrels.'

We finished our 'snap' (food) and tea, and finalised our details before setting off to the pub car park to get ourselves into position before the major arrived. His meeting was set for 8:30 pm and five of us were staked out around the car park in cars and on foot by 7:30 pm. I was alone in car 'Charlie' while Mike arrived a few minutes later with the major in car 'Delta'. We mingled our cars in with other vehicles around one side of the car park, but in a position where we could drive out easily enough if we had to. John, Bob, Dave and Ben were in 'Foxtrot', parked a few minutes away as backup if we needed them. Kev, Tug and Colin had quietly entered the area on foot and were positioned amongst the other cars in the shadows around the outer perimeter. No sooner had we taken up our positions than two other cars slowly pulled in, turning off their lights before they halted. The occupants just sat in their seats, waiting in the darkness.

Immediately, the radios crackled into life. Mike was on the air with the words, 'Stand by, stand by.' We could make out that there was one man in each car and that they were just sitting doing nothing, but we couldn't see any weapons at this time.

Everyone had a radio but Mike was the only one supposed to break radio silence prior to any 'contact' and it surely looked as if we were about to have one. I noticed through the haze of the mist that Tug and Kev were moving back towards me, weaving slowly in and out of parked cars, crouching behind others briefly as they went. Although well out of view of the 'players', they had decided to work their way nearer to me because they knew that otherwise they would be caught on the far side of the car park, in the line of fire, if any shooting started. Colin was OK in his position, kneeling behind a black car a few metres off to my right side, so he had no need to move. We all knew that the signal to open fire would be Mike opening his car door and stepping out of the vehicle, after positively identifying armed gunmen in the process to attack. Kev and Colin had unsuppressed SMGs and they were set in good firing positions. The rest of us had our 9 millies in our hands and were ready to go.

Just after Tug and Kev had taken up new positions around our side, both of the unknown men got out of their cars at once. They stood by their open doors for a few moments discussing something in voices too low for us to hear, and then went around the rear of one car and opened the boot.

Soon the car boot slammed shut and the two men moved round to position themselves between their two cars, which were parked side by side a couple of metres apart. There they crouched and huddled close together. I definitely saw them carrying two long weapons which I thought were a couple of Thompson submachine guns (known in the 1930s as Chicago pianos) or perhaps M2s. They were in a crouched stance with weapons at the 'ready' preparing to fire, between the cars and we had a very clear field of view and fire, about eight to ten metres across the open central area of the car park. I knew Mike was about to open his door and start to get out at any moment. We had all been working together so closely for so long that by now we could read each other's thoughts.

The familiar sensations arrived: my chest started to feel tight and I noticed my breathing was getting shorter and fiercer. I was low in my seat in car 'Charlie' but I could see Kev in the aim, and also Colin ready to fire. I wasn't able to see Tug but I knew he was aiming too. I could also clearly see, like the rest of our team that these two gunmen were in the aim and preparing to fire at someone. Perhaps they were waiting for our meeting to start or maybe for someone in the bar to come out. I glanced a little to my right and saw Mike's door start to open. He with the rest of us had clearly identified armed gunmen aiming and waiting to launch their attack. Then the whole place burst into what was like an 'in-your-face' fireworks display. The two SMGs were laying down some hellish firepower on those two gunmen. The shooting had started before Mike managed to put his foot on the ground and I was out of my car and firing before Mike was. Within ten to 12 seconds it was all over. Both SMGs had fired about 8 to 10 rounds each in short automatic bursts of three to four rounds at a time. I had fired two rounds and Tug fired about six. Mike only managed to get off a couple of rounds I think, but he didn't mind: the operation had gone off like clockwork and he was happy enough with that. I don't think the two gunmen managed to discharge a single round between them; it had all happened so quickly they never even had a chance to turn around and run. They had been transfixed by bullets where they stood and now where they lay: for them the lights had simply gone out.

Our backup car, 'Foxtrot', arrived within seconds and the guys took up positions around the car park in all-round defence to cordon off the area while we checked the victims, removed any weapons and reorganised ourselves. The major, still in Mike's car, didn't have much to say for himself and looked a little shaken up. His lady 'press' friend arrived in her car a few moments later as we were packing up to leave, and just before the Army unit we had called earlier to take over the situation from us and to clear up.

The feeling I got from the major as we dropped him off at his location was that he would prefer in future to stick to uniformed duties.

'Everything happened so quickly, it was over before I could catch my breath,' he repeated.

'It had to be that way,' Mike said quietly. 'We had to overwhelm them right from the start. They were ready and aiming and waiting for their unsuspecting victim to appear. To try and give some warning or challenge would put our lives in danger. Also, just firing a couple of rounds to frighten them isn't always enough. It's quite possible that an average gunman can be hit with a couple of 9 millies and still carry on firing for a few moments before going down. They had to be overwhelmed immediately, stopped in their tracks without allowing anyone a moment to fire back at us or anyone else around us. We also had to deny them the opportunity or time to detonate any bomb they might have placed nearby.

We zoomed off back to our base to hand in our weapons and again fill out our reports for the SIB over a pot of tea. Later we signed our section 'off duty' and settled down for the rest of the evening to watch a new-ish cop film that Tug had told us was great. After that I had a beer at the NAAFI before a long hot shower and bed, curled up in my little Army-style bunk. I laid awake there for about half an hour in the dark, thinking and talking to the others about that night's operation and the players involved. Then I slept soundly till 8:00 am. Next morning Kev, Tug, Colin and me got ourselves ready for our standby duty which began at 9:00 am and then spent our time checking some equipment until lunch.

None of us in the section was ever greedy to be in the action. It didn't matter to us if we were selected as backup for other members in our team. We were always in radio contact, so we were all involved to some extent. We didn't care which of us did the shooting, we just wanted the operations to go well and for none of our guys to get hurt. Being in the backup team was always just as important because everything could easily change at a moment's notice and we'd find ourselves in the thick of it anyway. We were all elated when ops went off OK, regardless of who did the shooting, and usually returned to base in amazing high spirits – probably part of the 'coming down' process after the adrenalin rush.

We undertook quite a few operations such as those involving the two majors, but most of the time they went off without any hitches or incidents. I retell here those that show what we were trained for and had to do when necessary. Our unit was far too small to attempt to make arrests, take prisoners or engage in any long term fire fight. The best we could do in situations such as this, was simply to hit extremely hard when it was required. We obviously challenged them or issue warnings if the circumstances allowed for that.

5

Blue on Blue

We undertook many operations where we had to follow a subject or a target in order to gather information on known or suspected members of the IRA. These usually involved tracking people through very hard areas like the Ardoyne, Falls Road and Andersonstown – which is a large council housing estate on the western side of Belfast. We made notes and tried, whenever possible, to take covert photographs of the places they visited and the people they met.

On foot surveillance, our team consisted of six to eight men, armed and in radio contact with each other. For mobile (vehicle) operations we used four or five cars. The procedure on both types of surveillance was constantly to change the lead position so as not to be compromised or noticed by the target. Team members driving at the rear or to the sides would be spread out, sometimes several hundreds of metres distant from the lead man, depending on the area and often the weather. At other times, we'd all be within fifty metres of the leader, which again depended on the situation, the area we were in and the weather conditions at the time. The rear members of the surveillance team would all be conducting a counter-surveillance operation to ensure that their lead elements were themselves not being followed or pursued.

One calm, sunny September Sunday afternoon, we had tagged and were now shadowing a suspicious vehicle around the city centre. During this time Tug had been talking about the recent dockers' industrial action on the UK main land: 42,000 of them had been on an all-out strike in the attempt to safeguard jobs.

Kev just said in his dry way, 'There's always someone on strike and I'm fed up with it all. They should send them out here to give us a hand.'

The streets at the time were quite busy and we had to stay close to stay with our target. He wasn't doing very much, just casually cruising around the general area of central Belfast. However, after 'calling it in', the V-check that came back on the radio revealed the vehicle to be a 'positive' – a stolen car. Suddenly, after 20 minutes tracking him in and out of traffic through the streets, he twigged us following him and tried desperately to accelerate away, jumping red lights and dodging around the traffic in a vain attempt to shake us off. After a few hundred metres of flying around, turning up and down side streets, we ended up chasing him full-on around Belfast City Hall square. He was jumping the lights at every corner while two of our cars raced after him 'on the pavement' with pedestrians screaming and diving for cover all over the place. We managed to weave about, avoiding the civilians during the chase, and eventually cornered the suspect, stopping him in a back-street.

Four of us surrounded his car while our two SMG men, Kev and Colin, covered us as we made our approach, pistols drawn. John and Tug wrenched his door open and dragged him out, forced him to the ground and searched him. Dave and me searched his car and found a variety of weapons and ammunition in the boot, plus some interesting maps in the glove box. In every circumstance like this, with a large 'find', we always called in some uniformed forces to make the arrest and take over the situation. We never arrested anyone; we just held them until some uniforms arrived. We didn't want to have to make a court appearance which would complicate things and compromise us.

Whilst out patrolling with Kev and John one drizzly evening a few weeks later, we picked-up on a stolen van at around 11:00 pm. We had spent most of the earlier part of the evening patrolling around Turf

Lodge, Divis and Shore Road. However, after noticing and following the van for a while, waiting for the right opportunity and place, we stopped it on Waring Street, a quiet area just off the city centre near Victoria Street. As it happened, a local Army patrol was in the vicinity and thought we were a terrorist group hijacking the van. We almost had a problem of a 'blue-on-blue' situation – a disastrous occurrence involving opening fire on your own side. We had just overtaken the van, pulled it in and stopped it. Covered again by our two SMG men, we were in the process of dragging the occupants out to check and search them, when I noticed someone in Army uniform by a street corner about a hundred metres away.

Fortunately for us, the young member of the patrol who watched me motionless as I pointed my pistol in the van driver's face and dragged him to the floor, then held him face down with my knee in his back, decided to look the other way and disappeared round the corner. He probably felt that the situation was perhaps a little too hairy for him to deal with. We were very fortunate that night: things could have turned really bad for us. If he had opened fire on us, all we could have done was run for it – obviously we could have never fired back. Blue-on-blue situations were forever in the back of our minds and we were always very careful when and where we drew our weapons. And we never drew them if we didn't intend to use them. Whenever we were on a specific operation in their area we always informed the local Army unit responsible. But if we were out and about on general surveillance we simply couldn't, because we covered and patrolled many areas of the city during our 'duty' period.

On this occasion we held the two van occupants until a uniformed patrol which we had called, arrived. This time it was a RUC (Royal Ulster Constabulary) patrol that turned up and took over the situation, leaving us once again to disappear into the night.

Earlier that summer of 1972 there was a period during which for a few days we didn't have any specific operations. Instead, I was on a general patrol with Kev around the central area of Belfast. It was July

21 and the weather was quite fine with light, high-level cloud. Kev was driving, with me next to him. We had been up looking around the Turf Lodge and Andersonstown area. It was drawing near lunch time and we were thinking of going over to the south side of the city to have a look around the Markets area and perhaps grab a sandwich on the way.

Suddenly we felt the whole city shake under us: an enormous bomb had just exploded, we couldn't see where but it was obviously close by. We carried on driving for a few minutes, trying to see where it was. Then another concussion rocked the car but still we couldn't see where either the first or second blast originated. Then another blast came, and another, and we began to see smoke billowing in dark grey umbrellas, towering over the roofs of buildings, as we slowly carried on. Then, gradually, the whole city came to a standstill as everyone stopped their vehicles, far too afraid to carry on in case they drove slap into the next explosion. All we could do was to stop, too, hemmed in by stalled cars and trucks and buses; we were trapped with everyone else. We couldn't move forwards or backwards in the gridlock, so we both hunkered down low in the seats and foot-wells of our car, taking cover and waiting. I sent a Sit Rep (situation report) back to base on the radio, warning the other members of our section what was going on around the central area of Belfast.

During that hour-and-a-half of mayhem and destruction during which 22 bombs went off all around us, we sat there huddled down in the middle of the street. Nine people died that day and 130 were seriously injured, many around the Markets area where we were origi-nally heading, and the city was crippled. This day was quickly named 'Bloody Friday' and was intended as retaliation for the chaotic con-frontation of 'Bloody Sunday' in Londonderry some six months earlier.

In the weeks leading up to this bombing spree, specifically on Monday 26 June, the IRA had called a bilateral truce as a prelude to secret talks with the British Government. The SDLP had made such a ceasefire possible when John Hume and Paddy Devlin held a meeting with members of the IRA in Londonderry on 14 June. At this meeting the IRA laid out their conditions for talks with the British Government, which included no restrictions on who represented the IRA; an independent witness at all meetings; no meetings to be held at Stormont; and political status to be granted to republican prisoners.

In London the next day, 15 June, the SDLP met with William Whitelaw, the Secretary of State for Northern Ireland, to present the IRA's conditions. Whitelaw accepted them and on 22 June the proposed ceasefire plan was announced.

Gerry Adams, who had been released from prison for the purpose, was part of the delegation that travelled to London for the talks with Edward Heath's Conservative government, on 7 July. However, the talks broke down, as did the IRA's ceasefire, after disputes over the allocation of housing in the Suffolk area of Belfast, together with IRA-British Army gun battles in Horn Drive. The 'Bloody Friday' bombings were part of an attempt by the IRA to bring ordinary life in the city to an end.

The first bomb exploded at **2:09 pm** on a footbridge over the Belfast railway line at Windsor Park, with no injuries. At **2:36 pm** a suitcase bomb exploded at the Brookvale Hotel, north Belfast. The area had been cleared and there were no injuries. More bomb warnings were being received by the police and Army every few minutes, some of them hoaxes. At **2:40 pm** a car bomb went off at a branch of the Ulster Bank in Limestone Road, just a few hundred metres from the first bomb. This area had not been cleared in time and many motorists were caught up in jammed traffic and injured in this blast, together with a local Catholic woman who lost both legs. At **2:52 pm** another car bomb exploded outside the railway station at Botanic Avenue but there were no serious injuries, and there were also none at **2:53 pm** when a car bomb containing 160 pounds of explosives detonated without warning on the Queen Elizabeth Bridge, badly damaging it. At **3:02 pm** a smaller car bomb exploded without warning in Agnes Street, again without serious casualties, and at the same time a device went off in the Liverpool Bar at Donegall Quay with the same result. Again at **3:02 pm** a 30-pound bomb exploded on a bridge over the M2 at Bellevue, north Belfast, and there were no serious injuries. A minute later, at **3:03 pm**, another suitcase bomb exploded at York Street Station before the station could be cleared and this time there were many horrific casualties. One minute after that, at **3:04 pm**, a large car bomb exploded in Ormeau Avenue without warning but there were no serious injuries. At **3:05 pm** another large car bomb of approximately 150 pounds of explosive detonated at Eastwood's Garage, Donegall Road, but with few casualties. Then, at **3:10 pm**, a very large car bomb in a VW exploded close by the Ulsterbus depot in Oxford Street. This explosion caused the greatest loss of life and most numerous mutilations of all. The area was being cleared but remained crowded when the device went off. Two British soldiers standing near the car were almost evaporated in the blast. Five minutes after that, at **3:15 pm**, an apparently abandoned bomb in Stewartstown Road exploded but caused few casualties. At **3:20 pm** a car bomb exploded next to some shops in Cavehill Road before the street could be cleared, killing three people and seriously injuring many others. After another five minutes, at **3:25 pm**, a device exploded on the railway line near Lisburn Road with no injuries. Simultaneously, two more bombs went off at the Star Garage on the Crumlin Road, but there were no serious injuries. At **3.30pm** a landmine was detonated on the road near Nutts Corner, West Belfast, narrowly missing a school bus which was passing at the time and was thought to have been mistaken for an Army vehicle. There were no serious casualties amongst the children. Also at **3.30pm** another bomb exploded at the NI Carriers depot on the Grosvenor Road but with few casualties, and at the same time a bomb on the Sydenham flyover was defused by the Army. There were two other bombs at Garmoyle Street and in Salisbury Avenue with few casualties, but I'm not so sure of the exact times of these explosions.

In the shocked aftermath of the devastating blitz, Kev and I managed to get the car moving again and we drove around the areas of the blasts to see if we could help in any way. But there was little we could do so we made our way back to base through the rubble of the destruction. We made out a report of the events that afternoon before going 'off duty' and grabbing a few hours' sleep.

Some days later I was casually listening to some tapes in our cabin with Tug. He had received them from his brother on the mainland a day or so earlier. Tug was dead keen on the Eagles and I was sat on my bed reading a motor magazine whilst he was freaking out, playing an imaginary 'air' guitar to 'Take it Easy' and 'Witchy Woman'. Colin and Kev were on the other beds reading, while they ignored him leaping around the room, twanging at strings that didn't exist.

Suddenly Mike appeared in the doorway and made an announcement. 'Everyone listen in a minute, we have a job. We all need to be in Lisburn HQ tomorrow by 10:00 am, so I want you all ready to go by 8.30,' he said. 'I'll give you more details before we set off in the morning."

The next morning, after a chat in the briefing room and having drawn our weapons and radios, we set off for a meeting with the GOCNI (General Officer Commanding Northern Ireland), apparently to discuss some problems a particular Belfast Hotel was having. The 240-room establishment off the city centre had only opened the year or so before; it was luxurious and modern, and consequently some of the Press covering the Troubles stayed in it. However, there had been various attempts to blow the place up over the past few months, and on one occasion a female terrorist posing as a mother-to-be had entered the hotel, gone to the ladies' toilets and placed in position the bomb she had under her maternity dress. She quickly disappeared and the toilet's outer wall was blown away, scattering debris over the adjacent car park, luckily with no injuries.

On arrival at Lisburn HQ we checked in with the gate guard like we had many times before, parked our cars out of sight from prying eyes and cleared our weapons. We kept our 9 millies on us but left our SMGs hidden in the boot of one of the cars. We all then made our way to the canteen for a coffee, as we were a little early for our meeting with the GOC. Over our coffees, Tug and John were cracking jokes as usual while Mike read some papers he had with him. Kev was playing around with his flick knife while chatting to Colin and the rest of us.

Relaxing and minding our own business, we encountered as usual some strange looks and whispers from many of the uniformed military around us. We had no right to be surprised at this, because we all looked like shit, as if we were a bunch of scruffy builders straight off a building site. The troops in the canteens generally never really bothered us much and we often sat and chatted with them if we had the time while waiting around for something or other. It was the officers that normally tried to make problems for us.

A few moments later, a chap in uniform came over to us and said, 'OK, the GOC is free now and he will see you when you're ready.'

'Thanks, we'll be over in a moment,' Mike replied, and then set off first while we all straggled along a few moments later when we had finished our coffees and popped our cups onto the tray racks.

We left the canteen and made our way over to the main building and into a long, highly polished corridor, passing office doors to our left and right as we made our way to the far end.

We were ambling along as a loose group, chatting like we had just gone on our lunch break from some building site. Then suddenly we heard a loud frantic voice: 'Hey! Stop there! Stop, who are you people?' We all halted in our tracks and turned around to see who was making such a racket.

Kev answered first, just as loud and demanding. 'Who are you?' he shouted. Kev knew exactly who the guy was but just enjoyed stirring people up, especially people like this. I could clearly see that the person was a staff officer, a Guards captain wearing very shiny shoes and Army barracks dress trousers with an immaculately-ironed shirt – a right stickler for the proprieties for whom we were a walking insult to HM Forces and the Crown.

'What are you people doing here? Do you have any identification?' said the Guards officer.

'Sure, but you're making us late for an important meeting, and you don't need to know why we are here,' said Kev while he took out one of his fake ID cards and I flashed my sports centre ID card. A couple of other guys were fumbling and searching for whatever they had on them, which included a variety of different faked identification cards.

The officer stood there for a few moments deeply scrutinising our documents front and back, not realising for a minute that they were all counterfeit. 'OK,' he said at last, 'Now what about the rest of you? Come on, show me.' Suddenly another voice rang out from up along the corridor.

'It's OK, Richard, I can vouch for them all,' the GOC himself called, leaning out of his office door.

'In future, when you arrive here, I want you all to check in with me first before you go anywhere,' the captain said as he gave us back our bogus ID documents.

'I'm afraid we'll not … Richard,' was Kev's parting shot to the officer.

Thankfully, Mike was busy in the GOC's office during this little incident. He never liked people interfering or being nosey about us or our unit – especially uninvolved staff officers who had no right to know anything about us. If Mike had heard the goings on, he would have surely given the chap a right mouthful, far worse than Kev had.

Mike, our section commander, really was a great guy, always cheerful and friendly. As far as he was concerned, we in our section were all one family. We didn't need his physical protection as he knew we could all very well look after ourselves. But he always supported any decisions we made and really didn't like people from outside the unit interfering. He'd been around and seen plenty in the Army and done a lot of stuff during his time when he was in the SAS years before and he really wasn't the type to mess with.

We had many interesting fellows like Mike with us, such as a couple of guys in section 81 that had recently joined the unit. They had been part of the team that 'jumped' into the Atlantic earlier that year, 1000 miles out to sea, and boarded the QE2 together with some bomb disposal experts. There had been a bomb scare on board the vessel and they went out to join the ship to check it out. Luckily it all turned out to be a hoax and the FBI later caught the culprit (the movie *Juggernaut* with Richard Harris, Anthony Hopkins and Omar Sharif was based on the incident).

It was only occasionally that we had little problems with some of the uniformed military people, especially officers who felt they had a God-given right always to know who we were and what we were doing. In fact they had no right to know anything about us: they knew it and we knew it. But they were always there, trying to gather information on us, wanting to know our business. It caused quite a bit of friction at times with derogatory and condescending comments directed at us and our unit, the MRF. As far as they were concerned, if they didn't know anything about us or couldn't find out anything, then we must be crap and deserved only ridicule. We felt this attitude was born of jealousy and frustration but we couldn't really care less and found these moments of friction quite entertaining.

Anyway, at the end of our meeting with the GOC our task was clear. We were required to act as a civilian security firm brought in from London, to live in and protect this Hotel during a very sensitive period and until they reorganised their own security measures. After our briefing and further lengthy discussions, we decided that we required eight men on this operation to offer a worthwhile security network in and around the hotel. The weapons we decided to take were Walther PPKs because they were smaller than our Browning 9mm pistols and easier to conceal in a hotel environment where we would be dressed in close-fitting suits and other clothes less bulky than those we normally wore. We decided to take two submachine guns fitted with suppressors which we initially planned to use at night in our observation positions inside the hotel. We also drew six Pye handheld radios.

The next day, three of us went out early to meet the MD of the Hotel to discuss the layout and carry out a security survey of the premises. We noted and took photos of all the vulnerable points, lighting, fences, entrances and exits, together with car parking areas within 25 metres of the perimeter. Part of the survey included possible sniper positions on other buildings where an RPG 7 (Soviet handheld rocket launcher) could be fired from effectively.

The front entrance included a security barrier along the main road and a security hut with a couple of men checking people approaching the hotel at the end of the short drive. The hotel was just off from the city centre with the a car park to one side and an open area to the rear, surrounded with tall buildings and not at all easy to secure. Our operation was planned to last for almost three weeks and it was going to be a lot of work.

After we had completed our security survey at the Hotel we all gathered back at base and filed into the briefing room for a discussion on how we could carry out this operation. We laid out the plans and photos of the hotel, which showed lots of detail including the thickness of walls and floors, across the briefing-room table. Everyone gathered around and involved themselves in the discussions about how we could successfully secure the hotel from attack.

Eventually we decided to operate a two-shift system. Four men would be on duty and four off, but ready on standby in the event of a full-scale attack, and each shift would last for eight hours. We planned to move into the hotel at 6:00 am the following morning, so as not to draw attention to ourselves. We had reserved two rooms on the first floor overlooking the entrance at the front. The only person that knew we had been tasked through military channels was the managing director of the Hotel.

After we had set our plans, the rest of the afternoon was spent checking weapons and radios and packing essential clothing and suits we felt we'd need, together with Tug's ghetto-blaster and selection of his Eagles, Neil Diamond and Crosby, Stills, Nash & Young tapes. Ghetto-blasters then were very different to those of today. We didn't have cassettes or CDs. We had those large old-style bulky twin-spool tape players into which we had to hand feed the quarter-inch tape, through the tape heads, before we could play it. Tug's brother often sent tapes over to him which he had recently recorded from his new LPs.

After a very early night we got up, had coffee, drew our weapons and equipment and were ready to go by 4:30 am the next morning. The duty section took us into the city at 5:00 am in four vehicles and dropped us off at different points a few hundred metres from the Hotel. The gatemen at the end of the driveway were expecting some new security people at about 6:00 am, but they didn't know who. They were ordered not to search us but to simply let us straight in after we gave the pass word, 'Exeter'. We arranged things this way as we didn't want anyone to know who was coming and what we were carrying into the hotel.

I was dropped off with Tug near Bedford Street, by the City Hall square, and we both made our way through the side streets a few hundred metres to the Hotel. I'm not sure where the others were dropped off but it wasn't far from the hotel. We all arrived within minutes of each other in groups of two at a time and the reception lady gave us our room numbers as we walked in. The rooms we were allocated were really very nice. They had large springy beds, spacious sitting/lounge areas, TV and radios – altogether different from the Army-style metal cots in cold portacabins we were used to. I said, 'This is nice, Mike. You can leave me here when it's all over.'

He smiled. 'You should be so damn lucky, if anyone gets to stay on it'll be me.' Then he stretched out on the bed and rang room service: 'Breakfast for eight, please.'

We had two adjoining rooms with long curtains draped all the way to the floor and four single beds in each. Over breakfast in our room at 7:00 am we decided that during daylight hours two men would be sufficient patrolling in or around the reception area together with a periodic check around the outside, front and rear, for any suspicious vehicles and packages. The other two could relax for an hour or so and then change over, but be ready to move and join the others at a moment's notice.

During the night all four would be active, two around or covering the reception area and the other two patrolling the hotel, while again periodically checking the rear and north side of the hotel which was our most vulnerable side. We agreed that each subsection had to keep in regular contact with each other, either by sight or by radio checks at least every half an hour during their active period. We also decided to start operating at 10:00 am, which initially gave a reasonable mix of day and night duty between the eight of us. Mike split us up into two teams of four: Colin, John, Dave and me in one team and Mike, Bob, Tug and Ben in the other. Kev was involved in something else for a couple of weeks and not among us on this operation.

After breakfast we arranged to meet the gate security men to introduce ourselves and brief them on the procedures we wanted them to follow in the event of an approach or trouble in their direction. Their orders were to inform us by radio, or through reception if not able to speak directly to any of us, if any suspicious characters appeared to them. They were to give us a full description and state how many suspects there were, and we would handle it from there.

Our aim was to stop any threat before it arrived in the reception area – in other words outside the front entrance. If by chance any gunmen arrived in reception through the entrance we were to challenge them first but if necessary, to neutralise them in the reception area if possible without injury to anyone else, which we felt was quite feasible given the open-plan layout. We planned that if a bomber got inside the entrance, we would wait until the bomb was placed before taking on the bomber. Afterwards we'd evacuate the hotel and call ATO (bomb disposal) to disarm the device.

In the 1970s, This hotel entrance had tall revolving glass doors, with the main restaurant to the right as you stepped through them.

The reception desk itself was straight ahead and a little to the right and was usually staffed by two or three reception girls in hotel uniform. In the open-plan central area there were some large lounge chairs and glass-topped tables arranged in a circle. To the left was a door leading to the bar, which ran along the building from front to rear and could seat approximately 60 people. Half left, leading up to and through the high ceiling and the first floor, stood a very large and wide marble spiral staircase with thick dark Perspex banisters. I felt this was an excellent vantage point to observe the entire reception area, and at night the top of these stairs near the ceiling was quite dark and so was the area behind it. I was able to scan the reception area from this position for quite some time day and night, without drawing too much attention to myself, and I spent many nights observing from this position with a silenced submachine gun. With its butt folded down it slipped nicely into a large black padded tennis case I had with me. The hotel was normally quite busy during the day, mostly with people gathered in the bar or loitering and chatting in the foyer. Nevertheless I casually wandered around the hotel all day long with my SMG tucked under my arm, neatly hidden inside its sporty case, and nobody suspected a thing.

During our 'off duty' time we normally stayed in our rooms, resting, watching TV or reading. Colin had some good books with him, including *Inside the Third Reich* by Albert Speer, plus a couple of new ones from Frederick Forsyth, *The Day of the Jackal* and *The Odessa File*, just the type of books to suit the occasion – and not forgetting Tug with his ghetto-blaster. But Tug was good: he never played it too loud. I found it quite relaxing, lying in bed in the dark and drifting off to sleep listening to the Bee Gees singing 'Massachusetts', 'Words' and 'Saved by the Bell', all very popular songs at the time.

We generally took our meals in the downstairs restaurant, relieving other members of our section periodically so they could grab a bite to eat. In our rooms, we had coffee-making facilities and the chamber girls used to supply us with plenty of sandwiches and biscuits to get us through the long nights. Sometimes the girls called in to see if we needed more sandwiches and occasionally one or two would stay a while, just chatting. They knew we were English but had no idea we were Army. We'd ask them where they lived, pretending we didn't know Belfast and that we had only been in Ulster a week or so. Most of the staff in the hotel were Protestants and lived in relatively quiet areas of the city but there were one or two girls from some of the fringe Catholic parts of Belfast. They generally seemed very friendly but we were always extremely careful about what we said to them and kept our weapons and equipment out of sight when they were around.

Over the time of this Hotel assignment, which turned out to be just under three weeks long, we had one or two little incidents when the odd drunk came in, wanting to get in the bar, but nothing too serious, except for one event that could have turned nasty. Kev arrived one afternoon to drop off some extra batteries for our radios. As I said, he wasn't with us on this operation, and it turned out this was because he had some other work to cover, so we had him as our link man to the outside world. He called in sometimes for a coffee and a chat or to drop off something we needed. On this particular day we were both in the bar quietly drinking a coffee and chatting, when one of the gate security men walked up to me.

He sat down with us and raised his eyebrows in the direction of a couple of blokes on the other side of the lounge. 'Those two men sitting across by the window are armed; I frisked them and felt the weapons but said nothing and pretended I didn't feel the guns. They didn't offer any ID and I let them through.'

'Thanks,' I said. 'Leave it to us and we'll check them out.'

Both Kev and me, just like the gate man, were almost certain they were RUC detectives here for a lunchtime drink. I was a little annoyed because they knew they were required to hand in any weapons to gate security before entering the hotel, so we decided to teach them a lesson as they probably thought they were being clever – or perhaps were trying to test our security and thought that they had breached it.

I was dressed in a nice suit but Kev didn't look so tidy. He was wearing jeans and a black donkey jacket frayed around the edges; he was also unshaven and his long unwashed hair was flopping down to his shoulders.

We got up, walked over to the two men and sat down at their table. They just looked at us in total surprise. We didn't say anything but Kev took out his eight-inch flick-knife and started nonchalantly cleaning his finger nails, periodically glancing up at these two guys.

While they appeared mesmerised at what Kev was doing, I drew my Walther PPK as a precaution as we weren't absolutely sure who these two were at that time, and I laid my hand with the pistol flat on the table between their two coffee cups. The weapon's ejection chamber was facing upwards and the muzzle was aiming directly at the chest of one of the men.

Both men turned white. 'Don't make any sudden moves and slowly with your left hands show me some ID,' I said quietly. Gingerly they opened their wallets, confirming they were two detectives. 'I know you are both armed,' I said. 'Why haven't you left your weapons with security?' They tried to give us some lame, bumbling excuse, but I interrupted them. 'You know you shouldn't do it,' I said harshly. 'If any of your people come in this hotel again with weapons, they'll have a big problem. Now drink your coffee, get out and don't come back.'

Within moments they gulped down their coffees and were gone and we never saw them or any other RUC again while we were there. I left the bar and walked outside to see the gate man.

'You did the right thing in letting them through and telling us,' I told him. I think this cheered him up, because I'm sure he didn't really know what he should have done in this particular instance, and whether or not he had cocked up.

Back in the Bar, Kev said, 'They looked really scared when you pulled the Walther. They had no idea who you were.'

'It wasn't the Walther that scared them,' I grinned. 'It was that dammed machete you keep waving around at people that gave them the shits.' We had a bit of a laugh about it while we finished our coffee and then Kev set off from the hotel, vanishing into the city streets and making his way back to base.

At the end of our stay we briefed the staff, offering a little advice to everyone on tighter security arrangements, and we said good bye to the MD, who gave his thanks to us and wished us well, saying, 'Take care of yourselves.'

Then, with our weapons and equipment bagged up, we simply disappeared, melting into the city streets in a similar fashion to when we arrived. I never managed to go back there again, and for the rest of my tour in Belfast the hotel never had another serious attack, only the odd stone-thrower or ineffective petrol bomb chucked from beyond the security barriers.

6

Duck, Dash, Get Down

Early one morning after a wonderful big breakfast of sausage, egg, bacon, beans and tomatoes, we piled into the ops room. Our section, 83, was due to take over as the 'duty' section at 8:00 am. While checking in with the Int. boys and drawing our weapons from the armoury, we were informed that we had the North Howard Street Mill operation for the day. After our briefing at 8:15 am, we got our weapons and equipment together and moved off at 9:00 am to meet the Intelligence and Operations officers at the North Howard Street Mill Army location, in a side street off Falls Road.

During our briefing with the area Int. and Ops officers, we were told the details of the operation. We were to be operating with cars and our full section, together with the regular Army OP (observation post), in a derelict house on the Falls Road. This OP offered a clear view of approximately 200 metres along the main road in the direction of Andersonstown. We were also provided with details of the 'Top Ten Wanted' players in the area, which included descriptions, photos, names and addresses etc., together with a dossier of their past record of offences listing their known and suspected involvements. Each wanted person was given a title code, Alfa, Bravo, Charlie and so on.

Our job was to wait just inside the main gate of North Howard Street Mill Army base in two vehicles on immediate standby, at a moment's notice to move. We couldn't even leave our cars to go to the loo and food was brought to us while we just sat and waited, sometimes for up to seven or eight hours.

Our third vehicle a few metres behind us was on reserve/backup in case we had a major problem out on the Falls Road. Plus, an Army Land Rover patrol with four men was also on standby if required. The entrance to the location was nicely up a side street and quite secure, hidden from general view. If the troops in the OP spotted any of the 'Top Ten' listed characters, they would simply come up on the radio net, giving the title code-letter – Alfa, Bravo or whatever – and details of exactly where the suspect was, what he was wearing and what he was doing (talking with two or three friends, in a shop, etc.).

Within seconds we would mark their exact position on our street maps and then we were speeding out of the location onto the normally busy Falls Road. On reaching the position of the suspect we would completely seal off the road with both cars, creating a temporary secure zone between the two cars. The two patrol commanders were covered by the SMG-man from each vehicle as they made the snatch. The third man in each vehicle (the driver) stood by his car with pistol drawn. Their job was to hold the secure zone we were working within and keep people back.

The essence of this type of operation, like many others, was surprise, aggression and speed. We had different procedures based on whether the suspect was walking, standing in a group or inside a house or shop. After hours of practice we calculated the whole operation from leaving the Army location, making the snatch and returning in the vehicles with the suspect, to be not much more than two to three minutes. Any longer and we ran the risk of an IRA ASU (Active Service Unit) being mobilised to confront us. Also, we never attempted more than two snatches in any one day. If we did, an ASU would almost certainly be waiting for us to appear on our third outing.

During the snatches we almost never encountered any opposition from passers-by or shoppers. They were generally surprised and stunned by the events in progress and then a little afraid and shocked.

We looked as rough as any IRA unit and we had a very aggressive approach.

I often felt that people in the street thought we were just some terror group kidnapping someone – which was happening on a daily basis on all sides at that time in the city. IRA gangs were kidnapping people from the loyalist paramilitary UDA (Ulster Defence Association), and the UVF and UFF (Ulster Freedom Fighters, Ulster Volunteer Force: both protestant terror groups) were kidnapping members of the IRA. Perhaps people were thinking we were the IRA or even the UFF or UVF.

However, on this particular operation, everything and everyone was ready and waiting by about 10:30 am. We were positioned just inside the gates, close to the wall of the Army location and our third car with Ben, Bob and Colin on backup was in position about ten metres behind us. I was commander in my car with John driving and Kev in the back with his SMG – and of course his flick-knife. Mike was in front of me in the other car with Tug and Dave. All seemed fairly quiet for a long time except for the regular radio checks with the OP crew.

We were all perfectly capable of working in each other's positions in the cars, but Kev usually preferred to ride in the back with the SMG or sometimes he'd drive. John always liked to drive and they normally left me to be the Commander, working with the radio and maps. But we always discussed everything together before making any decisions or plans which we always agreed as a group.

At about 3:00 pm it happened and we received an urgent message over the air.

'Hello all stations 83. This is Oscar 1 [Army OP] – shop – numbers one, one, eight, [street number] – Foxtrot [subject's code letter] in blue jeans, black jacket. Over.'

While Mike and me plotted the target's location on our maps, Tug at the wheel acknowledged the message and we were away like a Grand Prix start. Bumper-to-bumper we roared out of the gate, turned right and then right again onto the Falls Road. We managed to get straight out onto the main road without any delay at the junction. Had there been a blockage or oncoming vehicles we would simply have forced our way out. We only had to drive about a hundred metres or more up the road to the shop.

As we approached number 118, John let Mike open up a space between us to allow for our little secure zone. At the same time I heard Kev cocking his SMG in the back seat of our car, preparing himself for when we arrived. We braked and quickly swung half right, stopping diagonally, right outside the shop, and creating a kind of chicane in the road, temporarily blocking the traffic. Mike and I jumped out with our 9 millies in our hands, followed by our back-seat SMG men, while the drivers left the engines running and took up their positions inside the zone, looking outward.

The drivers were there to cover us and to indicate for the traffic to stop while we were busy. Our SMG men took up positions on each side of the shop door, keeping people back and covering us as Mike and I went in. Mike went first with me back-to-back with him, virtually pushing him in. This way we avoided getting separated as we entered and moved through the customers, looking for our target. As we pushed our way through the crowded shop my 9 millie was panning from side to side through a 180 degree arc, indicating for everyone to stay back while I simultaneously scanned the figures surrounding us for any aggressive movements. Mike was doing the same as he searched out for our 'Foxtrot'.

I felt him stop and take hold of someone; he grabbed hold of our 'Foxtrot' around the neck to prevent him resisting, showing him we meant business, while I continued to ensure that everyone else in the shop stayed well back. Then we reversed direction and began making our way back out to the street with me leading and Mike pushing me with his back. At the same time he was pulling 'Foxtrot' backwards with one arm round his neck, holding the target close and keeping him off balance while prodding his 9 millie in the guy's ribs in between panning the barrel around the shop.

One or two women screamed initially but everyone backed off from us. I've never known anyone (that was sober) come forward onto me while I was waving a 9 millie under their nose: they could probably see that I intended to use it given a reason.

Outside, as we were about to force our 'Foxtrot' down onto the floor in the back of Mike's car, we noticed that he was the wrong man. He looked similar but he wasn't our target. Mike instantly let the man go and told him to move on. This man was initially a clear and present threat to all in our section and Mike told his driver to watch him while we returned for our real Foxtrot. He turned to John:

'John, keep an eye on him until he moves on,' said Mike as he raised his hand, indicating for me to go back inside with him.

We both ran back into the shop, same procedure, followed again to the doorway by our SMG men, and eventually found our real 'Foxtrot' hiding behind a large lady near the far end of the shop. He was only a young guy, about 20 years old, slim and not very tall. Mike reached for him and with the same procedure he grabbed him, pulling him close like before.

On our way out to the cars I noticed a couple of old ladies on the verge of passing out and I couldn't blame them, really. I thought that if it had been my mum in that shop and all this happened to her twice in a few minutes, she would have had a dicky-fit. But there again, on second thoughts, my mum would have probably laid into us with her handbag, tough old lady that she was.

She had had a traumatic time in Europe during World War Two, spending a few years in a north German concentration camp when she was very young, narrowly surviving. She escaped after the Americans bombed it, mistakenly believing it to be a German Army camp. She met my father in Austria at the end of the war, and they got married and came to England when he was demobbed in 1947.

After a quick frisk, we piled our 'Foxtrot' onto the floor in the back of Mike's car as Dave, his SMG man, jumped in on top of him, trampling him face-down and binding his hands with some plastic ties we used for hand cuffs. Pressing his foot hard on 'Foxtrot's' neck, Dave slipped a bag over his head and held 'Foxtrot' firmly down with his feet, almost standing crouched on top of him while he roughly searched him again for any weapons he might have had hidden. Kev and I jumped into our car, and with John at the wheel we reversed up a little, spun hard right and sped off back to North Howard Street Mill, followed closely by Mike in his car with Tug, Dave and the prostrate 'Foxtrot'.

Back at the Mill, we quickly handed over our hooded and bound suspect to the uniformed troops there waiting to arrest him. Within moments of our arrival, he had been frog-marched away for questioning.

This time, our operation had taken almost five minutes before we were on our way back to our base location and we were lucky we didn't find ourselves in a re-make of *The Gunfight at OK Corral*. On other occasions we did get into confrontations, and we sometimes had to shoot our way out.

A few weeks later, we were back at North Howard Street Mill to carry out this same operation again, same format, same plan and same crews – but different target. We had been sitting there for about four hours when the radio burst into action.

'Hello all stations 83. This is Oscar 1 – house – numbers one, three, niner, – Charlie, in blue jeans and green jumper. Over.'

Again the front vehicle driver acknowledged the message while Mike and I plotted the target on our maps, and we were off. But this time – because a house will have back-door access – our backup third car drove with us to cover the rear street. Meanwhile the Army Land Rover patrol listening in to us on the radio moved up to immediate standby position.

As before, with the same crews in each car, Mike and I opened up a little and then swung our cars to a halt in the half-right position, jumped out with our SMG men and burst in through the front door of the house. However, at the same time, our 'Charlie' and another man were running out the back.

By the time Mike and I made our way through the building, checking and clearing the downstairs rooms while backed up by one of our SMG men on the landing, we reached the kitchen and back door. The target and his accomplice by this time were in the back street and one of them opened fire at us with three shots from a pistol as we emerged into the back yard. Luckily the rounds struck the wall to our left as we ducked and split up, taking cover in the back yard area. Mike and I quickly took up positions against the back yard wall either side of the gate. Then, almost at the same moment, we heard more shots – but they were not from us or from the enemy.

Colin with his crew had appeared in the back street. They had parked and got out of their car and Colin, with his SMG-man Dave, had crept along the street to cover the rear exit of the house. On seeing the two men run out of the house firing, Colin fired one shot into the chest of the gunman from a range of about ten metres just as the man was about to fire more shots at us in the yard. Then with a second shot, Colin fired at the other man who was also armed, whom he recognised as our 'Charlie', as he turned to run. The target was hit in the right buttock and both men tumbled to the floor.

Colin had intentionally aimed low at our 'Charlie' because, as always, the target was required for interrogation by our friends in uniform. Within moments, as arranged, our backup uniformed patrol arrived to take over from us and take control of the situation – one man dead and another seriously injured.

Both rounds that Colin had fired from his own personal .357 Magnum were armour-piercing and had passed right through each man. The rounds were so powerful that Colin knew very well how one for each man would be enough to stop them dead in their tracks at that short range. I'd seen a .357 Magnum armour-piercing round stop a car in the past. Aimed at the rear, the bullet passed right through the boot, then through the passenger compartment and cracked the engine block.

Before we left the area, Mike had a chat with us all and we packed up our equipment after we went back in the house for a quick check around for any other players who could be in there. Later we heard that a follow-up search on the house had produced quite a haul of weapons, including some ammunition, which made us feel quite pleased that the day had turned out so fruitful.

After the end of an operational day, we'd usually finish back at the North Howard Street Mill location and get some snap and tea before going into a debriefing. There, we'd discuss everything with the local Int. boys, then write our reports of the day's activities for the local unit and perhaps SIB before making our way back to our base. Sometimes we picked up fish and chips on the way home, after radioing in, to take supper orders from anyone present in our ops room.

Back at base, we'd clean and hand in our weapons and radio equipment, have a chat with the Boss and settle down in front of the TV or perhaps take a long hot shower, before a welcome night's sleep. The next morning we spent an hour or so getting our gear ready again for our next stint on 'standby', followed 12 hours later by our 'on duty' period again. For me, this routine went on day-in, day-out for almost three years.

Like all the others, I felt fear when the shooting started but I was never so afraid that I lost control of what I was doing. Your training kicks in and you do the very best you can at the time, firing aimed shots and supporting each other with fire and movement, using whatever cover is available.

If somebody didn't feel the fear, it would mean he was simply crazy and we wouldn't have wanted anyone like that with us. For me, it was only later, after a contact, that I used to suffer a little. Perhaps over a pot of tea, my hands would be shaking slightly. Then I'd look across at the others sitting around me and their hands would be shaking just the same. Probably it was just delayed shock, egress of adrenaline perhaps, but it would pass.

Sometimes we would laugh nervously at how lucky we had been to get away from a particularly dangerous situation – a kind of military black humour. But looking back, I feel training played a larger part than luck; our planning, preparation and execution was always meticulously polished to the finest detail, as it had to be if we were to stay alive.

In 'the book', the official reaction to effective enemy fire is Duck – Dash – Get down – Crawl – Observe – Return fire – Win the fire fight – Follow through – Reorganise. The first three parts of this sequence tend to come to you completely naturally and don't need much training. But the rest needs concentration and practice. If you can't keep moving under fire – terrifying though it is, and against the iron will of every cell and fibre in your body, which just wants to disappear in the earth and stay still – then you will be dead in moments. The average terrorist gunman when firing and fired at will indeed Duck – Dash – Get down ... and that's when you can get him. He or she will normally stay in the general area where they dropped for cover. Then you just fire at that area they are hiding in and firing from, or shoot at the object they're hiding behind.

To survive and fight you must always move, crawl away to a fire position, observe and return fire ... from a different place to the one you went down in. Fortunately for us all, in uniform or plain clothes during that period, many of the 'players' were not as highly trained in weapons and tactics as most people think. It was only on rare occasions when we or regular troops would be involved in a full-scale, toe-to-toe gun battle with the IRA. Most of the aggressive operations they carried out involved gunmen emerging from a rioting crowd, firing a few shots and then disappearing, some quick hit-and-run ambushes, bombing attacks and sniping incidents. Of these it was the sniping that was carried out by those IRA members who had some reasonable amount of weapons training – some of them courtesy of the British Army years earlier.

Another day about a week later, we were back at North Howard Street Mill. But this time the streets were very quiet during the day and we didn't catch anyone; after hanging around there for about six hours, sitting and waiting, we were planning to call it a day and go back to our base. The weather was clear and dusk was settling in on us, when suddenly we heard some gun fire, three or four rounds fired on automatic from out on the streets. Almost at the same time, the main gate uniformed guard collapsed like a sack of potatoes.

We all dived out of our cars and jumped into positions of all-round-defence and just watched and listened for a moment or two. The gate guard was flat on his back and didn't move. Mike indicated to me and the others to stay in position, while he and Dave, his SMG man, edged over to the soldier to see how he was.

As Mike and Dave slowly inched along the wall towards the prostrate soldier, the strangest and eeriest thing happened. First, the gate guard moved a little, and then he started to sit up and slowly got back onto his feet, in a kind of ghostly slow-motion way. Mike got to him and led him back to where we were, while Dave covered them both.

We sat him down against one of our cars and asked him what happened but the guard was quite shocked and couldn't say much. Mike and Dave started to check him out for gunshot wounds while we all held our positions, barrels pointing everywhere, but Mike realised he was unhurt.

A few minutes later the soldier gathered together his senses, and on closer inspection it was discovered that he had been shot in the chest but the bullet had lodged in his flak-jacket. The round, a .45 from a Thompson, had been a stray shot fired from quite a distance away somewhere in the streets – somebody else's argument – and it had struck him square in the chest, on the zip of his jacket. Those old flak-jackets used to have a pleat/fold-over in the centre where the zipper was. The 'lead' .45 round fired from far away had randomly hit him flush on the fob of the zip and moulded itself onto the zip with two layers of flak-jacket between the round and him.

It was obvious that it was just an unlucky, stray shot that had struck the soldier. He had a large bruise on his chest but was otherwise unhurt and was in fact very lucky that day. If the round had hit him in any other area, it would have undoubtedly caused quite a serious injury.

I felt that the whole incident was quite spooky, as we all saw at first that the gate man had clearly been shot and probably killed. It was almost supernatural to watch as moments later he slowly climbed and staggered back onto his feet as you might see in a horror film.

In the late summer of 1972, a uniformed company from my original parent unit was caught up in quite a long-running gun battle in the Lenadoon area of Suffolk, on the west side of Belfast. The exchange lasted more than a few hours, through the day and into the evening, fortunately with few casualties on our side. I remember one of my friends was shot in the hand but all he seemed worried about at the time was that his watch that had been blown off his wrist and destroyed. Another friend was shot in the back of his legs while he was running across the street and another lad, half his size, ran after him and hauled him over his shoulder before carrying him into some cover. Some weeks later, the smaller lad tried to lift up his larger friend again but found it impossible: it must simply have been the adrenalin rush at the time of the shooting that made such a physical feat possible.

Stories of such intensive battles were quite rare and most of the uniformed troops were mainly occupied with riot control, patrolling and bombing situations. They also had to deal with being sniped at and to cope with the odd hit-and-run gunman appearing from rioting crowds.

Some of my old friends in uniform did eventually realise what I was up to with Dave and Ben. Occasionally we came across members of our old parent unit whilst out and about in the city. If they happened to stop us randomly in the crowded streets to be checked, we indicated who we were and for them to treat us and search us just like anyone else. We immediately informed them that we were armed, but whispered to them not to pull the weapon out or make any fuss that we were carrying a firearm. Occasionally we passed messages and asked them to say hi to some of our pals in uniform back at base.

7

Lucky to Escape Alive

Weapon handling played a major part in our unit and we all spent many hours on almost daily weapon training. Some of our members had their own private weapons, which ranged from Smith & Wesson .38 Specials and .357 Magnums to Colt .45s. I don't know if these weapons were unauthorised or not and were used mainly on the ranges for practice. It wasn't my business and I presumed they were authorised as they were there together with the .45 Thompson. We had a job to do and all we were interested in was that the weapons worked, were accurate and not too big and bulky. We didn't mind what they were as long as they fired bullets, were easy to use and powerful enough. I don't know if the authorities were aware of these weapons, I just presumed they were.

One of our chaps in Section 81 was sitting on his bed casually cleaning his own personal .357 Magnum, which had interchangeable barrels and a variety of ammunition. After he had finished cleaning it and while he was putting it back together and screwing on the snub-nose two-inch barrel with its specially designed key, he had an ND (negligent discharge).

It used to be called an 'accidental discharge' a few years earlier, but the Army decided on a change of name because someone up high felt that it was more negligent than accidental. So, while he was tightening the barrel with its special tool, the weapon fired accidentally or negligently, depending on your opinion, inside the living accommodation we all shared. He had obviously had a couple of rounds in the cylinder and was gripping the weapon very firmly while putting the short barrel on. The round, being 'armour piercing' and made of tungsten steel, ripped its way through three prefabricated walls, two metal lockers, and a metal bed frame before embedding itself in the OC's desk while he was sat there and everyone else in the area was diving for cover. The OC was really not very happy, and quite visibly shaken by the incident. The man responsible came out of his room looking rather sheepish, was later charged and awarded a £200 fine – which was quite a lot in those days. At dinner that evening, the guilty chap apologised for shooting up our living accommodation and assured us all that it wouldn't happen again.

Another time, one of the Intelligence collators, a friendly tall blonde chap called Mark, also had an ND. He had been out and about with one of the sections for some familiarisation of the Andersonstown area and had been gone for about five hours touring the city – one of our regular general surveillance patrols. He'd met a few of the other Int. people on his rounds and had taken quite a few photos of different parts of the city while he was away.

We sometimes took them out with us to show them the type of areas we worked in and give them a break from the monotony of life in the ops room, where they would sit at the radio console for hours on end, listening in to us and tracking us on the large wall maps while we were out in the city. We liked to give them a flavour of what we did and where we did it, which they always seemed to appreciate.

On his return Mark had cleared his weapon, a standard 9 millie Browning pistol, in the usual gravel patch area near the vehicle park, before going into the ops room. There he put the loaded magazines and odd loose ammunition on top of the radio console and started to strip the pistol down for cleaning. A few minutes later, having cleaned the weapon and chatted to the other lads in the ops room about his trip into the city, he started to re-assemble it.

While he was checking and testing the actions (working parts) he inadvertently popped on the magazine, cocked the pistol and almost simultaneously fired off a round while standing beside the radio console. The radio operator at that time was a chap we had nicknamed the 'Colonel' because of his university accent and large curly moustache, who was unfortunately sitting in the line of fire.

Normally when you have cocked the Browning 9 millie 'without' a magazine on – perhaps after cleaning – you would usually push a finger up inside the pistol grip to depress the sear. This means you are able to pull the trigger to allow the hammer to rest forward. Some people, however, prefer to place the magazine back on the weapon after cocking it, which in turn depresses the sear, and then pull the trigger. This practice is or was generally acceptable, but if the weapon handler gets his sequence wrong it can easily lead to an accidental (or negligent) discharge of the weapon.

Luckily for him as the round was fired, the Colonel just happened to turn his head to the right and looked directly at the Intelligence collator. The 9mm round struck him almost flush in the face, just missed his nose and skimmed his cheekbone about an inch below his left eye and exited just forward of his left ear. The shock of the round being fired in such a confined space threw him careering back off his chair, bounced him off the wall behind and sent him sprawling across the floor. The effect was just like in a Western, when two gunslingers have a disagreement over a card game. The rest of us stood there stunned for a moment before moving in to pick him up and take a look at the poor Colonel.

After patching up his face and sending him to the medics for them to have a go at him, we calculated that if the Colonel hadn't turned his head at that precise instant, he would have been struck squarely in the side of the head and probably killed outright. Thankfully he moved and turned just as the round was being fired, and within a week he was back on duty, fully recovered from his little 'contact', even though it was 'blue on blue' – and he even seemed quite proud of his little battle scar.

I'm sure today, wherever he is, he'll undoubtedly have given many versions of what exactly happened that day when he received his little war wound. The Int. chap responsible got the customary bollocking and fine, together with a full apology to us all, once again over dinner. Incidentally, the term 'blue on blue' comes from Intelligence battle-planning wall maps, where friendly forces' positions are marked with blue pen and enemy forces are in red.

Also, incidentally, contrary to popular belief, when someone is shot they usually fall directly down – especially if killed outright. It's not like in the movies, where you see cowboys flying through the air or getting blown through a window. The reason is that the projectile is travelling so fast, it simply just cuts through anything in its path like a knife through butter, destroying flesh and tissue on its way. The human body can, however, jolt or twitch when hit by a bullet, and this can be for a variety of reasons. Firstly, if someone is shot from close range or in a confined area, like the Colonel, the body can make an involuntary jolt, or can appear to jerk away with hands rising up. This is mainly from the noise and shock of the weapon being fired at such close range. Quite understandably, most people will jump and raise their hands if surprised by a gun being aimed and fired at them at close range.

On the other hand, a person can receive a gunshot wound and not even realise it for a moment or two, and this in turn can also depend on the type of ammunition being used. In Gibraltar in 1988, some witnesses claimed that the IRA terrorists put their hands up just as, or a moment before, they were shot by the SAS team. Yes, this is very possible because of the shock of being confronted and shot at, from close range within a matter of seconds. The movement of the hands going up is an involuntary reaction to the surprise of the situation – a natural defensive action.

Again, when John F. Kennedy was shot (as seen on the Zapruder footage), the first round that hit him struck him in the back of the neck and exited frontwards through his throat. Or vice versa, whichever report you choose to believe. At the moment of impact, there was very little if any movement in his body at all. A moment later, Kennedy started to tilt forward and bring his hands up to his throat, obviously realising he had been hit by something.

Three or four seconds later, it appears he was hit again on the forward right side of his head and this time his head jerked back and to the left before he collapsed. The round that hit him in the neck had passed directly through soft tissue with little reaction from the body. However, the round to his head struck dense bone and probably deflected slightly or disintegrated, transferring much of the energy from the round to his head. This was more likely the reason his head jerked back and to the left. At the moment the shooting started, Kennedy had little idea he was being shot at. And incidentally, I'll never believe that any one person can fire three accurate, aimed shots from an old bolt-action rifle in less than six seconds.

There were many discrepancies that day, which anyone with some form of weapons or sniper training can see. The best shot from the book depository building would have been when Kennedy was approaching it. He would have been a much easier target moving towards the gunman rather than away from him after the presidential motorcade turned down Elm Street on Dealey Plaza. With a frontal target, the target grows larger as it gets closer. But after the target has passed, it gets smaller as it moves away.

Even though all members of our unit were extremely well trained, with most of us being expert weapons instructors and highly competent in the use of many weapons, NDs still sometimes happened, which we ascribed to the day-in, day-out constant stress of the job. A momentary lapse in concentration or a slight distraction of the mind is all it takes. Weapon handling is a drill which we all do automatically and probably the most dangerous time is the moment of unloading where you're distracted for a split second. The drill you have practiced for perhaps many years misses a beat and you slip out of sequence – something that very easily can happen.

We had just arrived back at base early one evening from a task near the city centre. We parked our vehicles up against the fence inside the gate as we did every day, and went about unloading and clearing our weapons. Mike and the others had arrived a few minutes before us and were in the briefing room drinking tea and cleaning their weapons. I had cleared my 9 millie and so had Kev, together with his SMG. John, however, was busy in the boot of the car fiddling with the radio. He later walked around to the gravel patch to clear his weapon, in a bit of a hurry to catch us up while we walked down the path to the ops room.

As we were about fifteen metres along the path, over halfway there, I suddenly heard a loud crack from John's weapon being fired. Kev and I both instinctively ducked and I looked around to see John going through the unload procedure once again. But somehow he had the sequence totally wrong. He had managed to fire off three rounds before I could get to him to take his weapon and clear it myself. Instead of the sequence of Safety catch – Magazine off – Cock and clear, he was cocking the weapon first, checking the chamber, releasing the slide and then taking the magazine off, thus firing it as he thought he was clearing it. And he was doing this repeatedly, in his flustered state, due to being out of synchronisation.

The best thing to do in a predicament such as John found himself in is to simply put the weapon on the floor and step away from it. He was so fixated on the idea that he had to clear the weapon that he just kept making the same mistake. There was no danger to anyone because he was firing directly into the gravel area we used by the path. I just stopped him, took the weapon, cleared it and gave it him back. Luckily no one in the operations room heard anything, so we just put it down to experience after we picked up the empty cases. All of us in the section understood how and what happened and it made us all that little bit more careful with our weapons in future.

A couple of months later, the 'Colonel' had another lucky escape. He was out on general surveillance with one of the other sections, patrolling the fringes of Andersonstown, west Belfast. Many of the streets around the city had 'sleeping policemen' built on them, especially near Army or police locations, to help control passing traffic. These ramps were quite large and if we were not careful while passing over, we could catch the exhaust pipes or damage the underside of our cars. Therefore, when we drove over them we turned diagonally, just like everyone else.

The Colonel was in the front passenger's (commander's) seat as his vehicle made its short turn to the right, preparing to pass over one of these security ramps. As the car rose up and rolled diagonally over the top of it, a shot rang out and the windscreen fractured with a small bullet hole right in the centre. Immediately, they sped off away from the area and reported the shooting as they made their way back to base.

Once there, a close inspection of the damage to the car revealed that there was a short crease or groove just off centre on the car's bonnet, perfectly in line with the hole in the middle of the windscreen. We all felt that the round was probably a .22 calibre, based on the shape and size of the mark on the bonnet. And the hole in the screen was right in between the driver and the commander.

If whoever fired the weapon had done so a moment or two earlier, we were sure that someone in the car would have probably been injured or perhaps killed. But fortunately the vehicle was making its turn as the shot was taken and it missed everyone. As they say, sleeping policemen save lives.

People taking pot-shots at passing cars did occasionally happen, not very often but it happened. We figured it was probably some youths having a bit of fun, rather than an ASU launching a specific attack. Nevertheless, the Colonel was pretty well shaken up when they arrived back at base after the shooting and I don't think I ever saw him out on patrol again after that incident.

Periodically we had to keep a low profile or even to stay off the streets for days on end, spending our time just keeping ourselves busy with training. Often this was during major operations, such as 'Operation Motorman' at the end of July 1972, when the Army was out in force clearing away barricades from the no-go areas of Ulster's cities. Or it occurred when large operations were in progress, gathering up suspects for internment. It was a very busy time during the early 1970s, when the province was moving ever closer to civil war, seemingly on a daily basis.

Operation Motorman started at 4:00 am on 31 July and carried on all through that day in Belfast and Londonderry. The Army deployed around four per cent of the whole of the British Army's total strength during this operation and unfortunately a 15-year-old youngster and an unarmed 19-year-old IRA member were shot dead while Motorman was underway. A few hours after the end of the operation, a massive coordinated car-bomb attack was launched in the village centre of Claudy, County Londonderry. Nine people died in this attack, five Catholics and four Protestants.

During these restrictive periods, however, we did occasionally go out on the streets. Usually this would only be in a general surveillance mode, staying away from sensitive areas where the Army was out in large numbers. We often cruised around the city, looking out for wanted players and hoping to bump into an armed group milling about. We occasionally called into out-of-the-way Army locations for a chat and a pot of tea with the local Intelligence boys, to see if we could help with anything they were planning. Usually we would spend an hour or so doing this, and then move off to another Army location for another chat and a brew.

It was during one of these periods that one of our patrols was heading back to our base after their day shift in the city had finished. It was early in the evening and they were making their way home, passing through the area of Dee Street-Newtownards Road, on the east side of Belfast. It was a lone vehicle with just two of our lads in the car.

Driving out of the city along Newtonards Road, they suddenly came across a large group of UDA men in the street. Their vehicle slowed to negotiate its way through the group like we had done dozens of times in the past. But as it drew closer to the crowd, the UDA attacked with stones and bottles. During this attack something large smashed through the windscreen and hit the driver, Len Durber, in the face, forcing the car to swing out of control and crash.

The UDA afterwards claimed that the car attempted to run them over – which I found ludicrous. We never generally felt any great threat from the UDA; they were an accepted Protestant organisation at that time and the area of the incident, Newtownards Road, was a relatively safe area. If we ever came across one of their groups in the street, we always slowed down and they never bothered us and normally just let us pass.

A couple of us checked and inspected Len's car the next day. Given the amount of blood and what looked like pieces of brain on the dashboard, he had been hit by something quite heavy, and it wasn't the steering wheel or the door frame. The vehicle commander, Rick, who just suffered bumps and bruises, later told me that something the size of a Crown Green bowling ball had been thrown at the windscreen as they slowly approached to pass through the UDA group. Len was reported to be very ill for quite a long time and I heard months later through friends that he had died in a mainland hospital, leaving behind a wife and young family.

Another of our patrols, from section 82, again alone but with three occupants in the car, were caught out one night, again during a period of general surveillance. They were taking a look around an estate off Shore Road, north Belfast, and came across a crowd near Dandy Street. The crowd started to get agitated and blocked the road with a barricade, forcing the patrol to stop. They then launched an attack on the car with stones and sticks which grew in ferocity until the group tried to force the occupants out and roll it over. The rear door was eventually wrenched open and one of the patrol was grabbed and pulled from the back seat and hurled to the ground by the crazed mob. Fortunately, as he was being pulled out, he dropped his SMG and kicked it under the driver's seat so it was left on the floor of the car in the darkness. Two men then climbed into the back of the car and tried to drag the driver and the commander backwards over their seats into the rear, to get them out. The commander, Tim, while being hauled backwards in the struggle, managed to fire an un-aimed shot back over his shoulder, into the rear of the car in the darkness. At the same moment the driver, Mal, noticed an armed man moving towards them through the crowd. As the two attackers in the back seats jumped out to escape being shot, the vehicle managed to ram the barricade and race away. They then contacted the local Army unit and asked them to send in a uniformed patrol to rescue their SMG man. The Army patrol managed to arrive within minutes and after speaking with the group, they succeeded in taking our guy away from the crowd. This must have made the crowd feel they had helped in the capture and arrest of a wanted man and it eventually calmed the situation. The man concerned was unhurt, but was subsequently taken off the streets for a few weeks and instead spent most of his time helping the Int. boys in the ops room until the dust settled.

That night our people were very lucky to have escaped alive. They were trapped and the situation was turning very nasty. It was only due to the calm courage and experience of the driver and commander that all three of them were saved from almost certain death.

This was very similar to another situation which occurred many years later and was televised live around the world. Everyone looked on in stunned amazement while two soldiers caught up in an IRA funeral. They were trapped, dragged out of their car, mobbed and stripped, and within minutes they were driven away for execution on some lonely piece of waste land. When I saw the incident on TV, I could hardly believe what was happening, although I quickly realised that the two men were not part of 14 Intelligence Company.

If it had been Kev or John and me in that situation, our 'procedure' – which we had all discussed, planned and agreed many times in the past – was to quickly send a 'contact' over the radio. Our plan then was; we'd open fire directly at some of the nearest rioters, shocking them and forcing them back momentarily, creating some space to allow us to get out of the car. Being sprayed with the brains of the person in front of you is a powerful incentive to back off from a man with a gun. We then would have tried to make our way over to the nearby wall and put our backs against it, holding off the rioters by shooting them if necessary until the Army could extract us.

We would have had an SMG and over 100 rounds of 9mm ammunition with us for our two Browning pistols; and for sure, we would have used them all up if we had to, to get out alive. Sadly, as we all saw, simply firing a warning shot in the air is just not enough in that type of mad mob situation. In the middle of a frenzied riot when everyone around just wants to get at you and kill you, you really must do whatever it takes to gain some form of control over the situation – even if that means shooting directly in the face anyone that approaches you. Simply sitting there, reciting the Yellow Card - Rules of Engagement will get you nowhere in a crazed situation like that. Thankfully, I've never been in that kind of situation; but believe me, we all knew exactly what we would do if it ever happened. Most of us had spent almost every day for years thinking about it. I fully appreciate and totally agree with the Yellow Card - RoE, but when stuck in such a desperate situation or working under cover, usually alone, constantly surrounded by terrorists, their supporters and sympathisers.' At any moment, you may just have a split second to make a choice.

I know that this may appear to be a very aggressive and perhaps an over-the-top approach. But in a situation like that, when you're totally alone with nowhere to go, I'm afraid that all you have is the choice of life or death. There is no middle ground or the opportunity to issue warnings or try and negotiate your way out. I'm sure that Kev, John and the rest of our guys, wherever they are today, would agree with me. We were often told never to be caught alive with any ammunition on us if we were cornered. If we were ever trapped with no way out, we knew we would almost certainly not survive and the only chance was to shoot our way out. We constantly discussed all the scenarios we might find ourselves in and agreed amongst ourselves our best actions in such a situation.

I soon realised watching the whole episode unfold on TV, that those two poor soldiers trapped at the funeral were probably not part of 14 Intelligence Company the moment they fired that warning shot into the air out of the window. We never fired warning shots. Even though the crowd flinched momentarily, unfortunately it just didn't allow them enough time to get out of the car, and staying in it was simply a death trap.

A couple of weeks after Operation Motorman finished we were on normal patrol duties again and back to some of our regular operations. One of our earliest was a CP (close protection) job. But this time it was an RUC detective meeting with some people from the UDA which was an accepted Protestant paramilitary organisation at that time, although prohibited much later, in 1992.

They apparently wanted to talk about some peace plans they had for the area and needed to discuss them with the RUC. The meeting was scheduled to take place about lunch time in a coffee bar off the Shankill Road, by Tennent Street, not far from the RUC station. It was between the RUC and the UDA in a Protestant area of the city and we felt that the threat level was quite low.

However, we didn't want to take any chances because it was possible that an IRA ASU could slip through from a Catholic area – basically just along the road – and try to launch an attack on this group meeting. In addition, we discovered it was to be a meeting between two high level members of the UDA and two RUC detectives. During this period of great unrest, we never took any chances. We never gave the IRA an inch to play with and we covered all our CP operations the same way and with the same possible high threat level, wherever the meeting took place.

After an early breakfast at 6:30 am we gathered and checked our weapons and equipment and then made our way at about 8:30 am to the Tennent Street police station to meet the RUC people involved. It was a crisp clear morning with a light patchy mist in the air as we set off from our base HQ a few miles outside Belfast. By the time we arrived at Tennant Street, the mist had generally cleared but the sky was still a little grey and the streets were beginning to get busy with people wandering around the area. We radioed ahead as we arrived and the gate people let us straight in without delay. After parking our vehicles out of sight, we unloaded and cleared our weapons and made our way to the meeting after concealing and locking the SMGs in the boot of one car.

During our briefing, which began at 9:30 am, we decided to have four of our men in the coffee bar and three cars close by with five men on backup a couple of minutes away. Mike, with the radio, was to be in the coffee bar and three others, Dave, Ben and Colin, all armed with 9 millies. I was together with Kev in car 'Echo.' Kev liked to drive when we were in Echo because it was a tuned-up, super-fast Ford Cortina 1600E and he used to say that it suited him.

John, Bob and Tug were in the other cars, 'Delta' and 'Foxtrot,' all of us ready to move in to back them up if required. Our briefing was finished by 11:00 am and the meeting was set for 1:00 pm. Mike and his team made their way there on foot. They were in the coffee bar by 12:30 pm. I didn't know exactly where they were inside the bar but I had a good idea. We were spread out in our three cars and parked up along the road a little, near the RUC station. In fact we were out of the cars, a couple of metres away, mingling with the shoppers and passers-by but ready to move at the nod of a head. Whenever we were waiting around in the street, I always preferred to get out of the car and move around a bit. I always felt safer out of the cars when parked as I could observe the area much better than I could just sitting inside. If things began to look a bit dodgy for us, we could always see it much earlier from outside the car.

At approximately 1:30 pm we received the message from Mike that all wasn't so good in the coffee bar, so we all loaded up in the cars and moved in closer to the target area. On our approach we noticed a suspicious vehicle parked near the coffee bar, about fifty metres along the road with two men inside, so we pulled up and watched these guys for a few moments. Kev and Tug got out and ambled up the street on the opposite side to observe from a little closer while Bob stayed with John in their car. I quietly told Mike on the radio of the situation outside. A couple of minutes later Mike and Colin emerged from the coffee bar with the two RUC chaps, followed a few moments later by Dave and Ben, making their way across the busy road and covering each other as they walked towards Bob's and John's cars.

The two men in the car we were watching, together with another armed man further up the street, whom we hadn't seen earlier, started to move in on Mike's group as they made for our waiting cars. We now saw that all three of the unknown men were armed with handguns at the 'ready' and aiming, making their way towards our guys. Kev and Tug were closest and opened fire almost immediately from behind a couple of parked cars while John and I got out of our cars and joined in with them, with a few rounds. The four of us managed to fire about four to five rounds each at the gunmen while they only managed to fire approximately three or four rounds between them in return. Mike and Colin were busy bundling the RUC chaps into John's car while Dave and Ben, on leaving the bar, effectively switched their roles and became our backup, opening flanking fire on the attackers with a couple of rounds each. Everything happened very quickly, and we had been surprised when the other gunman from further up the road joined in the attack with the two from the car. They obviously knew who their target was because they started to move in very quickly when the two RUC chaps appeared in the street.

However, we were always prepared for eventualities such as this and we had practiced such procedures many times while training. Just fine tuning a procedure which is well known and widely used even in security CP training today.

In this manner we totally wrong footed the gunmen; they didn't expect to be taken on from the side and the front as they approached the coffee bar. As a result they were caught in the open with no cover, right in the middle of the road, and had little chance of escape. Again we used overwhelming accurate fire power, as always for two main reasons: one, to quickly overcome the gunmen and take control of the situation, and two, to reduce the amount of wild inaccurate fire at us from the gunmen and so to stop innocent passers-by from being hit.

We cordoned off the area and removed their weapons. Moments later as we were loading up and moving off, the Army patrol we had earlier radioed for, appeared. They took over control from us moments before we left the area.

Later over a coffee Tug and I asked Mike, 'Why did you feel so uneasy in the coffee bar?'

'I felt suspicious of the whole situation,' he explained, 'but I couldn't put my finger on anything or any person in particular, just lots of whispering going on in the bar. I sensed something wasn't right and decided to close the meeting down and pull out, especially after you told me the situation outside.'

8

Lying in Wait

I was watching the news on TV one evening with Dave, Ben and Tug as it was reported that President Nixon had just announced a cease fire for the US forces in Vietnam. As usual there was a lot of coverage of the conflict – choppers with troops firing from them, flying around the jungle.

Kev arrived in the cabin with Colin: 'Mike has just seen us and we've got a big job on tomorrow. It's another CP operation and we have to be ready to go to Lisburn by 7:00 am.'

'No problem,' answered Tug. 'Mike will probably give us some idea of who and where it is in the morning.'

We were all in bed by 10:00 pm, as we didn't know how long the next day's job might last. It could have been for a couple of hours, or all day and into the night.

As usual, at 5:30 am we collected together all our weapons, ammunition and radio equipment – not forgetting a hot mug of coffee, organised by the Int. boys, when we walked in the ops room.

Standing behind the console, Mike explained: 'Today we have a CP op involving the GOC himself; he's visiting Belfast later this afternoon. But first we have to check the route for him. So just take your normal weapons, we don't need the silenced SMGs.

By 6:00 am we were all loaded up. The day's operation involved five cars split between two sections, as most of 82 Section would be with us on this job – a total of 14 or 15 men. We set off individually in the vehicles from our base and split in different directions as we pulled out. Immediately Mike came up on the radio, giving out a radio check which we all acknowledged in alphabetical order. This was followed moments later by Tim, 82 Section's commander, and we could hear his section going through their acknowledgements.

The clearing and escort operation along the route planned for the GOCNI (General Officer Commanding Northern Ireland) was another classic type of CP that we were sometimes tasked to carry out. This time the GOC had scheduled a visit to Belfast later that day and we were required to check the route from Lisburn via the M1 motorway to Belfast for any suspicious activity, and then later in the afternoon to act as escort to his convoy.

By 9:00 am we had already reached Lisburn and been through the briefing. Everything was done and dusted, even though it was very crowded, with our two sections huddled round a large table that practically filled the room. We had covered the usual points, such as Ground, Situation, Mission, Execution, Admin support and Communications, and from the briefing room we all went off for some breakfast and to chew over our plans based on the GOC's earlier briefing. The route was fairly simple: straight out of Lisburn, onto the M1, down the motorway to Belfast Grosvenor Road, then on to Donegall Square and City Hall. There the three car convoy, with us escorting, was to meet up with a uniformed Army mobile unit and carry on from there before we peeled off and away.

Our plan was that in phase one (route checking) three of our cars would concentrate on searching around the area between Donegall Road-M1 roundabout and City Hall. They were to check the areas of Broadway Industrial Estate, the hospital playing fields opposite and the Linfield Industrial Estate, together with any roads or bankings overlooking the motorway in those areas.

Our second team of two cars had the task of patrolling from the Donegall Road roundabout, Junction 1, out of town to Junction 3 along the M1. Some other unit was checking the Lisburn sector to Junction 3. We didn't know who; we didn't need to know.

I was commander in one of the two cars checking the M1, and what we had to look for were any possible ambush positions, explosive devices or abandoned vehicles by the roadside. Uniformed units had been checking along the motorway culverts and bridges for any devices over the previous couple of days. The GOC planned to leave Lisburn at 4:00 pm that day and the total journey time would be 30-40 minutes depending on traffic entering the city. It wasn't much use, us checking the route two or three days before as the situation could easily change in a couple of hours. We needed to be checking the route constantly throughout the day itself, making notes of any suspect activity along the way; for example, a man loading a van, people hanging around by the motorway hard shoulder or on a rise above, and packages left by the roadside. We had to just keep on the move and continually monitor the area, checking out anything we felt was suspicious.

By 3:30 pm two of our cars had to be back at Lisburn, ready to join the convoy as escort while the other three cars had to be in position at the motorway junctions 1, 2 and 3 respectively. These cars would act as backup and an early warning of any new suspicious activity; they were then to follow on and link up behind it as the convoy passed them.

After the briefing we talked about how we didn't like the idea of three very nice, gleaming cars travelling nose to tail together in the GOC's convoy. They were all identical, very clean and shiny. Anyone could have seen them from a distance, approaching in convoy. We suggested that our two cars (which weren't so pretty) should mingle among them, opening things up a little, with the GOC in between us. Our other three cars could tag onto the end of the convoy later as we passed them at the junctions. The Special Branch boys, who were there with us at the briefing, were not too happy about that idea but the GOC liked it and that was that.

Doing this type of work, you tend to call on all the military skills you've ever learned, developing them to fit in with the current scenario. In Camouflage and Concealment, the idea isn't to totally hide an object but to change its shape and appearance, making it look a little different to what it really is. The main points to remember are Shape – Shine/Surface – Shadow – Spacing – Silhouette – Movement and Aircraft. Eliminating as many of these factors as possible is the main objective. We couldn't eliminate points like 'movement', and 'aircraft' didn't apply. Neither could we hide a gleaming three-car convoy, but we could surely change its shape a bit and rearrange its silhouette. This could possibly pass a little of the element of surprise over to us in the event of an incident. All we would require was a few seconds' warning, if anything looked suspicious, allowing us precious time to act first.

We finished what we called our 'sunshine' breakfast (sausage, eggs, bacon, beans, fried bread and tomatoes) by 10:00 am. Kev and Colin had been chatting to a couple of their uniformed Royal Marines buddies sitting at a table across from ours as they ate. Next, we stuffed our jackets and jumpers with sandwiches and filled our flasks with that delightful Army tea, which had been stewing in the urn since 7:00 am. Then we all made our way out of the canteen, checked our radios and weapons and piled into the cars, setting off for the M1 and Belfast. Once again initially heading off in different directions, we carried out another radio check.

'Hello all stations 83, this is 83 Alfa, radio check. Over.'

'Bravo OK.'

'Charlie OK.'

'Delta OK.'

'Echo OK.'

'83 Alfa OK. Out.'

Although we comprised two sections, 82 and 83, we used our radio call sign 83 as the operation was actually given to us and only a few guys from 82 were helping us out for the day.

Cars Alfa, Bravo and Charlie cracked on to the city centre to check out that area, while I in Delta, with Echo, peeled off at the Junction 1 roundabout just outside the centre. We both pulled in at a lay-by, to once again go over our plans and finalise the details amongst ourselves.

Our task was quite straight forward, but we didn't want to look suspicious driving up and down our piece of motorway, which was only about a five- or six-mile stretch. We felt it was best if both our cars worked independently of each other as we didn't want to drive around in a convoy attracting attention. We would only join up together if we decided to check out some suspicious activity.

I set off first, cruising up the motorway away from the city in the direction of Lisburn, while Tug in car Echo waited a few moments before he too set off.

Some of the time we spent parked up by a junction or lay-by, just observing for a while, having some snap and a sip of tea before driving off again. Often we appeared that we were checking a wheel or looking under the bonnet while the others in our car would be observing with binoculars and a sandwich, making notes and taking photos of activity in the area.

During this period in the Troubles, abandoned cars were always treated as suspicious because usually the only reason they were abandoned was that they were stolen and/or rigged up as a bomb. During our patrol that day we found the odd cardboard box lying around by the roadside, but they all checked out to be nothing. We also spotted one or two vans loading and unloading in car parks near the motorway hard shoulder so we took some photos and made notes, but they eventually went away.

At about lunch time, however, while again heading out in the direction of Lisburn, we noticed some men on the opposite side milling around in the back garden of a house in the Ladybrook Estate. Parts of that area were elevated from the motorway on top of a cutting and offered good views up and down the road; it was an ideal ambush site. We kept these men under observation for a while from various points along the M1. There appeared to be one man inside the garden who was chatting over a low fence to two other men with their backs to the motorway below them.

After an hour or so the situation hadn't really changed very much and we decided to go and check them out, so I radioed Tug in our other car to assist us. 'We'll pull up on the hard shoulder,' I told him. 'You and me will go up the banking and see what they're up to while everyone else keeps watch.

'OK Sy, no problem,' Tug acknowledged.

We both approached from the south and pulled up on the hard shoulder about 15 metres apart and adjacent to the garden. Tug and me emerged from our vehicles and casually made our way up the banking while our two drivers and rear seat men got out and stood casually chatting by the vehicles, observing us and the men in the garden area above them. None of our weapons was in view at this point.

As we climbed, our main view was the head and shoulders of the men, in line with the bedroom windows of the houses beyond them. Neither of us was very happy about this whole situation and we hoped it would turn out to be quite innocent. My stomach was tight and I was concentrating on keeping my breathing calm and regular, trying not to look nervous and casually chatting with Tug. He was being his usual comical self, but I noticed a note of tension in his voice – he knew we might be walking into a problem in just a couple more moments.

We were on our own walking exposed towards what could easily be an IRA ambush 'lying in wait'. Our backup was our mates, some twenty or thirty metres away and below, watching for any sudden movement. All we had was a couple of 9 millies hidden in our waist bands: it was not the best of situations to be in, but it had to be done.

We needed to approach these characters and find out what they were up to and why they were hanging around the area for so long. In a situation like this, if we were forced to confront someone and speak to him, we made sure that only one of us would ask the questions while the other observed.

The men in the garden noticed our approach but simply glanced over at us a couple of times and made no attempt to turn to face us or come near. Then as we breasted the banking, only a few metres from the fence, all hell suddenly broke loose. The two men on our side of the fence ducked down and quickly scurried away to one side. At the same instant the man in the garden bolted to his left into a wooden shed, and right then from two or three bedroom windows a colossal amount of automatic fire opened up at us from about ten to 12 metres away. As soon as we saw the men run, we knew they were running for a reason, and both Tug and me had instinctively dropped to the ground as the windows sprang open.

There were perhaps three or four gunmen in total – I'm not too sure – and they had begun shooting at us simultaneously. Within a split second, though, our lads by the cars had drawn their weapons and started to return fire with two SMGs and two 9 millies, giving us covering fire which allowed Tug and me to scramble down the banking and get back to the cars. First thing, we rolled and dropped into an area of 'dead ground' where we couldn't be seen, just below the brow of the banking.

We both lay there safe for a moment, two metres apart. We looked at each other and knew we were both thinking the same thought: How the hell can we get out of this mess?

We heard the shots from both sides cracking over our heads as we began to clamber and roll down the banking toward the roadside.

'Don't stick your bum up so high, it'll get shot off,' Tug muttered to me on the way down.

As we slid and skidded down the banking off the top of the ridge the gunmen lost sight of us, and for the moment we were in a reasonably safe position. We knew, though, that as we moved closer to the cars, we would again emerge into view and make a couple of extra targets for them.

About five metres from the cars we both stopped and waited for a signal from John, my driver, to tell us the moment to sprint to the vehicles. There were shots bouncing all around us but we managed to get back, in between the fearsome exchanges. I scurried around the rear to the driver's side, passing Kev firing out from the back of the car. I positioned myself crouched down behind the engine and managed to get a few rounds down as we prepared to make a quick exit when the moment was right. It was horrendous, like being in the middle of a Chinese street carnival, cracks and thumps all around us, and the adrenalin was racing. The vehicles were taking lots of hits and most of the windows were out. I clearly saw the rounds chipping and zinging off the road inches from my face, just in front of the car.

John was right next to me by the engine as we took turns at returning the fire. One of us bobbed up for a couple of seconds and fired three or four rounds, and then the other would do the same. He had fired more rounds than me and I noticed him quickly changing his magazine while sat on the floor with his back against the car. He simply pressed the magazine release button with his right thumb, and with one hand slipped the empty magazine out and slotted a fresh one on. He then flipped the lever on the left side to allow the working parts to spring forward ready to fire ... all in the blink of an eye.

He looked up at me as I crouched onto one knee, bellowing over the noise of the gun fire something which sounded like, 'I wish we were all back at base.'

Kev, the 'big bear', was lying on the back seat of the car with his feet and SMG pointing up towards the banking, firing automatic bursts of three to four rounds every few seconds. I noticed the man that had run to the garden shed stumble out again and collapse, as Kev riddled its thin panel walls. The guy had obviously seen too many movies: a wooden garden shed, with panels not much thicker than a figure eleven target, would never stop 9mm rounds from an SMG on full auto.

Tug in the other vehicle team shouted to me, 'OK Sy?' and gave me a wave to indicate they were ready to move.

We all discharged a final group of bursts of fire and then the drivers jumped in the cars first, followed by the commanders and then the other SMG gunner, covering each other with fire as we moved. Kev didn't have to move, he was lying on his back on the back seat, feet out the open door giving them hell up the banking with his SMG.

This whole contact lasted only four or five minutes and it was so intense that we hadn't any time to give out a contact report on the radio until we were speeding out of the area, with Kev still blasting away as we left. We made our way back to base, while our HQ Operations assigned two other teams to take our place and join the escort run. They also informed the local uniformed unit to get over to Ladybrook and have a look around the area of the contact. We knew for sure we had hit the man in the garden shed, plus perhaps a couple more in the bedroom windows. The Army would find out. There might not be any bodies or weapons lying around by the time they arrived, but for sure there would be signs of a firefight and they could gather any useful evidence that might be lying around.

We were very lucky that day, not one of us had a scratch, but the vehicles were a mess and they were what saved us. My car alone had 21 entry holes in the metalwork, not including the windows, but thankfully none of the tyres were damaged. I think this was because of the angle from us to the gunmen: they couldn't really see our wheels from their positions as we were directly under the banking.

Between us all we had perhaps expended over a hundred rounds of 9mm with four pistols and two SMGs. The gunmen must have fired 60 to 80 rounds at us during the few minutes of the contact. Our main aim at the time was to get away. The enemy was above us on high ground, we had very little cover and all we could do was to try and put down a superior amount of fire power while we made our exit, hopefully dropping as many players as possible on our way.

Under normal circumstances in an ambush, such as in a jungle, the procedure is to go forward and fight through it. When caught up in a well-laid ambush, running away is simply not an option. All exit routes will be covered by heavy machine guns in an SF (sustained fire) role, in fixed firing positions and locked onto the killing zone. Or there could be Claymore mines placed along the exit routes to prevent anyone from escaping.

In our situation, in an urban area like Belfast, to try and fight through the ambush was impossible and even suicidal. We would have had to dash over open ground, uphill to the garden fence, clamber over the fence, then run across the garden area to the house. Next, we would have to break into the house and clear the downstairs area before fighting our way up to the bedrooms. If we had grenades or something like those small, telescopic, throw-away hand-held LAW 66mm missile launchers with us, we could perhaps have gone forward and fought through. But unfortunately we didn't have any. Only the IRA was allowed to use weapons like those.

In a situation like this, when we had been involved in a firefight, even if the cars weren't damaged they were sent away to be re-sprayed and have the number plates changed. In this matter we had to take much care. We needed to ensure that the new registrations and colours were correct for the model type and the manufactured year of each car. The IRA would soon twig that a Ford Cortina registered in, say, 1970 could only be one of perhaps seven different colours – especially the 1600E model – and that the number plate also had to belong to that particular period. There were a few times when we drove along Falls Road or into Andersonstown that we saw our own car types and registration numbers painted on a house wall for everyone to see, which tended to make you a little twitchy, driving past it.

I was in the briefing room late at night with Dave and Ben, just updating some of the mug-shots which covered the walls. We put a red line through the photos of those terrorists who had been arrested and a red cross over any dead ones. We usually left the dead men's photos on the wall until we replaced them with new 'players', which was normally on a Monday morning, the start of a new week at the office.

While we were shuffling around the photos we heard the phone ring in the ops room and one of the Int. chaps took the call. It turned out to be a call from the Army unit Intelligence officer based at Palace Barracks, Holywood, a few miles south of Belfast.

Our Int. chap shouted for us, explaining, 'One of the uniformed lads from Palace Barracks has been approached in the village pub by some guy asking if he can get some ammunition. The guy said he will pay for it. The young lad said he probably can and he's going to meet the guy again tomorrow night, same place.'

I popped my head around the door and said, 'OK, I'll tell Mike about it in the morning and we'll see what we can do.'

The next morning over breakfast, I told Mike the story and he in turn called the Int. officer at Palace Barracks. Mike asked the Int. officer exactly what had happened, and then explained what we could do to help. By 11:00 am, we had a job on for that night. A few of us went over to Palace Barracks after lunch to interview the soldier involved, who was only a youngster about 19 years old. He said he had been in the bar with a couple of friends and gave us lots of details and a good description of the man asking for the ammunition. He said he was about 40 with greying collar-length hair and quite a slim build. He stood about five feet eight inches tall and had been wearing an old, dark suit. We showed him some photos but he didn't recognise any of them.

The lad had arranged to meet the man again, and Mike told him, 'Fine, that's great, we'll give you some 9mm to give to him. We'll put about ten rounds into a fag packet and you just hand it over when he asks for it or takes it. But make sure he asks for it first and gives you the money before you give it to him. If not, he may try to claim entrapment.' The kid understood, and Mike continued: 'We'll pick you up tonight in one of our cars at 7:30 pm near the side of the NAAFI building. Just you – and don't talk to your friends about this.'

The Kid said, 'OK, no problem,' and seemed quite excited about the whole project. We set off back to our base after going over our plans with the Int. officer.

Once there we got the rest of the section together in the briefing room and explained the situation to everyone, including a full description of the kid and the suspect.

Mike said we'd need to have Special Branch involved to make the arrest. 'We'll be in the pub observing and protecting the kid, making sure he's not being set up to be kidnapped, and that the handover goes OK.'

'Yes,' Tug interjected. 'We'll check the handover goes OK. We'll get the kid out of the way then give the nod for the SB boys to take over and make the arrest when we know the suspect has the ammunition.'

The pub involved in this CP operation was quite large and situated on the edge of Holywood village along the road, just a short walk from Palace Barracks. We decided to have six members of the section spread out in the pub armed with 9 millies, and three others with SMGs waiting in their vehicles in the car park, acting as our backup.

As Mike was on the phone organising things with SB, we all decided to visit the canteen to get something to eat. On returning to our compound at about 6:30 pm, we drew and checked our weapons and radio equipment.

Then we all piled back into the briefing room and Mike gave us a final brief – who was doing what and our procedures and timings. 'OK ... Tug, Dave, Ben, Bob, Sy and me, we'll be in the pub while Kev, Colin and John, you three are to cover the car park and grab the kid when he comes out.'

Mike and Bob went off to pick up the kid at 7:00 pm while the rest of us set off to the pub to meet up with the SB boys in the car park and get into position. We were all inside by 7:30 pm, having entered singly or in pairs a few minutes after each other. I was with Tug by the bar and the other guys were dotted around in various positions. Dave was sitting at a table near the door, covering our exit, and Ben was over near the snooker table sitting watching some people playing. The bar wasn't particularly busy at that time, but there were quite a few people clustered around the counter and at the snooker table. A few minutes later, Mike and Bob turned up and sat at a central table near the two SB boys who were with us that night.

The kid came in a few minutes after Mike and Bob arrived; he had been outside discussing his procedures with Kev and Colin in one of the cars in the car park. He went up to the bar, ordered a beer and sat there waiting on a stool.

Nothing happened until about 8:30 pm, when our player came in. Initially he ignored the kid and went to speak to another man. Ben managed to get a covert photo of this other chap a little later on, after our suspect had finished talking with him. Then after a few minutes our suspect came to the bar to sit with our kid. They shook hands and said a few words as the man sat down. The kid placed the cigarette packet, containing ten rounds of 9mm, next to his beer while the player was discussing something with him.

Mike had told him earlier: 'Place the cigarette packet on the bar and tell the guy that the ammunition is in it. Wait till the guy takes it and pays you before telling him you've got to leave, as you're on duty later.'

Outside, the kid was to be met by Colin and put into one of our cars to wait until it was all over.

Soon after, the guy placed another cigarette packet on the bar, which was some money for the ammo. Then the suspect took the ammunition packet while the kid put the money packet in his pocket as he got up. He smiled and shook the guy's hand, saying he had to go. The guy smiled and gave a brief wave as the kid made his way out and left the pub, to join Colin outside.

Almost immediately, the two SB boys got up, moved to the bar, identified themselves and quietly led the guy outside. We filtered out a few minutes later, after the SB boys had made their arrest and left the area with the suspect. We met up with our vehicles and made our way with the kid back to Palace Barracks.

Back at the Army location, the kid asked, 'What should I do with this money?'

'How much did he give you?' asked Colin.

'Fifty pounds.'

Mike smiled. 'Keep it, have a few beers on the IRA for the time being,' he said. 'When the SB boys ask you later – and they'll want to see you – if the 'player' paid for the ammunition, just tell them the truth and he gave you fifty pounds, as you may need to produce it later.'

'OK, thanks,' the kid replied. He was dropped off at his location and told not to discuss the operation with any one.

The SB had to keep our ten rounds of 9mm ammunition, as it was later required as evidence, along with the kid's statement. We didn't mind about the ammunition, we had plenty more in our stores.

During my time in the unit, I, like everyone else, had very little time off. We had our off-duty time but it was very unusual to get away totally for a few days. Only once did I manage to have a few days' holiday and that was to go to my brother's wedding on the mainland.

I learned of the wedding in May 1973 over the phone and the Boss said I could go for a few days, but that I couldn't go unarmed just in case I was followed across the water. I decided to take the ferry across: if I was being followed it would be much easier for me to spot someone on a boat as opposed to scrutinising the constant through-flow of people at a busy airport.

The next day a couple of guys from the duty section took me down to the ferry port in Belfast and stayed with me until I boarded. I caught the lunch-time ferry because I preferred to make the journey in day light hours, while being alone. The crossing to Stranraer was only just over three hours and was a little bumpy due to the fresh north-west wind running down into the main part of the Irish Sea. Most of the journey I spent in the lounge watching TV and reading newspapers, seated in a position where I could observe the entrance doors to the lounge and bar area. On the news there were still reports of President Nixon admitting responsibility and taking the blame for the Watergate scandal. There was also coverage of the 1.6 million UK workers who had joined the one day strike which the Trade Union Congress had called over pay and prices. Welcome home.

At Stranraer, I saw as I walked down the gang-plank that my parents were there to meet me in their little Ford escort. They hadn't seen me for over a year and were quite surprised at my appearance, but they didn't say very much about my long hair and were mostly just happy I was home. I told Dad that I'd drive but didn't say why, and we set off back towards Carlisle, down the M6 and onto the M62, crossing the Pennines to North Yorkshire for a welcome pot of Mum's tea when we all arrived home. Mum was born in Holland but moved to the UK with my father after the Second World War when she was 19 – she had been staying with relations in Austria. Despite being foreign she always made an excellent pot of English tea and faultless Yorkshire puddings.

During the drive, they both asked a few searching questions about what I was doing in Northern Ireland, but I smoothed things, saying, 'I just work at HQ behind a desk and sometimes I take the OC around in a civilian car when I have to.' The main reason I didn't tell them what I was really doing was not to let them worry too much. Mum was always a bit of a worrier, like all mums, and wasn't happy with me being in Northern Ireland with the Army in the first place.

After a great dinner that evening I enjoyed a good night's sleep in a familiar bed and surroundings. The next day I quickly checked around and under the car before we set off for the wedding ceremony. This was to be held in Leeds in the morning, followed by the reception party in the afternoon at a wonderful lakeside hotel-restaurant on the edge of the Yorkshire Dales.

Again, I drove my dad's car throughout the day, and when I met my brother and his bride-to-be before the ceremony, they also gave me some strange looks. I had a nice suit on, but my rock-star hair-do was most unlike the last time they saw me over a year ago, when I'd had a normal, short Army hair cut which they were used to. It's interesting to wonder what they did think: who in the Army would have had hair like mine? What sergeant major would ever have stood for it? However, they were very busy with the wedding and said little about it after Mum explained to them that I worked in an office.

I really enjoyed the reception, which included lots of family and friends from all sides. But it was particularly good to see the many old school friends of my brother. He's a couple of years older than me but I knew most of his friends as we went to the same schools together. I spent most of the afternoon and evening chatting with them all. I'm sure most of them thought I had left the Army and was doing some local civilian job. I was just happy to let them think whatever they liked.

Occasionally I took a 'casual' walk around the outside area, telling people who asked that I was going out for some fresh air. In reality I was looking around the cars and the bins to check for anything suspicious that might be lying about or going on around the building and car park area. At that time UVIEDs (under vehicle improvised explosive devices) were very popular with the growing IRA units.

As it happened there were no problems: nobody had tried to follow me from Belfast to Leeds; I didn't notice any suspicious activities taking place outside the hotel; and the wedding party went without a hitch. One of my main concerns had been that if my brother realised I was carrying a loaded Walther PPK in a shoulder holster. That was not quite the thing to bring to a wedding, at least not outside of Sicily, and he would have gone nuts and given me a really good beating. He's bigger than me and can get quite stroppy at times. I would have preferred to mix it with the IRA – or even Kev – before getting into a scuffle with my brother. Luckily for me, he didn't notice the slight bulge and I was back on the streets of Belfast patrolling with Kev, John and the lads before everyone back in Yorkshire had fully recovered and cleared up after the party.

With my brother being a little older than me, he always played the boss when we were out and about together as kids. We usually got along quite well but our friendship soured a little and we didn't speak much after I joined the Army. He always thought I was stupid for joining up and we didn't really communicate during that time. However, he was much happier after I finished with the full-time Forces around the early 1980s and we've got on much better ever since. Looking back on it now, I can guess that it was not so much dislike as worry for me that generated his disapproval.

Another time, not long after my brother's wedding, I was out and about on general surveillance with my section in three cars, Foxtrot, Delta and Echo, patrolling the Falls Road and Andersonstown district. It was an unusually clear and quiet evening. We had been up onto Glen Road, down Kennedy Way and Stockmans to Musgrave Park Hospital for a brew with some of the uniformed lads down there and a chat with the Intelligence section. As usual, after we pulled in we parked out of sight and left our SMGs locked in the boot of one car. Then we cleared our 9 millies before going into the location building.

At about 10:30 pm, we decided to go out again and have another look around Andersonstown off the Falls Road after a run back up Kennedy Way and up around Turf Lodge. We drove around the general areas but we were always close enough to be in a position so we could support each other if required, especially in 'hard' areas.

As a section patrolling out in the city we normally split into various cars, staying in constant radio contact, and we always knew where the other guys in their cars were. We moved around spread out and we very rarely split up totally. We only went off on our own when we had finished and were heading back to base or to meet up with someone else for some reason.

What we were looking for in and around the dark, dismal streets on these general patrols were opportunist targets, such as car thieves in action, suspected weapon movements, armed vigilante patrols and wanted persons – which we had a long list of, in our operations room.

This night, however, was fairly quiet and little seemed to be going on until we turned off the Falls Road onto Donegall Road. There we noticed some people milling around on the darkened street corners in the murky area of St James's Estate. It was quite a small estate and backed up to St Louise's College between the Falls Road and the M1. So we decided to take a look into the estate – a bleak, depressing place with many derelict and burned-out terraced houses, with rubble in the roads.

Most of the street lights had been shot out on previous occasions by the Army, because it assisted them for when they moved around the streets or to and from various locations while patrolling at night.

We continued to tick along through the estate, and just as we passed a group of two or three men near the junction of St James's Road and crescent, Kev, in the back of our car, piped up.

'Look Sy, I'm sure one of those guys over on the corner is armed.'

He was certain he had seen a weapon, so I immediately radioed this information through to one of our other cars, a few hundred metres away towards the other end of the estate.

'Hello Foxtrot, this is Delta,' I said. 'Colin, can you come over this side, around the junction of St James's Road and Crescent and have a look at some players to try and confirm Kev's weapon sighting?'

During this early period of the Troubles, we usually gave out street names in 'clear' as the IRA were not sophisticated enough to be able to tune in to our radio frequencies. At other times, we gave nicknames to areas we were working in, or we often used 'veiled' speech when speaking about various areas. But this all later changed, after they acquired equipment to enable them to listen in to us or uniformed Army and police units.

Colin in the other car immediately confirmed. 'OK Sy, no problem. I'll be there within figures five minutes.'

We turned away, down Donegall Road to the M1 roundabout. We would hang around there in a quiet dark lay-by while the other team with Colin moved in to take a look around the area, check out the group of men Kev had spotted and report back to us.

Mike was in Echo further away on the Falls Road but confirmed on the radio that he was close by if he was needed.

Even in many of these hard Republican areas it was quite feasible for us to drive in and have a look around without being stopped or challenged by the locals. That is to say, once or twice at a push was OK, but no more. The few people around would look and stare, not sure who we were. Perhaps they were initially a little afraid or apprehensive that we were simply another terror gang from a different part of the city just having a nose around. But if we stayed around the area for too long, they would throw up a barricade or otherwise block the road to trap us and check us out. Had we been a uniformed patrol in a Land Rover, we would probably have been shot at or stoned as soon as we showed our faces.

Our other car made its pass by the men and Colin came on the radio to confirm. 'OK Sy, we have two men on that corner with one rifle, possibly an M2 carbine.'

'OK, out,' I acknowledged, as Colin and his team moved away from the immediate area. Heading back up from the M1 roundabout, we turned onto Donegall Road, left into Rodney Parade and right up St Katharine Road. We wanted to come up to the group slowly from behind with lights off to surprise them, catching them momentarily off guard and try to provoke some reaction.

As we slowly turned right onto St James's Crescent, we killed our lights and wound our windows down. None of us in the car spoke a word to each other, with the radio turned down as we gently, silently crept up to our targets at about four or five mph. Kev in the back seat cocked his SMG. They were there, two people chatting to each other, standing a little sideways to us but mainly facing away, on the corner about 15 metres ahead. We closed in on these two unsuspecting players until, when we were just a few metres behind them, they turned and saw us. One started to run away as the other lifted his rifle to aim at us. We all (him and us) opened fire almost simultaneously at each other. The man possibly managed to fire off his first shot as we drew level with him, just before we opened up.

By the time they saw us, I had already forced my 9 millie across the front of Tug, my driver, making sure the gun was just out of his window. This was to stop the ejecting empty cases hitting him in the face while he started to accelerate. I fired two or three rounds with one hand at approximately three to four metres range. Kev, at the same time, was aiming and poised to fire his SMG at the group. As I fired, he too fired a short burst of three to four rounds out through his side window and then quickly spun and turned on his knee to fire another burst of four to five rounds out through the car's back window as we passed by the group and carried on accelerating away.

We carried on and sent a full report over the radio as we drove off directly back to our base. Our ops HQ informed the uniformed forces of the shooting and as far as we knew, they went over to St James's to take a look around. After we arrived back at our location, we parked the vehicles and un-loaded our weapons before handing all our gear into the stores … but not before checking our car for bullet holes. We couldn't see very much that night but in the morning we noticed that Delta, a Hillman Hunter, had some holes in its driver's side, the one nearest the gunmen.

We took three hits on the car (front wing, rear door and rear wheel arch). We saw both men fall as we drove away and heard later from the Army that only one had survived. We had no casualties except for the rear window which Kev fired out through as we passed the men. But unfortunately, the press had a field day with this incident, with ridiculous claims like *Army murder gangs are out on the streets murdering innocent people*. We always fired controlled aimed shots when we had to.

A couple of days later, Kev went back to the estate posing as a member of the press. He went to the house of the dead gunman to have a look and interview the parents of the dead man, while the body was there lying in a coffin in the front room of the house. No one knew about this except a couple of us in the section. We took him down there in a car and dropped him off near the estate so he could walk in. Then we waited around for him for about an hour or so, until he returned to the car after the interview.

Kev always seemed to have a strange, even morbid sense of curiosity, especially when he was involved in the shooting. However, he got round to paying his respects to the parents and managed to get the interview to help keep his cover intact.

I can only imagine what would have happened if all the players in the house had realised that Kev wasn't really from the press and that in fact it was him that actually shot the deceased. It took nerves of steel and the courage of a lion for Kev to go in that house, but that was Kev.

It was about this time that we all began to feel some distinct changes in the atmosphere. It was not an unhappy feeling, but it just seemed that a little more tension and urgency was in the air. The streets of some of the most desperate areas of Belfast had become like a war zone. Every night and most days were filled with explosions and gunfire. Many people in the city were not living; in fact they were barely surviving, what with the constant gun battles running in some of the toughest and direst streets in Britain. All over the city people were far too afraid to even leave their homes after dark.

Another good friend of mine had recently been gunned down and killed while on one very successful long-term operation.

He was part of the Four Square Laundry operation, which was run by another small independent section of the MRF. They operated with a small team of three or four members and had been extremely successful for a very long time; much longer than most people think.

They operated from a vehicle made up to look like a genuine laundry van and they used to regularly visit the fringe areas around Suffolk and Dunmurry, on the outskirts of Belfast. They collected laundry from various houses in the estates to be taken away for cleaning. But first they sent it to forensic testing for explosive residue, gun oil, lead and powder-burn traces.

After the testing, they'd record and register any positive clothing and have the laundry washed and returned. Later, the uniformed forces would make follow-up spot searches of the whole area including the suspect addresses and would usually find weapons, ammunition or explosives in the houses.

It was a wonderful well organised little operation, worked very well for a very long period and was fully instrumental in the finding of hoards and hoards of weapons and explosives. Unfortunately, the Four Square Laundry needed a lot of business to be successful, and as a result had to pitch its prices quite low. It could have been this that attracted attention to them but I very much doubt it, due to its longevity in its activities. It was also strongly rumoured at the time, and was more than likely, that one or two of our own IRA informers who had 'turned back' to their masters and given the IRA details of the operation, probably in some vain attempt to save their own skins. It didn't work: the two informers were found slaughtered soon after my friend's murder and the end of the Four Square Laundry.

When the Four Square Laundry op was eventually blown, my friend Telford (Ted) Stuart was making notes in the driver's seat of his van. He was murdered without warning, sitting right there. It has been rumoured that other MRF members were hidden, observing, in the van roof. But this is not true and Ted was alone when he was machine-gunned to death at point blank range. His female colleague was across the street collecting laundry from a house at the time, and although she was deeply shocked she was fortunately unhurt. Needless to say, this particular operation ceased to exist then and there, but we had many strings to our bow and other operations forged on relentlessly.

This small section was part of our MRF unit but operated totally independently of us. They had the laundry business, together with an office, and also a very popular 'information gathering' massage parlour which was wired for sound, just off the city centre. This was also raided soon after the shooting but without any casualties. The whole section (or troop) consisted of only a handful of members. I knew many of them and we often met up for a coffee and chat, in between operations. The murder of Ted Stuart was a great shock to us all, not that it made us afraid for our own lives. We were shocked because of the loss of a very good close friend: a generous, cheerful and genuine person. I can still see him to this day, laughing as we walked together down the path in our compound, with his big thick hair and bushy beard.

The main responsibilities and duties of this section were being regularly and deeply involved in observation/surveillance and information gathering, working closely with our MRF Intelligence section and that of other uniformed units throughout the city. Other methods they used included working with informers, whom some people outside the loop called 'MRFs,' 'Smurfs' or 'Freds'. It's well known, they were taken around in covert blacked-out vehicles, pointing out known and suspected terrorists. Other responsibilities included a great deal of OP (observation post) work, much more than carried out by us in 81, 82 and 83 sections. Our main duty was to be out and about day and night in the city, gathering information, trying to spoil and interfere with IRA plans and operations, and when possible; confront active terrorists.

If the MRF was known as a top secret operational unit, as it was, then this other small section was a double top secret sub-unit of the MRF that even fewer people knew anything of.

9

Firing on Automatic

An old friend of mine, from my original parent unit but working in a different, unrelated plain-clothes outfit, was caught late one rainy night in the Falls Road area. He was in a dangerous part of the city, driving back to his base from being out on public-relations duties.

After turning off the Falls Road to take a short cut through the streets, he was forced to stop the vehicle by a group of armed men waiting in the shadows. A man travelling with him prior to his capture managed to jump out of the car and disappear into the back streets before he came to a halt. The armed vigilante group dragged my friend out and forced him against a wall while they searched him.

While he was held at gunpoint, his 9 millie pistol, which he carried for his own protection, was found. They beat and kicked him to the floor then dragged him into a derelict house in one of the dark and bleak streets off Falls Road.

He was relentlessly tortured and savagely beaten for a couple of hours before the group decided to throw him head first down the cellar steps of the burnt-out house. Fortunately, despite having landed heavily on the hard cellar floor, he had the peace of mind to crawl away to one side as fast as he was able. Above him, he heard the gunmen laughing and preparing their weapons to fire down at him in the darkness. As he struggled and crawled into a corner he was hit in the legs by three or four bullets from two or three automatic weapons, which fired between 10 to 15 rounds down at him. After the shooting, he again heard the gunmen laughing and chatting so he lay still and quiet, in the dark, cold room, playing dead for several hours until he was sure the gunmen had gone.

Four or five hours later, in the early dawn, he managed to drag himself back up the cellar steps in what must have been horrendous pain – one of his kneecaps had been blown off. From the top of the cellar he clambered and crawled, picking his way through the back door and into the alley. Out there he slowly edged along, close to the walls, quietly passing the backyard gates of the other buildings, stopping himself from crying out in pain, not wanting any local 'Catholics' to see or hear him while he inched along through the deserted streets for about half a mile.

If any locals had seen him crawling along injured, the likelihood was that they would have finished the job themselves. Dragging his legs behind him, no doubt losing plenty of blood, my friend made his way to the near-by Royal Victoria Hospital; he just managed to reach the hospital gate-man before passing out. That man, realising what the situation was, immediately called some assistance to get him into the emergency department.

I went to visit him a few days later, after he had been transferred to the Musgrave Park Hospital (military wing.) Initially he looked in a terrible state, with his bruised face and both legs bandaged and held up by a kind of trapeze system. I spent a few hours with him, cracking jokes about his situation and telling him that he was lucky to be alive.

From his descriptions of the terrorists, I was quite sure of who the main character was that tried to murder him. He was a local psycho we thought was hiding away in the South at the time, as he was wanted for a variety of killings. A few more days later, I had an evening meeting down in the city with one of our more reliable informers. I asked him to have a quiet check around to see if this particular character has been around the area recently.

Not very long after that I was contacted by the informer. 'Yes,' he told me. 'He's back in the city, he's been back a few weeks.' He also confirmed that the fugitive had been directly involved in the incident concerning my friend, along with three or four other men.

Over the next few days we managed to forge a plan within the section to draw this particular crazy out of the shadows. We knew that he knew of our existence, that he had a deep hatred of us, and that he would also take much pride in getting the opportunity to slot a couple of us if he could.

We made it known through various channels, that a military plain-clothes section would be operating an observation post in a house roof in the Ballymurphy area on a particular day and time. When we received confirmation that this psycho – James Bryson – was preparing an attack on our bogus OP, we informed the local Army unit of a possible attack.

Our target, together with two or three armed friends, arrived in the area cruising around, up and down the streets in one car. The Army made their plans and was lying in wait in various positions and we were observing the scene from an area where we could follow up if things didn't go to plan. However, exactly as they planned, the Army opened fire on the ASU, claiming the terrorist kills and leaving the streets of Belfast a little safer. All we in fact did was to pass on some vital intelligence of a possible terrorist attack and the Army formed their own plans. We were effectively just doing our job. We weren't interested in claiming the kills ourselves, we never were. We simply wanted all hard core terrorists stopped. It was irrelevant who actually stopped them, along with this particular psycho and a couple of his sidekicks taken off the streets ... permanently. As it was, Bryson lingered a few weeks and finally died on 22 September, 1973.

Most of the terrorists gunmen we were directly confronted with, were not of much Intelligence value anyway, especially with the developing 'Cell' structure they were operating with... It was the boys further up the line who had some Intelligence value, not so much the average inexperienced gunman. Our office was in the gutter and our job was to gather information while interfering and spoiling IRA operations. The IRA physical structure was our target and main focus. We had no contact or association with any of the Loyalist organisations.

It all sounds simple and straight forward but in fact it took quite some time to plan, organise and co-ordinate. We never went out to directly target any specific individuals or focus on any one particular player. There were so many armed terrorists running around the streets at this time. It was very much a 'target rich environment'.

My friend managed to make a full recovery and carry on with his military career, after losing a kneecap and having to undergo more than 12 months of recuperation. But this didn't stop him from taking part in the many sporting activities he was regularly involved with. Many years later we both enjoyed a weekend water skiing together at Lake Windermere, north of Manchester, and you couldn't really see that he'd had his legs so badly shot up.

Things didn't always go our way all the time. Together with a colleague, I was on a static OP observing a house off the Falls Road near the Royal Victoria Hospital. It was quite a clear sunny day with a few billowing white clouds in the distance. We had been there, with our car parked at the roadside, for quite some time and we were expecting our relief to arrive very soon in the area to take over the surveillance. The streets were quite busy with lots of people shopping and passing cars scurrying about. We occasionally got out of the car and mingled with the pedestrians wandering up and down the street and looking in the shop windows. We didn't feel or look out of place and nobody was taking any notice of us because there was plenty going on around us.

Back in the car a little while later, I was sitting in the driver's seat and Bob, my colleague on the operation, was in the front passenger seat next to me. We occasionally glanced through a newspaper and fiddled with the radio while continuing to observe the area. Our car was parked, like many others, with the driver's door on the kerbside.

I'll always remember very clearly; it was as if in slow motion. I saw what in a split second was going to happen – an old blue Audi 100, mingled among the traffic, was coming towards us along the street at approximately 30 mph. As it drew closer it slowed down and I saw a gun barrel showing through the rear passenger window. There were three men in the car and it slowed even more as it closed up to us.

Before I could say anything or even reach for my 9 millie under my lap, the air was filled with blinding flashes and deafening cracking. Our windows were blown out and there were bullets flying everywhere. The smell of cordite was very strong in the air: they must have opened fire on us from a range of only a few metres as they slowly slipped passed. Within only two or three seconds, it was all over. I was, amazingly, OK. Then I looked at Bob who was slumped on me, slowly falling onto my lap. I knew he was hit but I wasn't sure how badly, and all I could do was put my arm around him, bash a clear hole in the windscreen and drive like a man possessed to the hospital, just a couple of hundred metres along the road.

As I set off, I swung out into the road and noticed people running and cowering behind other cars along the street. They looked bewildered and not too sure what was going on or who had done the shooting. I quickly made my way the short distance along the Falls Road, weaving through the cars and people until I reached the RVH.

I flew screeching through the main gate and carried on weaving my way up the driveway in and out of parked cars. At the casualty department entrance, I pulled in and stopped. Two men in white quickly took control and put Bob onto a stretcher. I felt helpless and a bit frantic and could see he was in a very bad way if not already dead. He had taken two or three rounds through the lower part of the car door and sill into his hips and lower abdomen. His passenger seat looked like a grenade had gone off under it. Bob died a couple of weeks later.

While he was being wheeled through the florescent corridor into the emergency ward I contacted our base on the car radio and informed them what had happened. They said for me to wait there and they would send someone down to pick me up as soon as they could.

Bob was taken into a cubicle and the doctors and nurses worked on him for about ten minutes while I watched over them. They put a drip in his arm and an oxygen mask over his mouth, while trying to shock him into life. I was a real mess, covered in blood, so the nurses took me to another cubicle to check me out and were relieved to see that none of it was mine. When they finished, I asked if I could wash my hands and arms and one of them smiled and indicated, pointing to the sink in the corner. I had to use the nail brush to clean Bob's blood off my hands and wristwatch before it dried too much.

One nurse gave me a cup of coffee to settle me down and a doctor approached me to give me Bob's 9 millie pistol which had still been tucked in his belt. Even though he said nothing, I'm sure the doctor and nurses had a good idea of whom or what we were. He handed me the Browning together with Bob's magazines and spare ammo, wrapped up in a pillow case which he took from a cupboard.

I kept out of the way and felt that it was best to wait in the gents' toilets until Tug and Dave arrived to pick me up. After they found me we went out to my car and picked up all the equipment which I'd wrapped in a jacket and locked in the boot earlier, while the doctors were taking care of Bob. We waited for about 15 minutes there until the car was picked up and transported to Lisburn Army HQ. Little was said during the 40-minute drive back to our base. I sat quietly in the back just staring out of the window most of the way. I must have looked awful, covered in Bob's blood.

Back at base, I had to go straight in to see the OC for a debriefing of the events while they were fresh in my mind. Before I went in, I handed in mine and Bob's weapons together with the vehicle documents, maps and radio equipment. The atmosphere in the ops room was very sombre as everyone knew what had happened and just nodded to me and tapped my shoulder as they walked by me. I was still shocked and couldn't say very much at the time; but there was little to say anyway, except for general descriptions of the gunmen and the type of car they were driving. The Boss said he would write out the report of the shooting which I could check over and sign the following day.

'OK, Sy,' he added, 'You go and get yourself cleaned up, have some rest and something to eat and I'll see you in the morning. Take it easy tonight and we'll see how you feel tomorrow. If you'd like a bit of time off, just let me know."

As I left his office, I said, 'I'll be OK in the morning, no problem.'

After dumping my jeans, shirt and jumper in the bin, for burning, I had a long hot shower and spent most of the evening on my bed listening to some easy music on Tug's tape recorder. Some of the other guys popped in occasionally to see how I was or offer me a pot of tea and have a chat.

We had been very unlucky that day, just in the wrong place at the wrong time, perhaps overstaying our welcome. We were sussed and the IRA did a number on us, and I was just very lucky to survive. I lost three very good friends from the unit in my three years and all were in very dramatic circumstances. I feel that casualty rate was rather high, at ten per cent, considering the size of the unit at the time.

If any other Army unit lost ten per cent of its strength during its stay in Ulster, there would have been hell-to-pay all the way back to Downing Street. But in many ways, our job was many times more demanding and dangerous than that of the regular soldier on the streets.

It has been mentioned, in other recent books, that it was much later in the 1980s that the first undercover agents were killed in confrontations with the IRA. But in reality, the first under-cover agents were actually killed during terrorist activities in the early years of the 1970s and not later.

It's was my understanding now, that the Army and government went to great lengths to keep the activities of the MRF tightly under wraps during 1971-74 and there is very little or almost nothing accurate published about the MRF operations during this period, except for some media extracts from some previously publicised incidents we were involved in. It was not until it was confirmed in Parliament in March 1994 that the MRF actually existed. Even though there are many people around, some of them quite influential, making assumptions and claiming or pretending to know all about the MRF, in fact, over 40 years later, there remains only a small handful that truly knows anything of this secret undercover unit and its activities.

During our off-duty 12 hours we almost always stuck together playing cards or reading. Sometimes a small group of us borrowed one of the cars and went off to Bangor to sit by the shore, just relaxing as best we could. One time I went out for a drive in the country with Kev and Colin, the two lads in the section. Off-duty we always travelled fully armed and ready in case we had a call-out while we were away from base, so we were able to go directly to the incident in question and link up with the rest of the section, without wasting precious time.

The weather was quite clear and sunny and we had a really lovely day out, initially heading off towards Bangor then tootling into and around the country side, visiting some local beauty spots and a couple of country pubs where we had a beer and relaxed over some lunch. Later, on our way back, we suddenly realised that we had spent most of the afternoon over the border in Eire. The actual border wasn't specifically marked on most maps and it was very easy to simply wander over to the other side if you were close.

Had we been stopped by the Garda, we would have had a very difficult time trying to explain away the reason for the maps, radios and weapons we were carrying. Not to mention Kev's eight-inch flick knife. We would have probably been arrested on the spot, perhaps causing quite a problem for the Army and government in the north.

However, we kept the location of our little afternoon jaunt to ourselves. The OC would have gone shitless if he had known where we had been that day. He couldn't have done much about it but he would still have gone nuts.

Some days, while on standby section, we'd all slope off in two or three cars to the nearby 30-metre firing range about two miles away for some practice with the various weapons we had in our armoury. We'd load up the cars with all the guns we could get our hands on, including Browning 9 millies, Walthers, SMGs with and without silencers, plus some of the other weapons – .357 Magnums and Smith & Wesson .38s. We also took the Thompson .45 whenever we could, just to play with.

I always enjoyed those range days; the atmosphere was relaxed and the banter was good. Mike usually played the range officer, checking the safety procedures and setting out the plans for the day's shooting. Tug normally controlled the ammunition, splitting open the boxes and setting the bullets out in batches for us to load into the magazines, while Kev, Colin and me would be checking and lightly oiling all the weapons, getting them ready for firing. John, usually helped by Dave, was in charge of making sure we had some food and tea available for lunch break while at the same time organising some targets for us all. This left Ben complaining, as always, that he had nothing to do but sit and watch us.

We didn't bother to use regular targets like figure 11s or 12s, and instead just threw some tin cans or cigarette packets on the 'butts' (sandbank behind the target mountings) and practiced on them. After a few months handling and practicing with a 9 millie, my best score was nine out of twelve rounds within the area of a cigarette packet (6 x 4cm) at 30 metres, which I felt was pretty good shooting with the 9mm Browning pistol. The rounds that missed were only an inch or so off the packet, which seemed good enough to me as they would all have been kill shots. The overall grouping spread was about four to five inches in diameter, which I felt was good enough for a hand-held pistol at that distance.

I remember one day, one of the lads in our section brought with him a flak jacket he had picked up at one of the Army locations a day or so earlier. It had a bullet hole with dried blood around the upper chest area and the lads in the section wanted to test the weapons on it to gauge the effect different types of ammunition would have on the body armour.

I wasn't too keen on the idea, though, and didn't fire at it, because I couldn't help thinking that some poor guy had probably died wearing it. However, the lads threw the jacket onto the range target area and the tests went ahead using 9mm, .45, .38 and .357 rounds, which clearly proved that flak jackets weren't much use against gun fire and their main protection was from bomb blasts or nail bombs. Perhaps that's why they were called flak jackets and not bullet-proof jackets. Many years later, an extra armoured ballistics plate was inserted in the frontal section so the more modern jackets offered at least some protection from gunfire.

We also practiced firing from various obscure positions, such as from out the rear window of one of the cars, over the bonnet and boot, or across the front of the driver's face from the passenger's position. It can be naturally unnerving when someone fires a 9 millie pistol about two or three inches from your nose, especially when you're trying to drive at the same time. The empty cases eject out from the upper right side of the pistol and you need to force your firing hand across the driver's chest and out through his window, otherwise the cases of the spent rounds would hit the driver 'oven ready', right in the face – not to mention the eyes. (In the USA or Europe where they drive on the right the cases would bounce off the windshield and into the driver's lap: only a slightly better scenario.)

During one of our practice sessions we also developed a technique where we could fire a semi-automatic Browning 9 millie pistol so it appeared as if it was firing on full automatic. What you have to do is turn sideways to the target and hold the pistol tight in one hand, preferably the right. Hold it close to your body, horizontal at about waist height and forward on your leading hip. Then, with the other hand, placing your index finger straight through the trigger guard, you move it forward and back horizontally in a rhythmic fashion. If you get it right, you can fire off a full 12-round magazine in about five seconds. It's not a very accurate method and is best used in an emergency situation where you have to fire into a group or down a small passageway. If you didn't hit anyone, you would sure frighten the hell out of them, allowing you a few valuable moments to escape.

Another trick with the quite bulky Browning 9 millie pistol was to take off the plastic pistol-grip side panels to make them a little slimmer and easier to conceal under our jacket or in our waist bands. We did have shoulder holsters but very few of us used them, as they were also quite bulky and we preferred to just slip them in the waistband of our jeans. With the barrel pointing vertically down the back of the hip and the butt end pointing forward, you could almost feel it wasn't there. The only problem we had with this method of carrying the pistols was that we had to give the barrels a good scrub and light oiling every day. This was because the heat from your body would cause some condensation, resulting in a build-up of a rust film in the barrels.

When we were travelling in a car, we normally slipped our pistols under our thigh with just the tip of the grip showing so it was easy to get at even if using the radio or the maps. However, with the Walthers (the James Bond pistol) we almost always used shoulder holsters. These guns could easily slip out of your waist band if carried this way as they were smaller, slimmer and less bulky. We normally carried Walthers when we worked in a hotel or restaurant environment, where we operated close to people and needed to wear closer-fitting clothes or suits.

Occasionally while on the ranges we used a 'willing volunteer' from our section to act as a guinea pig to practice 'fire and movement' drills. We threw a few tin cans on the butts in different places, moved up close to within a couple of metres and took our guinea pig 'hostage' by grabbing him around the neck. Then with the other hand we'd fire double taps at the targets as we backed away. Again, it was not a very accurate method, firing with one hand, but it was an effective way of backing off from a dangerous situation in an emergency. The main idea is to put fire down on the targets, while you increase your distance from them and escape. You try to keep a constant blanket of suppressive fire on the targets, forcing them to run or hide and allowing you a few valuable moments to make your move.

Another type of fire and movement we practiced was as a half section. We lined up with two full magazines of 12 rounds each for our 9 millies and the SMG man also had two full magazines of 28 each – the Sterling SMG mags took 30 bullets, but we would never fully pack them because it would fatigue the springs and could lead to jams (stoppages). The two or three pistol men quickly moved forward a couple of metres beyond the firing point and dropped down onto one knee to fire three or four rounds each, while the SMG man moved forward through and between us. He then took up a firing position a couple of metres forward of us, in his turn firing eight to 12 rounds, double tapping. And as he was firing we moved forward past him and so on until we were on top of the targets.

The aim was to keep a constant flow, a blanket of fire going down on the targets while members of the section are moving to new positions with no halts in the shooting. We all had to quickly change our magazines halfway through the sequence by counting our shots. That's not so difficult on the range, but it's a whole new ball game trying to count your shots when you're live on the streets and being fired at by terrorist gunmen.

However, it proved a very effective method of moving forward onto the targets while keeping up constant fire. It takes a lot of practice to be effective, and we also practiced it in reverse – an excellent way of backing off from a target or group of targets and keeping accurate covering fire going down at the same time.

The Sterling SMG and the 9mm Browning pistol have similar actions and characteristics in many ways, except that the SMG has a fixed firing pin. Therefore, with the SMG, when the working parts (breech block) are cocked back, they stay locked back. Whereas the 9 millie breech block slides forward when released from your grip and feeds a round into the breech, or chamber, and is only discharged when the trigger is pulled. The SMG breech block is only released from its locked-back position on pulling the trigger when it's set on semi-automatic (single shots,) feeding a round into the breech and firing, all at the same time because the firing pin is fixed and solid on the block.

The recoil (re-cocking) system is virtually the same in both weapons and that is a 'blow-back' system. The SMG blows back to its locked-back position to fire single shots when not set in the fully automatic mode, whereas the 9 millie breech block blows back and immediately slides forward, placing a fresh round in the breech ready to fire. The round being fired in the breech chamber ejects the spent case on both weapons to restart the cycle. Both weapons have a safety catch but the 9 millie pistol has a secondary safety system on the hammer itself. After cocking a 9 millie, the hammer can be released forward under control to rest on the firing pin and then gently pulled back to a first stage click, resting two or three millimetres back off the head of the firing pin.

When the magazine of the 9 millie pistol is empty, the working parts automatically lock back, like most other similar handguns, which allows for a quick and easy magazine change. When complete, you simply flip the lever with your right thumb, allowing the working parts to slip forward so you can carry on firing with a fresh clip. However, if you count you rounds while firing you should know when the last round is fed into the breech. Then you change the magazine and keep on firing without any interruption.

It often surprises me when, in films, the bad guys are told to drop their weapons and they happily toss them off to one side, bouncing and tumbling onto the floor. In reality it's the worst thing you can possibly do with a handgun or SMG. Because of their design, they can easily discharge when dropped on the floor. With the SMG, this can happen because the breech block can 'half cock' itself, meaning it is not fully cocked and locked. In turn, this will feed a round into the chamber and fire off at the same moment of impact with the floor. The 9 millie pistol can fire off if the head of the hammer strikes the floor or if the concussion of the weapon hitting the floor disturbs the sear in the trigger mechanism.

The holding and aiming of these two types of weapons is obviously quite different. If you can't hold and aim a weapon correctly, you're not going to hit anything; it's as simple as that.

I remember one time when John, driving with a couple of other lads in the car, stopped at a junction in the Andersonstown area late one night and a young boy came out of the shadows up to his side of the car. John turned to look at the boy, but came face to face with the wrong end of a pistol barrel. The boy was only about 12 or 13 years old and very nervous.

A moment later John saw a bright flash in front of his nose, perhaps less than a metre away, as the boy fired in his face. John's reaction was to put his foot down to get away fast, not knowing initially if he had been shot. Fortunately neither he nor any others in the car were hurt and later, after checking the car, there were no holes to be found or any damage at all to the vehicle.

The young boy had aimed the relatively heavy pistol with one hand directly at John's face from perhaps two feet away, fired it, but totally missed the car. Therefore, correct holding and aiming is essential for accurate shooting. We decided that the boy, being quite small and nervous, must have pulled the pistol in an upward direction as he exerted pressure on the trigger. This, combined with a strong recoil action, meant that the round passed right over the top of the car and probably struck a house wall across the street. I don't think we reported this. We very rarely bothered to report incidents such as this. We discussed them amongst ourselves, but never normally bothered to make out any official reports. The police had enough on their plates and something like this was just another minor occurrence, of many.

The SMG is held in the conventional way, as a rifle. In the standing position one hand, normally the left, is a cradle support under the stock of the barrel with that side of the body turned a little towards the target and feet open about shoulder-width apart. Meanwhile, the firing hand holds the grip, with the elbow kept high to keep the butt in the shoulder. If the elbow is down, the weapon can jump out of the shoulder when it's fired.

The recoil from the SMG isn't much of a kick; it is more like a rocking feeling. Firing on automatic, it's best to fire in bursts of two to three rounds at a time. Anymore and it's most likely that after three rounds the rest will be off target due to the recoil action, which kicks up and to the right. Your breathing pattern is also important as the weapon's barrel will move up and down in the aim as you inhale and exhale. Therefore, when firing the SMG – like all weapons – I always found that it's best to take in a deep breath, then exhale about a third of your breath and hold it, check your aim and fire.

The 9mm Browning semi-automatic pistol, like most others, is a totally different weapon to hold and aim, and generally speaking, the shorter the barrel the more difficult it is to be accurate. Again, in the standing position, the cradling hand and body is turned slightly towards the target. The firing arm and hand is held almost straight, forced forwards into the cradling hand towards the target with the pistol barrel like a direct extension of the arm. The firing hand grips the pistol grip with the middle two fingers, with the little finger just resting but not gripping too much. If you grip and pull in with the little finger the barrel is pulled downwards and the rounds will strike low on the target. Therefore, with the pistol held in a direct line with the firing arm, the barrel becomes like a pointing finger.

For example, if you sit at home, stretch out your best, firing arm and point your finger at objects randomly around the room, in a natural way with both eyes open. You'll notice that at least 90 per cent of the time you will be spot on target with the object you are pointing at. This is how you aim a pistol, pointing at the target as if the barrel is your pointing index finger. The cradling hand cups and holds the firing hand and helps to keep the aiming position as stable as possible. The Browning 9 millie, like most other pistols of a similar calibre, has quite a powerful recoil action 'kick' and requires quite a firm grip with both hands. To fire this weapon and most other pistols with one hand, unless in an emergency, is very much a waste of time and ammunition.

10

First, Fast and Furious

On many operations we had to man our own observation posts. These took many different forms – from standing on a street corner or sitting in a vehicle to hiding in the roof of a building; or simply setting up a conventional OP out in the countryside overlooking the city. Sometimes, as mentioned earlier, we would take up a position in house gardens, provided they were large enough and that there was plenty of cover and good avenues of escape.

Periodically, I manned an observation post in an old church roof by Crumlin Road, taking photographs of the Sunday morning worshipers. Two of us usually 'infilled' – moved into position – very early in the morning. Then when it was all over by around 1:00 am the following day we would 'exfill,' in the middle of the night, leaving no trace that we had been there.

We'd have our cameras on motor-drive, set on tripods, and plenty of film for all types of light, together with camouflage nets to put over ourselves in the darkened area of the roof. We took our 9 millies with us and normally a silenced SMG for a little reassurance, together with plenty of sandwiches and flasks of tea. And there was always at least one of our cars a few minutes away, on standby if we needed them as extra support.

It was a nice little operation, simply clicking away, taking lots of photos and registering them on a timesheet as the Catholic worshipers entered and left the church during the day and evening. We'd make a full register of all the photos of the people that were there on a particular day and time.

We were in effect collating a picture library of who was and wasn't there, which also came in handy if some player was picked up and tried to use the church last Sunday as his alibi, as they often did. It was known as 'The Gathering of Information'. Many items of data, gathered together, will produce an 'Intelligence Picture'. It's never totally complete, but will be good enough for other experts to build on and fill in the gaps. Intelligence isn't the information, it's what you can deduce from the information to hand.

For example, most people walking into a single person's house can generally see if it's a man's or a woman's home. What you see – clothes, pictures, ornaments, magazines and the style of furniture – is the information, but the picture all this information gives you is 'Intelligence'. The rooms will often show that they are occupied (information) but the items you see will tell you (intelligence) if the occupant is male or female, perhaps even their age group and also things about the person: smoker or non-smoker, size and weight, books and hobbies.

It's a matter of training in observation techniques and practice, of being able to analyse accurately the information on hand. Like when you enter a bar and you see at the table where you sit how many chairs and glasses there are and how many cigarettes are in the ash tray. Simply the types of glasses and chairs can tell you how many people were there together, and if they were male or female. Good Barmen will often give males and females different styles of glasses, even if they are drinking the same drink. Also, the ash tray can tell you how many people were there smoking, the sex of the people (lipstick traces), the different types of cigarette and probably how long they were all there.

None of this is foolproof or totally reliable but it all adds up to build the Intelligence Picture. You could also take it one step further and remove items for finger printing, except that gathering glasses and cigarette ends everywhere you go isn't easy when you're working alone undercover. But you could take a glass for printing if you knew for sure one of your targets handled it and you needed his or her prints. Today, the experts can get DNA from a cigarette butt – it is legal to extract such information from a discarded item.

We had set up an observation post in the bushes, high in the hills above Suffolk and the Ladybrook Estates near the area of Andersonstown. It was quite a calm, sunny day with some light wispy high clouds and a gentle northerly breeze. There were chest-to-shoulder-high thick, bushy hedgerows running along both sides of the road, offering an ideal quiet place where we often set up an OP for a few hours at a time, observing the estates below. We were in two cars parked on the grassy hard shoulder, off the Upper Springfield Road on a slight bend near some old quarries.

One car had its bonnet up and our two drivers, with their SMGs out of sight, were positioned by the front. Periodically, one of the cars would move off to have a look around a few hundred metres up and down the road. Then they'd come back and park while the rest of us had set up and manned the OP in the bushes.

That particular day we only planned to be there for a few hours, as we had arrived quite late in the morning from our briefing with the Operations and Intelligence officers responsible for the area. The local Army unit knew we were in the area and had arranged for their patrols to keep out of the way for us. Our task was, like always on this regular operation, to observe the housing estates below and record any weapon movements around the streets from house to house, and to take photographs. Afterwards, we would give the details to the local uniformed forces to make follow-up searches later that day or early the next morning.

Frequently, weapons were moved around different houses and luckily for us these movements tended to occur when, as arranged, the uniformed patrols were not so prevalent in the area for a certain period. It was a good operation which we often activated, with great results. But on this occasion everywhere was very quiet, with little or no movement. I had been up and down the road with Kev a few times while John stayed with the other car and Mike, Tug and Colin were observing in the bushes. But there was no-one around. Dave and Ben were off in a third vehicle patrolling nearby, in case we needed some help or support.

After about three or four hours we decided to call it a day. We informed the local Army unit responsible that we were going to move out of the area so that in about an hour they could resume their normal pattern of patrols through the estates below us.

Our plan, after packing up our cameras and tripods and cleaning the whole area, was to drive west, initially about 25 to 30 metres apart, moving away from town along Upper Springfield Road. Then we would turn left, opening up our gap a little and dropping down a narrow lane to Glen Road, which was parallel a few hundred metres below us down the hillside. At the junction with Glen Road we'd turn left again towards the city centre and head off back to base.

We had packed everything up and erased all evidence of our presence, and were ready to set off west along the top road. I was in the lead vehicle with Kev driving and Tug in the back, and we were approximately 100 metres ahead of our second car by the time we got to the lower junction with Glen Road. Arriving at the corner I turned east towards the city and onto Glen Road with the wide, rolling fields rising to my left, up to where our OP had been just a few minutes earlier. The Suffolk housing estate sloped down to my right, like long terraces dropping away in the distance as we moved off towards the city centre. On approaching the bus terminus, which was a few hundred metres further along the Glen Road and on the right, I clearly saw in the distance some men standing and moving around by a car.

As we drew closer and were almost about to pass them, Tug in the back said, 'Hey look, these guys on the right are armed.'

I looked up from my map folder and both Kev and I registered the men standing by a car holding binoculars and weapons. They were just loitering there, grouped together and looking up directly at the area we had just left. I didn't feel they notice us because they were holding up their binoculars at about 45 degrees, four or five metres from our car, so we carried on past: it was too late to do anything anyway.

As we cruised by at about 30 mph, I radioed a quick Sit Rep back to Mike, who was behind us with John and Colin in our second car. In fact, the Sit Rep turned out to be more like a Fire Control Order: (Group-Range-Indication-Type of fire ... or GRIT as it was known):

'Hello Mike – 100 metres – two o'clock – bus terminus – three armed men.' I didn't give the 'Type of Fire' ... I left that up to Mike to decide.

Mike acknowledged simply, 'OK, Sy – out.'

The gunmen were still looking up at where we had been as our other vehicle drew closer. They seemed totally oblivious to Mike's car quickly closing in on them. I pulled in and stopped by some other cars parked about 100 metres further on, to try and observe and act as backup in case I was needed. As far as I could see; Mike's car drew nearer still, slowing down, and I saw a barrel poking out though the rear side window. Mike was in the back and he gave the gunmen two or three short bursts with a machine gun at about four or five metres range, spraying ten to fifteen rounds into the group. I'm not sure if any of the gunmen fired at our other car, it looked like they did as their weapons appeared to be held up in the aiming position, but I'm not sure, I couldn't see clear enough into the terminus from my position. All the three gunmen collapsed tumbling and sprawling around the floor with their weapons by the car. They had little idea what had suddenly happened or what hit them. Mike carried on past me and I moved off to follow on behind him, making our way back to base to fill out our reports. As we left the area we immediately reported the shooting to the uniformed forces based in that area.

Soon after, in fact within a day or two, we heard of a fourth casualty – a chap in a house, actually in bed, who had been in the line of fire. The houses beyond the road and bus terminus were lower and the bedroom windows were in line with the road. This fourth chap had been released from internment a few weeks earlier and turned out to be a suspected terrorist member of the IRA.

One or two of the men at the bus terminus had most likely opened fire, while holding their weapons, getting ready to come up to our observation post and launch a murderous attack on us. I don't think they hadn't fully realised we had already packed up and left, but could have spotted us as we past-by first. The 'Rules of Engagement' in Northern Ireland were and are very clear: in general, you are only allowed to open fire at a person actively shooting at you or someone you are with. Also, you can open fire at someone 'aiming' a weapon but who hasn't yet fired. However, it's not necessary to have to correctly aim a weapon, to fire it and most weapons can be easily fired from the 'ready' position or from the hip.

Our role in Northern Ireland was very different and more dangerous than that of the regular uniformed security forces. Our tasks were far more demanding and we had very little backup to rely on. If there was going to be any shooting about to begin, we always planned to initiate it ourselves whenever possible. Disguise and surprise were our main forms of defence. And our method of approach, if there was a possibility of any shooting, was to act 'First, Fast and Furious' with surprise, aggression and speed foremost in our minds. We were a very small unit, no more than eight or nine on duty at any one time, regularly split up in different cars and totally alone. Often working out on a limb and totally surrounded in Republican areas and we had to use 'maximum force' when it was required, just to survive. If we hadn't … we would all be dead now.

Ulster at that time was very much a lawless state. Everyone was desperately fighting for control and the police had little idea of how to control the situation – they were just like empty uniforms walking around. People drove vehicles around freely without licences, insurance or road tax, and the police were very apprehensive or nervous about approaching anyone or issuing summonses in the strong Catholic areas, for fear of being killed. Therefore, the only way to come up with any form of a result and survive was to be ready to act quickly, obviously in line with the Yellow Card - RoE, which we did.

I was with Colin in an OP in the roof of a large building overlooking some streets in the Ballymurphy Estate. We had everything set up just the way we liked it: our SLR cameras with long lenses were mounted on tripods and lots of film for day and night photography was stacked nearby. We had our 9 millies and an SMG with suppressor beside us in case any unwelcome guests turned up, together with our sandwiches with flasks of tea and coffee. We planned to be there for 24 hours, after which time another section would take over from us.

The operation was to last seven days in total and our task was to take photographs of anyone entering and leaving a certain house in the estate. As always in OPs, we had to keep our movements down to a minimum, and if we did need to move around in there, we went very slowly so not to draw any attention from the outside. After our shift finished, we normally took away all the film we had shot for developing back at base by the Intelligence boys. They checked and collated them and later sent copies off to the Special Investigation Branch (SIB) – the military Special Branch – to look over.

During our stay, we had both taken approximately 50 photos each of the comings and goings. But I remember one particular photograph I took: it was of a man acting quite suspiciously by the house. He hovered about, moved up to the door then moved away – I managed to get a couple of shots of him as he did this. One photograph I took, I found out quite a few weeks later, had helped to land him in prison. This was the one I managed to get just as he took hold of the door handle and had one foot inside the door. This photograph associated him with the owners of the house, despite his denying throughout the police interrogation being there on that day or even knowing them. In the end the photograph broke down his defence.

That one photo out of hundreds taken over days sitting and waiting helped to dissolve the case for his defence. That photo, together with other evidence, helped land him and his associates in prison for ten years for illegal possession of weapons.

I often found it quite intriguing how little snippets of information could turn out to be so important in building a case against someone. And from that moment on, I was especially careful with every piece of information I had the privilege to handle.

Another type of OP operation we got involved in was providing protection for prominent people who had been directly threatened, such as ministers or police officers. A well-known senior police officer had asked if the military could offer some form of protection over the coming week.

Following this request, we were tasked to devise a protection plan for him and his family. They lived in a semi-detached house in the area of Castlereagh on the outskirts of southeast Belfast. In our briefing we were informed that this police officer had been threatened on a number of previous occasions, but that he felt the threats were now becoming more serious and would appreciate it if we could offer him protection.

After a lengthy meeting with the officer involved and a reconnaissance of his house and the surrounding area, we all got together back in our briefing room. We filled our pots with tea and got stuck into the sandwiches while Mike briefed everyone about the situation and the task. Mike placed some photos on the backboard, together with a large sketch of the house and surrounding area. He covered all the relevant points and, as always, threw the whole subject over to us for discussion, to put forward any points we felt relevant to the task.

We decided that we needed the whole section, to cover the house, with one more half section acting as backup, periodically patrolling around the general area. We decided to take two SMGs fitted with silencers, together with our own 9 millie pistols and radios to be in contact both within the house and also with our backup team and base HQ. We planned to have four men on duty at any one time, the other four being on reserve in the house, covering the rear but resting. The house itself was part of a terrace and had two large front bedroom windows overlooking a small garden and waist-high brick wall fronting the pavement and road. We felt it would offer some cover and a swift exit for any attackers from the street.

We agreed on one sub-team of two to be set in positions in each front bedroom, covering the street-facing area of the house. We didn't bother with any specialist equipment as the streets were quite well lit. We agreed on infill at 8:00 pm and exfill each morning before first light at around 5:30 am, and planned to carry on this operation for seven days.

Two of our sections had to alternate each day, operating in a four-hour shift pattern between the eight of us in the house. The officer's family stayed at a hotel during this period although the officer himself was in the house with us and slept on a couch in the kitchen.

The rear of the house was quite secure, with high panel fences and a large open-plan garden with shrubs around the borders. We all felt that the weakest point was the frontal area. However, we did place some early warning devices around the back garden in the event of an approach from that direction. We assigned each bedroom at the front its own code name and 'arc of fire', and we knew thoroughly our procedures in the event of an attack – by either petrol bomb thrown at the downstairs windows or an approach to the front door.

There was little activity during the first two nights except for the odd drunk making his way home. But on the third night at approximately 2:00 am in clear moonlight, we saw two men in their mid-30s. They were long haired and dressed in black donkey jackets and jeans, walking casually down the street on our side. As they reached our house they suddenly stopped and looked around, up and down the street. Then, after a moment or two, they bobbed down behind the low wall at the end of the small garden, only five or six metres from the house. I cocked my SMG and Kev quietly reminded the other half of the team on the radio in the other bedroom:

'If they stand up with some form of explosive device or aiming a weapon and are a direct threat, that will be the signal to open fire on our designated targets with the SMGs.' He also contacted our backup car to move in a little closer, but to stay off the main street and await instructions. The lads downstairs took up positions to cover the rear area and the guys at HQ acknowledged, as they all could clearly hear our conversations while they listened in on the radios.

The air was still and what seemed like hours going by were only a few moments. My window was slightly ajar and the muzzle end of my SMG was just inside the opening. My heart was pounding in my chest while I held my aim at the point where the men had ducked down. I was controlling my breathing, trying to keep it slow and calm, preparing to open fire and straining to listen to what they were doing or saying, although I could hear nothing. Kev, who was with me, slowly moved back into the room, away from the window and huddled down in the corner furthest from me, whispering on the radio. He was on the air informing base HQ, together with everyone else listening in, of the possible attack, and noting the time and the descriptions of the two men.

Then without warning they jumped up side by side, looking very confident, one man holding a petrol bomb in his right hand and leaning back preparing to throw it at the lower windows just below us. The other, with a large nail or pipe bomb in one hand and a pistol in the other, just stood there as if to innocently observe what was about to happen. There were no vehicles or other people in the area; they had arrived on foot and were alone. Just as we had practiced a thousand times, I drew my breath with my eyes fixed on my target, exhaled about 30 per cent, held it, checked my aim and opened fire from the bedroom window at the same time as the other SMG at a range of about six or seven metres. They fell and the petrol bomb was on the floor, still alight but not broken, as I could see from the glow of the device. It was all very quick and over in less than four or five seconds.

I whispered to Kev while he was moving back towards me at the window: 'Two men down. One man has managed to crawl away up the street behind the wall on hands and knees but I'm sure he's badly hurt.'

We both had a clear view and we could see that the man lying on the ground wasn't moving. Nonetheless, he was still there and still a threat, if only a minor one. We didn't know for certain of his condition and he could have jumped up with the gun or bomb he had, at any moment, or perhaps be calling in some support on a radio.

We slowly and gently closed our windows a little way and I waited and observed in case he made a move, while Kev transmitted his contact report. The four-man team downstairs with Mike were covering the rear of the building in case a secondary attack was launched from there. Kev also contacted the backup car to stay in position unit all was clear and await instructions. We didn't feel it was worth them showing themselves to search for the injured terrorist. He was obviously in a bad way and would turn up sooner or later.

Our procedure after a contact was to silently wait and observe in case of follow-up by an ASU. We were using silenced SMGs, producing little more noise than if you were tapping a wall with a pen, more like a tap than a bang. The only disadvantage with silenced weapons is that they lose much of their hitting power, although at six or seven metres range and firing four to six rounds each they'll stop any man: they might not kill him outright, but it would ruin his day in a big way.

Within moments of the shooting, the streets were silent again, not a movement or a light going on anywhere. Nobody heard or saw a thing ... just the way we wanted it. A few minutes later, a uniformed patrol arrived in a Land Rover, pulled up, checked the body and lifted it into the back of the truck, with the devices on the floor. It all appeared very matter-of-fact. To any innocent onlookers, it would seem as if the Army had simply picked up a drunk from the streets and taken him away to sober up. The troops didn't even look in our direction. They flushed the pavement with a bucket of water and then left a few moments later.

Mike came up to see us. 'Well done lads, that was nice and quiet. We'll just hold our positions and observe till we pull out.'

We held our positions until just before first light at about 5:30 am and then with our radios and SMGs bagged up, one group covered the other as we moved out through the back gardens. We RV'd about half a mile away, near the junction of Castlereagh and Knockbreda roads, to be picked up by the standby section in the area, which had been waiting near there in case everything went pear-shaped.

On our return to base HQ, after cleaning and handing in our equipment, we piled into the operations room for a debriefing to make out our reports over some hot tea. Later, we signed the section off duty before going to breakfast at 7:30 am. We spent the rest of the day lounging about discussing the events of the previous night, reading and sleeping, and then we all piled off to the canteen at 6:30 pm for a good feed before we signed ourselves on as standby section and drew our weapons at 8:00 pm. The rest of the evening was spent relaxing and watching TV, in between periodically checking with the ops room in case we were needed.

A few days later, we were informed that the body of a man was found in the boot of a car in a side road out of town towards Newtownards. He had four 9mm gunshot wounds to his chest and shoulder. As for the player the troops took away, little was known or said and perhaps it was just listed as another body found or as somebody who had simply disappeared, as happened to quite a few people during that chaotic period, but I doubt it, he'll be registered somewhere.

This type of operation was successful for more reasons than just destroying the enemy: it also made the IRA nervous of mounting such attacks. They knew we were around, operating in the area of Belfast, but had little idea of who we were and when and where we would strike at them – especially in such a deadly silent, deliberate way. They really didn't appreciate the way we operated and often voiced complaints of our so-called underhand, cloak-and-dagger methods.

We didn't care. We had a job to do and if the IRA didn't like the way we did it, that was just tough on them. We were really far too busy to be answering snivelling complaints from the so-called Irish Republican Army. They took great pride in killing, maiming, and destroying people's lives, but they felt totally cheated and insulted when we covertly and aggressively hit them back as hard as we could.

Earlier, when I was in training for the MRF, one of the instructors regularly told us, 'You have to be like, and think like a terrorist in order to beat one.'

Those words have stayed with me ever since, and I soon learned how true they really were after seeing how conventional, uniformed military methods simply don't appear to work very well in a restrictive, urban guerrilla-warfare environment. Even today, terrorists seem to screw the system. They play on the security methods we use and turn those methods to their advantage. I feel that the best way to eradicate terrorists is to obviously always try diplomacy and negotiate a lasting peace. But if that doesn't work, I feel it is best to send out small, specialised hard hitting units to literally hunt them down and hit them extremely hard. But I know it's not easy in today's environment but we're slowly getting there.

11

A Faceless Enemy

We were involved in many types of surveillance operation and a lot of them were very uneventful – like so many other operations we took part in. We spent hours and sometimes days just sitting around, doing nothing and waiting. That is similar to operations in other conflict areas … 95 per cent of the time consists of hanging around twiddling thumbs and then for the remaining five per cent all hell is let loose and everything is happening at once. That, though, is the five per cent when your training really shows and when everything clicks and falls into place, as best it can in the chaos. The four of us in our subsection discovered that we moulded together and automatically acted and operated as one. Almost being able to read each other's thoughts, we moved and covered each other with almost nothing being said.

Like all military units, we had our successes and also our occasional failures. Battles and fire-fights are fluid environments and everything can change at a moment's notice. Having access to reliable information and being well trained and flexible enough to bend with the situation is absolutely essential.

Thankfully we had far more success than failure and this can be seen by the lack of detailed, accurate publicity and information that arose regarding MRF operations. Very few people knew anything about us, our operations or our successes. Even the few operations we were involved in that did create some media and public interest remained pretty much secret, and very few people knew for sure who was really involved.

It was the Army itself that eventually weakened and compromised us, allowing the Press and public to pick up on a small element of our activities. We were tasked with far too many commitments and way too much 'in-your-face' active. The government allowed the Army to feed us to the wolves by claiming we were to be soon disbanded, but this in turn only resulted in a shuffle of name changes during 1973 and 1974, creating confusion everywhere while, in fact, 14 Intelligence Company was developing in its shadows. Many MRF personnel were part of the newly forming 14 Int. and very few actually departed for anywhere. We just underwent a period of changing identity while continuing with our ongoing commitments. To us in the sections, there was little change except a toning down of some of our operations.

Perhaps we in the MRF were a little more successful than was originally anticipated. Perhaps we really were being used as 'cannon fodder', as my brother said to me some seven years earlier. Perhaps the Army was testing the water with us to see what happened and not expecting us to survive or last so long. Perhaps that's the reason why we were, for years, such a very small unit.

A larger unit is anyway far too difficult to hide away in the shadows of the military system. Perhaps they were using us to evaluate and analyse the best way to evolve and develop 14 Int. at a later date. Who really knows? I don't know, but one thing I am quite sure of ... it wasn't Oswald alone that shot Kennedy.

In a place like Ulster in the early 1970s and on, into the 90s, you tended to build a special kind of friendship when every night there were gunfights or bombs going off all around you. Some people call it camaraderie but I think it's more than that. Camaraderie is normal in the long-term close environment of a barrack room in the average military unit. But in a conflict zone like Ulster, and later the Falklands, the Gulf wars or Afghanistan, when you can be literally blown to bits or shot dead at any moment, something more profound develops.

You and your friends become totally reliant on each other for everyone's survival. That's a different kind of camaraderie altogether, quite an emotional feeling that non-combatants will never understand. It stays with you for life.

You can see this almost every day, when World War Two and Vietnam veterans are seen on TV programmes or parading in the city streets wearing their regimental badges, medals and berets. This display of loyalty and lifelong friendship is much more than the normal unit camaraderie most people understand and accept. I personally don't parade in the streets, except on the eleventh hour of the eleventh day of the eleventh month (Remembrance Day). When I'm in UK and I have the opportunity, I'll join the onlookers and mingle with the crowd. When I'm not, I'll usually watch the ceremony on TV. However, I do have a little corner of my home where I keep some things as a personal remembrance and sometimes I stand and look at them.

You probably think that the Ulster conflict wasn't or isn't the same as the Falklands or the early part of the Gulf wars and you would be right. The main difference with Ulster, in some ways similar to the cities of Iraq and Afghanistan now, is that the enemy was everywhere and faceless and wore no uniform. Very rarely would they stand and fight, although they were always ready to strike at a moment's notice. Also, Ulster is British soil and very close to home, which means the Press and cameras are on top of you, constantly hanging on every word or action: it was very frustrating.

I know that the Falklands was a hard slog and had its own set of problems and setbacks – I was there too. I appreciate that the Gulf had its difficulties with the hard living conditions, wide-open deserts and the Yanks hitting us from behind without warning. I also had an involvement in Desert Storm. But generally speaking, in the Falklands and early stages of the Gulf wars, the enemy was to the front and wore a military uniform that was quite recognisable.

During my time with the MRF, we were involved in and tasked with some quite dangerous and hair-raising operations, but I can't remember any one in any of our sections ever refusing an operation. Occasionally we had our concerns, but none of us ever refused a job.

Often I felt lucky not to have to be in uniform, walking the streets like a figure 11 target – which I had done in the past – just waiting for a sniper to take a shot at me. Working in plain clothes, we could quickly slip out of sight and blend into the shadows if a situation turned dodgy. We'd wait and observe until the right time to make our move.

When I was operating undercover in plain clothes I looked as rough as any of the worst IRA players. I blended in with my surroundings and usually felt quite secure. If I came across some bad boys and they looked me over from across the street, I just looked back at them the same way. They wouldn't know for sure who I was and they normally avoided close contact, at least initially, because of their uncertainty. Perhaps they felt I might even be part of an ASU operating from another area, on a mission and not to be interfered with. All that worked in our favour. On the streets, we had to look like and act like the terrorists, pretending to be one of them, because if we didn't we were dead.

I saw much death, pain and misery during my time in Ulster, like many other soldiers over there – surely far more than the average person on the UK streets could ever imagine. It's strange, but thinking back I very rarely felt any great fear or concern for my own life. I was usually more concerned about others in the unit and being caught up in a bomb blast and being crippled, perhaps losing a leg or an arm. Being bedridden or wheelchair-bound for the rest of my days was my greatest fear. Death was a simple final solution but being crippled or disfigured, with the concomitant never-ending pain and misery, was the one thing I didn't want to happen to me. I think many of us felt this way. I was always far more concerned for my colleagues lives rather than my own; but that's not to say I, or any of us, were reckless. We all knew the risks and we planned all our operations meticulously and down to the smallest detail.

An interesting little surveillance operation I was part of started in the area of Andersonstown and was initially mobile surveillance (in cars). The operation lasted for some four hours and ended up with a change to foot surveillance around the city centre.

All we had to do was follow a chap, make notes and try to photograph anyone he made contact with. We had four cars involved, Alfa, Bravo, Charlie and Delta, with our team shared out amongst them. Mike and Tug were in Alfa, I was in Bravo with Kev, Colin and John were in Charlie, with Dave and Ben in Delta.

In our briefing we were told that our target would be driving a maroon-coloured Hillman Minx. We had the registration number with a description and photographs of the driver. We were to make our pickup ('first contact') in the area of Glenhill Park, and from there we were simply to follow, writing notes and taking photographs.

We drew our weapons, radios and map-books and set off individually, performing radio checks as we left. We made our way to the pickup location and were all in position in good time in the general area of Glenhill Park and Fruithill Park. We had spread ourselves so all the roads in and out of the area were covered from a distance, and once again we carried out a radio check. We had no idea which direction our man would be coming from or where he would be going. Any one of us might have had to take the lead when he appeared, so we all had to be on the ball and ready to move when he showed up. We had been waiting around for almost an hour, moving around from position to position, when suddenly he appeared driving northwest along Kennedy Way in the Minx.

Colin, with John driving, was in the best position and off we went with them in the lead. The traffic at the time was quite light, and the weather was cloudy but calm with a chill in the air. Colin in car Charlie was approximately a hundred metres behind the target with the rest of us strung out another few hundred metres behind him. Colin was giving us a good commentary on the radio as they moved towards the city centre.

The target car stopped by the school opposite Broadway and the driver spoke to another man. By this time Dave and Ben had taken over the lead position and Dave got about three photos of the other man as he and the target chatted.

When our target set off again, Kev and I assumed the lead and we followed him around the Markets area of the city. Meanwhile, our other cars closed up and moved nearer, we all moved into various positions so we could cover the target from all sides and directions as we entered the main part of the city. From there Mike with Tug took over the lead until we were over near the Europa hotel on Great Victoria Street. Moments later Colin took over again and before we knew it, he came up quickly on the air saying: 'On foot, on foot, on foot!'

The target had parked in a car park near College Square North and was now walking. Immediately we all moved up much closer while Colin and John locked up their car and followed him. John was in front with Colin backing him up until the rest of us managed to deploy around the area. I was already out and on foot with Dave while Mike was still parking his car. Our drivers stayed with the cars and periodically brought them forward as we moved along. The streets were quite busy with shoppers and the weather was still clear and calm.

When Colin saw us closing on him, he radioed for John to go back to the car and join in the follow-up while he took the lead himself. The target then went into a large shop, so we all moved in closer again, taking up positions all around the shop. Dave was on the target and I moved up much closer than normal, following Dave into the large shop.

In a busy department store it's best to have various members of the team up closer, moving closer to the target and observing from various distances while mingled in with the crowd. If we just had a one-on-one in the store, it would be quite easy to lose the target in the crowd.

The target stopped again. This time he went for a drink in the coffee lounge and was joined there by another man. I sauntered in to buy a coffee and then sat down near the entrance where I had a clear view of the target. Dave entered and bought an orange juice and sat at another table on the other side of the room. In the 20 minutes we were in there, the target was joined by two other people and an envelope was handed to him, after which he soon got up and left. We only managed a couple of photographs of the group from the cameras we had with us in our bags as it was risky with so many people close around us, but we managed to radio back to the lads in the cars a full, detailed description of the others at the meeting.

Mike was outside, ready to take over the lead, and I followed on behind Colin while Dave followed behind me. The man quickly made his way back to his car and set off back in the direction of Anderson-stown. I was quickly back in my car with Kev so we took the lead while the others organised themselves.

'So, did you enjoy your coffee?' Kev asked sarcastically as I settled back into the car.

I turned to him and replied enthusiastically, 'Yes, thank you very much.'

And with a horrendous scowl on his twisted face, he sneered, 'You little twat.' But then I handed over a couple of biscuits I saved for him, which made us both smile as we followed on after our target.

Back at his home, the target parked his car and let himself into his house, which ended our little surveillance operation for the day. An hour later back at base, we all cleared and checked our weapons, handing them in to the armoury, and settled into the briefing room where we collated our notes and arranged for the Intelligence boys to develop our films.

Car surveillance was a type of operation that was demanding but relatively straightforward; but when it turned into foot surveillance our co-ordination had to be spot on and everybody had to move very quickly to stay on top of things and keep control of the situation.

Compared with any surveillance operation undertaken on foot or in vehicles, or both, the counter-surveillance operation is generally far more complicated – but just as important as following the target. If we felt at any time that our lead man has been compromised or was himself being followed, we immediately called off the operation and all broke off in different directions to meet up later at a pre-arranged RV.

Our lead man would be watching the target and people close to him. Meanwhile, the other members of the team are involved in counter-surveillance, watching everyone else. Believe me, for that you really need eyes in the back of your head. You're looking for signs that someone is watching or following your lead man. Also, if the target gets a little suspicious, he might try to pull a trick, like 'boxing' around a block of buildings, to see if he's being followed. If this starts to happen, the lead man position must change, perhaps more than once, and another team member has to be waiting for the target to finish his circuit around the building. Other methods the target can use to shake a tail, mentioned earlier, is to walk into a shop and then immediately turn and walk back out again, or simply speed up, slow down, stop suddenly or turn around and go the other way. The target will do this to observe the reactions of anyone else that's following on behind him. In this type of close-up situation, you as the follower must carry on as normal, without blinking or getting flustered.

The weather was changing and winter was just about on us but we had work to do. The whole section was out and about in the city on general surveillance, just taking a look around areas like Oldpark by the Ardoyne, together with the Springmartin, Turf Lodge and Suffolk estates around Andersonstown. We had been cruising around independently looking for vigilante groups and opportunist house and car break-ins. We would drive into these estates, have a look around for a few minutes and then leave and go to some other area. A while later, another of our cars would do the same and then move off. It wasn't a problem going into these areas at night as there were always some other cars milling around. Belfast is a large city and there is always someone around, on foot or in a car.

I was with Kev in car Alpha with him driving. We had spent about four or five hours cruising around but everywhere seemed quiet, perhaps because of the rain.

On occasions, if the city was uneventful, we'd cruise around looking at the estates for a few hours and then zoom off back to base for a break and some tea and snap. We'd stay in base for a couple of hours discussing where we had been and what we had seen, then go out again until 4:00 or 5:00 am. In the very early hours, at about 6:00 am, we'd make our way back to base again, have a debriefing over coffee and then hand over to the next duty section at 8:00 am before going off to have some breakfast and a few hours' sleep.

We would eat dinner and by 8:00 pm in the evening we'd be back on as standby section, drawing our weapons and loading up the cars that were available and sitting around in the briefing and ops rooms until midnight. We just waited around to be called out to assist the duty section if we were needed or required to assist them on some operation. By midnight or 1:00 am we'd go off to bed but just sleep on top of the blankets fully dressed before starting our own duty section at 8:00 am, after a shower, change and breakfast.

It was approximately 4:00 am one morning and Kev and I had been patrolling around the area of Ladybrook. There wasn't much going on so we decided to call it a night, and go down Kennedy Way to Musgrave Park Hospital Army location for a pot of tea and a chat with the uniformed lads before heading off back to base.

After some tea and a chat with the guard commander, we informed the rest of our section and set off back to our own location at about 5:00 am. We turned along Stockmans Lane and onto the M1 motorway towards the city centre. There, we made our way right, along Divis Street, then Castle Street to Queen's Square and the Queen Elizabeth Bridge, onto the Sydenham Bypass.

The weather had been quite miserable, foggy and drizzling with rain showers for most of the night. Perhaps, as mentioned, that's why it had been so quiet. The IRA was normally a fair weather terrorist group and didn't like to play out in the wet with us.

As we made our way along the Sydenham bypass, about three or four miles out of the city where the building line dropped away to grassy fields and a few houses to both sides, I saw a man at the roadside. He was wearing a long dark coat with a baseball cap and seemed to be just sitting there at the side of the dual-carriageway. He had his arms draped over his knees and his head bowed down between them, looking down at the ground between his feet.

I said to Kev, 'What do you think about that guy sitting by the road up ahead, shall we check him out in case he's sick or hurt?'

"Yeah OK, sure, let's take a look at him' Kev replied in a sleepy grunt. 'But keep a look out in case he has some friends around.'

We were always very careful if we checked out someone in this kind of situation and we very rarely did it. It could be a genuine situation but it was always possible that it could be a setup and there might be some others lurking in the shadows waiting for someone to pull in, so they could hijack the car – a very common occurrence back then. However, we were pretty well armed with two 9 millies, an SMG and big Kev next to me with his huge flick-knife.

Kev slowed down as we drew near the chap to give us both a little time to have a look around the area. He then pulled over and stopped next to the guy, who was about two metres from my door. He didn't move until I wound my window down and shouted at him.

'Hey you, you over there, are you OK?'

The guy slowly looked up and in a drunken stupor replied: 'Who the fuck wants to know?'

Charming. 'We're the police and we're just checking to see if you're OK,' I replied.

The guy slowly staggered onto his feet and looked at us as he swayed from side to side. Slowly, he stepped towards our car, put his hands on my open window door frame and poked his head in towards me. I didn't want him to get too close and see inside the car, so I quickly said, 'OK, stop there and show me some ID.'

The guy said nothing but started to push his head further in through my open window, half forcing his way in and half falling in. It was very dark so I think he couldn't see anything and was just curious to have a look at me.

Within moments he was so far in my window, with his head and shoulders and his hands on the frame, that I was being forced over onto Kev's side of the car. I pulled my 9 millie up and stuck the barrel under his chin, but again I'm not sure he even realised the gun was there. By now the guy was pushing himself so far into the car that I was being forced up both against Kev and the steering wheel. Kev quickly climbed out through his door and moved around to my side of the car, taking hold of the drunk by his shoulders and dragging him out of my window and away from the car. As I jumped out, keeping my 9 millie hidden behind my leg, Kev was holding the guy up and forcing him against the car.

'Come on you, just show us some ID, then you can go home,' said Kev to the drunk.

The guy's head rolled from side-to-side and as he looked at us both with his intoxicated gaze he replied, 'Piss off, who are you? You show me your ID.'

You almost had to admire his attitude, but he was being abusive and it upset Kev, then as quick as a flash Kev grabbed the guy tight around his throat. 'Here's my fucking ID,' said Kev.

The guy froze, threw his hands in the air and started to apologise. 'OK guys, I'm sorry, I'm sorry, I didn't mean any harm. I'm just on my way home, no problem, I'm going, no problem.'

Kev let him go and the guy quickly staggered and stumbled away in the darkness towards some houses about two hundred metres away. We both shrugged our shoulders and jumped back into our car and set off as if nothing had happened. A few moments later, I said to Kev, 'I don't think we'll check-out any more drunks in future, what do you think?'

He answered with a smile: 'Yeah, I think that's a very good idea, Sy.' We both burst out laughing at what had just happened.

I must admit that this was the first time I had ever seen Kev move so fast in an aggressive way. And he was damn fast with his throat grab, fast enough to frighten the life out of anyone.

Back at base we told the other lads in the section what had happened. We all had a good laugh over it before packing our gear away and wandering off to our beds, where we flopped down as Tug put on his tape recorder, playing some new Bob Marley releases his brother had sent him, 'I Shot the Sheriff' and 'Get Up, Stand Up'. They seemed somehow relevant.

12

Cut It Off and Kill It

Christmas had come around again. It was the winter of 1973 and the situation in Northern Ireland had over the past two years grown more and more intense and desperate. The IRA bombing campaign of the UK mainland had been in full swing since soon after Bloody Sunday, early in 1972.

The latest atrocities had been several months earlier, in September, and Scotland Yard was still hunting the culprits after two bombs at mainline stations had injured 13 people and brought chaos to central London. The first explosion at King's Cross injured five people after a youth had thrown a bag-bomb into the booking hall. Fifty minutes later, a second explosion tore through a snack bar at Euston station, injuring eight.

No group at the time of the bombing admitted to setting the devices, which weighed two to three pounds each, but the police were confident that the mechanisms were of typical IRA design. The King's Cross blast occurred at around 12:25 PM, shattering glass throughout the old booking hall. One witness said, 'I saw a flash and suddenly people were being thrown through the air – it was a terrible mess, they were bleeding and screaming.'

The second occurred just minutes after the Press Association received a phone warning from a man with an Irish accent, leaving very little time for the police to act to clear the station. As an employee in the Euston station bar put it, 'Police officers were running up and down the platform shouting for people to get out of the station,' he told a reporter. 'A few moments later, the bomb went off.'

The police said they received over 100 bomb hoaxes that day and were also forced to evacuate three other London railway stations. They issued a photo-fit picture of a five-foot two-inch-tall youth they wanted to question regarding the King's Cross bombing. The IRA later admitted to the bombings, which came during one of their more sustained periods of activity on the UK mainland.

A couple of days earlier, on 8 September, bombs had been detonated in Manchester city centre and at London Victoria station. And two days after the King's Cross bomb, more blasts rocked the area of Oxford Street and Sloane Square in London. These random bombing sprees seemed to come to an end after the Balcombe Street siege in December 1975.

Within a couple of months, in November 1973, six men and two women had been convicted of being involved in two London car bombings they had carried out earlier, in March. One person died and almost 200 were injured in the two explosions, one of which was at the Old Bailey court and the other outside Scotland Yard, the Metropolitan Police headquarters. They were all active Provisional IRA members at that time. But a ninth defendant, Roisin McNearney was acquitted.

If it was starting to feel unsafe on the UK mainland, the province of Ulster was by now a mess and on the verge of civil war, if not already in one. The Government at the time knew it, but appeared to be running out of ideas to try and quell it. Talks failed, negotiations collapsed and thousands of people on both sides took to the streets in Londonderry and Belfast in demonstrations, as the shooting, bombing and killings increased daily.

In Belfast, driving through and around those 'hard areas' of the Falls Road, Divis Flats, Unity flats, Andersonstown and the Ardoyne, was just like driving through the streets of Beirut; burned out, derelict houses passed by me row on row. Most that still stood were boarded up. Rubble and glass covered the roads while clouds of smoke billowed over the city from houses and burning vehicles destroyed in rioting the previous night. It was a desperate place to be and to work in. I often wondered if I was ever going to get out of the place in one piece, to see the sunshine and flowers in some peaceful park back in North Yorkshire, on the blessed mainland.

Back at our little 70 by 15 metre compound life went on, although we were told that a few of our regular operations were being shelved due to new commitments. The word from 'high up' seemed that instead they wanted us to adopt a much more active and robust role when we were out on the streets. Then hopefully, they'd all get fed up and call their own mutual ceasefires, leaving the way open for the Government to step in and try to negotiate with all sides a long-term, peaceful solution – which all sounded very good, in theory.

Our whole unit together began to have daily briefing sessions and updates of the general situation. It didn't matter if we were on duty, off duty, on standby or even taking a shower, we all had to attend these regular briefing sessions. In the past we just had section briefings amongst ourselves and the Intelligence boys, at the start of our duty shift. It was during these new briefings that we noticed the format started to change a little and phrases such as 'deal with' and 'eliminate the threat or enemy', were being used far more often. We were given comprehensive dossiers of the most dangerous people in Ulster and told to study each of them and memorise as much information and detail as possible. We now had to commit to memory names, addresses, photographs and past histories of the most vicious terrorist killers in far more detail than before. Anyone that's ever worn an Army uniform knows exactly what is meant by 'eliminating the threat or enemy'. We didn't need it spelling out to us.

We were indirectly being tasked to go out on the streets, find the enemy and deal with it. In normal Army terms, the words would have been 'seek out and destroy'.

But we all felt that the word 'destroy' was a little too aggressive and strong for the politicians to stomach, so we went along with 'eliminate' as an acceptable alternative. We didn't really care which words they used, the end product would still be the same as far as we were concerned, at the sharp end.

But we were in Northern Ireland, very close to home, and the world's Press was paying very close attention, some of it revelling in the perils of the fading British empire. The British government and Army do, at times, tend to be a little fussy with the words they use. Unlike in the US, with those famous words of Colin Powel during Desert Storm: 'Cut it off and kill it', he said, referring to Saddam's tank army.

I couldn't imagine Willie Whitlaw or Ted Heath saying something like that, not in public anyway. But on the other hand, I can see Maggie saying it. Her husband Denis said with a smile to the SAS team after the Iranian Embassy siege in London 1980, 'You let one of the bastards live.' One of the terrorists had managed to hide himself amongst the hostages, pretending to be one of them, during the SAS rescue mission. It's hard to imagine Cherie Blair saying anything similar; she'd probably end up defending him in court.

As it was, we were left to work out the details and our methods of the 'eliminating the threat' ourselves, which we discussed regularly as a section. One thing we made very clear amongst the eight of us, was that we had to be very careful in our planning and preparation, much more so than normal for this type of project.

We decided that if we were ever seen dealing with anyone, we knew that we would be on our own. We were all volunteers and most of us had been operators and worked together a long time; we knew we were there to carry out an important task, and we understood the nature of that task. The Army didn't supply us with silenced submachine-guns because they expected us to act like the uniformed services. It appeared that the terrorists had to be stopped one way or another. Getting caught wasn't a big issue or great fear for us, we knew the area and how to operate. Most of us felt relieved that our leash appeared it was being loosened, at long last.

We felt we were indirectly being sanctioned to go out and specifically hunt down the IRA. 'Seek out and destroy', 'cut it off and kill it' – whatever phrase you preferred, we knew it wasn't going to be easy.

In the past, we opened fire at anyone seen to be carrying and aiming, or firing a weapon in a threatening manner, in the 'hard areas'. Now, it seemed that guys in the unit were discussing and planning to go out on patrol, occasionally stirring up a little trouble and targeting selected groups in the street – not every night, but occasionally. If we were out and ran into vigilante groups late at night patrolling in hard areas ... then as far as we were concerned they were up to no good, assisting and supporting the terrorists, most likely armed. Then the general idea was that they were a legitimate target and we were there to punish them.

The situation down in the city was an ongoing nightmare, night after night. Perhaps the politicians were getting desperate, and it certainly looked that way. One thing was certain, the policy was definitely changing and we felt it.

It wasn't only the people of Northern Ireland who were suffering at the hands of the terrorists. On the mainland 12 people, soldiers and their loved ones, were killed on the M62 when the IRA blew up the coach they were travelling in back to an Army base at Catterick, North Yorkshire, spreading mutilated women and children 200 metres along the motorway behind the wrecked vehicle. Six people had previously been murdered in another IRA bombing in Aldershot in February 1972. Many other atrocities were to follow.

It was occasionally discussed within our sections to work to some strict rules, mainly for our own benefit and security. These were, if we ever got involved in a contact in daylight, we played it strictly by the book. Our main areas of operation were in the hard Republican areas of Belfast and our main target was the IRA and its structure. We weren't too concerned about the UDA, UVF or the UFF unless we bumped into them as they were committing criminal acts. They were Loyalist groups and mainly involved in defending themselves against the IRA, along with some 'tit for tat' killings which were mainly carried out by the UVF and UFF.

We didn't feel we would last very long simply driving around the city, indiscriminately blasting people from our cars during daylight hours, like Los Angeles-style drive-by gang shootings. The IRA was probably one of the best terrorist organisations in the world at that time and we didn't fancy our chances using that tactic.

We had to be like them and think like them, but also be a little more subtle in our method of approach.

Over the next few days, we all got together during our standby shift to discuss these ideas of one or two possible methods. Firstly, it was felt that if possible, we would avoid all contacts in daylight hours. But late at night if we came across manned barricades, masked vigilante patrols or suspicious groups milling about in the most dangerous notorious areas and streets, we could possibly initiate a contact. The idea was, we'd make a pass, checking them over, then perhaps open fire and let them have a short burst of four or five rounds from our SMG. This would make them think they were being attacked by some other terror group.

In our planning, if we decided to go ahead; we would only fire aimed shots at groups of more than four people on barricades or patrolling vigilante style and never at anyone wandering around in the streets, alone. This was an important rule, as anyone on his own could well be someone working undercover, like us. We didn't know of any other specific undercover units in our area, but we knew that some local Army units had people on the streets in plainclothes in their areas for short periods. We didn't want to take any chances.

We discussed these ideas and thought we could target specific groups manning barricades or patrolling the unforgiving hard areas in the darkened streets late at night. These groups were always up to no good, usually masked and had some form of weapons on them and constantly looking for trouble. Now we thought it was up to us to deal with them.

If these groups were stopped or confronted by the uniformed Army, they'd quickly hide their weapons or get children to carry them away. These groups always claimed to the Army that they were only patrolling and guarding their own areas from Protestant attacks. But on the barricades or in the vigilante patrols someone was always armed – perhaps not all of them, but there were undoubtedly always some weapons among the group. As far as we were concerned these people were just as guilty as the most hardened terrorists gunmen or bombers. They would have quite joyfully killed us or any of the uniformed troops without hesitation just the same if given the chance, as such groups had done on many occasions in the past.

Types such as these probably didn't have the balls to go out and join an IRA Active Service Unit but they were nonetheless sympathisers and supporters, assisting the movement.

Another method, which some in the MRF felt would be useful to the task, was to carry out 'lifting and snatching' operations, again late at night or in the very early hours. This time lone men aged between 20 and 40 could be targeted, again in the most dangerous areas. They would be 'lifted' and taken out of the city a little way, following a quick ID check and search in the back of the car for weapons.

Not so dramatic or colourful as what the IRA did with their captives. Their victims would be hooded when first accosted, then driven out into the countryside and shot. The terrified prisoner would be sure from the moment he was taken, what was going to happen to him.

It was different with the MRF. Our general idea was, if a 'lifted' person checked-out clear, unarmed and not on our wanted list, he would only be reprimanded or warned a little – just pushed around a little and thrown back in the car – then taken back into town and dropped off near the city centre. So when the lucky ones got back on home ground alive and relatively well, they never knew for sure who it really was that actually snatched them. The shadowy figures of the MRF would appear to have been any one of a number of terror groups which were actively running around the cities at the time. The general idea was to sow even more terror among the terrorists, and that is what was planned.

Over those few weeks everything was regularly changing. The unit's name was changing almost daily and many of our operations were being toned down and our section didn't actually get around to putting our ideas fully into action. In our section, we decided not to follow this earlier discussed direction and didn't get involved in going after any vigilante groups or snatching anyone in particular in any of the hard Republican areas late at night in this way, as we had thought about earlier.

However, one incident which comes to mind and the Press managed to get their hands on was a shooting one night. I wasn't involved in this as I was only on standby section at the time and only heard of the shooting while listening in to the action on the unit's car radio in a different location.

Our duty section had been in the city for most of the evening on general surveillance patrols and it had been a fairly quiet night. However, in the early hours, between about 12:00 or 2:00 am, I heard over the radio a report of a brief shooting taking place. It must have lasted at the most half a minute. I don't know if the members of our unit were fired at first, or if they saw weapons on the vigilantes.

The one detail that stirred up the attention of the Press with regard to this incident was that someone on the street claimed that the people in the car had used a Thompson submachine gun. As far as I know we had one, perhaps a couple of Thompson .45s in our armoury. We occasionally used them on the ranges for fun but I personally never saw anyone in any of the sections take them down into the city on operations.

The people on the barricade had no idea who it was that shot at them, until some seven weeks later. Following their interviews with the police, one of the injured men was asked by a detective, 'Do you know who shot you?'

The victim replied, 'No.'

The detective then told him: 'It was the Army who shot you. We have four sworn statements from the occupants of the car that they were returning fire after they had been shot at.'

It was following this revelation from the police detective that the Press grabbed hold of the story, which previously they had been either unaware or uninterested in (just another shooting). Now the big story was that one of our sections had 'perhaps' fired on an unarmed vigilante group with a supposedly unofficial weapon, but I personally very much doubt it.

To us, of course, it was no big deal: the incident was just one of similar shootings we as a unit were involved in. There were just so many nightly shootings taking place all around Belfast during this very dangerous period that nobody could really know for sure who on earth was involved in what, or who was shooting at whom. Most often, the majority of the shooting incidents and exchanges of fire, with us involved or not, weren't fully reported or didn't even reach the pages of the newspapers – they were very much 'dog bites man' stories in Ulster at that time. Obviously today it's very different.

If someone is shot or stabbed in the streets of London or Manchester it's all over the media the next day. But in a place like Belfast in the 1970s, when there were perhaps ten to 20 shootings and between two to four bombings incidents almost every night for weeks and months on end, the marginal news value of minor tragedy steadily declined. The Press tends to get a little blasé at times, sifting through the incidents and picking only the most interesting examples to build a story on. If they tried to cover every single one, each day or night, they would have to have been marathon runners to keep up with it all. As it was then, much of the time, the Press relied heavily on the Army and police to give them information and leads.

That particular night, when the patrol returned to base soon after the shooting, I didn't notice a Thompson among their weapons. The lads all came into the ops room together, told us that they had been fired at first which appeared very plausible, and filled in their reports.

To me it was just another adrenalin-filled day at the office spent cruising around in enemy territory – one day out of very many similar days.

However, in our section during this changing period, we perhaps stopped and checked a couple men in the city, of whom neither of them were found to be illegally armed, or were on our special 'bad boys' wanted list for terrorist activities. We simply just checked them out and dropped them off in the city centre area. We never normally discussed our general patrols with the other sections just as we never asked what the other sections were doing ... and nobody asked us. These earlier ideas were just that; ideas, we never put them into action and I'm sure none of the other sections went along this path. We always stood by the Yellow Card – RoE.

There are quite a few reports in other books referring to the 'disappeared,' a few people who have simply vanished without trace during the early troubles and never seen again. I'm not saying that the MRF was responsible for any or all those disappearances – it was a very hectic time and I honestly don't know for sure. However, it is quite possible that we may have been indirectly responsible for some of these missing terrorist activists who perhaps decided to move far away and begin a new life in a better place – or a much worse destination.

As for terrorists who are known to have died, I have noticed mention of them in one or two books that list all the killings during the The Troubles. Frankly, I am quite surprised at the apparent accuracy of these listings, which seem usually to be collated by journalists using information 'given' to them through various sources, reliable or not.

Also, to my surprise, they categorically state who the victims were: whether they were terrorists, Army or civilians; where and when they were killed; and who actually killed them. They state, for example, whether the deceased were killed by the Army, police, IRA, UVF, UFF or the UDA. I find it quite unbelievable how anyone can categorically state a murky fact like that, or make such bold statements, having had first-hand knowledge of what was really going on around the streets of Belfast at the time.

These authors appear to my mind a little naïve and with very limited knowledge and understanding of what was happening on the ground in Northern Ireland during this early part of the 1970s. The whole situation in Ulster during that decade, and even into the 1980s, was not so clear cut as many people would like to think. Many dark and shadowy, secret things were going on and many strange, mysterious events were taking place on a daily basis.

It has been loosely mentioned that the MRF was a rogue unit, which is absolutely ridiculous. The streets of Belfast during the 1970s were heavily patrolled by uniformed Army and police units. If we had been some kind of rogue unit, operating totally independently, driving around randomly blowing people away (which has been implied), we would not have lasted very long, as the uniformed forces would have easily caught up with us and either shot us or arrested and jailed us all. At that time, we only operated in the boundaries of Belfast itself. We needed their co-operation and their manpower – for keeping their patrols out of the way when required and then taking over from us and cleaning up and 'disinfecting' the scene after us, if for nothing else. Had we been a rogue unit, out of control, we would have been caught and after our arrests we would all have been publicly charged and tried before the court-martial. As I said earlier, it was the Army that supplied us with silenced SMGs: what did they expect us to do with such weapons?

If you were issued with a silenced SMG, and told to go and patrol the murky unforgiving streets of Belfast at all hours of the night during that period, what would you honestly expect was required of you? Likewise, where are the file boxes filled with our innumerable incident reports from every day over a period of a few years? They should be somewhere – or perhaps not.

The facts are these: we operated out of an Army location – Palace Barracks – on the outskirts of Belfast. We were issued with civilian vehicles and specialist items of equipment, radios and some unconventional weaponry. We worked from an office/compound that held an operations room, briefing room and sleeping accommodation. And we often sat and ate our meals with the uniformed forces within the barracks and in other places.

I have never been court-martialled and after my time with the MRF, I returned to general uniformed duties, as did all the other members eventually. However, there was one strange point I recently noticed during the later stages of writing this book. In my army 'red' discharge book, my listed service dates are partly broken, showing that I was periodically serving in Germany during 72-74, when in fact I was in Northern Ireland with the MRF and I have proof of that. My discharge book had been at my parents' home, sat in a draw gathering dust for the last 30 years, and I had never noticed the anomaly concerning these dates before. This manipulation of dates in my discharge book could well be an innocent mistake, or it could have been done purposely for some reason. I don't really know, but it looks quite odd.

There are never any hard and fast rules in undercover work, chasing terrorist killers. It can all get very strange and mysterious, dirty and messy at times. We were a new unit, a new idea, and we just had to make up our procedures and methods as we went along. We obviously kept strictly in line the Yellow Card – RoE, for our own security and survival. But we also had a relatively free hand with regard to spoiling and compromising IRA activities and occasionally tracking down and dealing with terrorist baby-killers the best and most efficient way we could.

Our role in the MRF was to mainly to spy on and interfere with terrorist operations and to hunt down, when possible, vicious hard-core murderers and to protect innocent lives. I'm a great lover of animals but sadly, whichever way you want to look at it, the best way to protect the sheep is simply to kill the wolves.

13

Hunters of Men

It was spring 1974 and we had just heard that the miners' strike had come to an end. They had called off their four-week action following a 35 per cent pay offer from the new Labour government, which was seen as an enormous victory for the miners.

At this time I was recovering from my little going away gift from the IRA of a GSW (gunshot wound) to my left knee. It took me almost two months to walk again with any degree of stability. I was also back in uniform, with my unit, again in Germany. But in truth I wasn't very happy and soon began to feel despondent about the regular military lifestyle.

It was back to regimental duties, standing to attention and 'Yes sir, no sir, three bags full sir', which by now seemed totally alien to me. I had been away for years working undercover, being treated as an equal among what was basically a unit without rank, and where, Special Forces-style, we were expected to all chip in and formulate our own tactics and solutions, and then execute our plans. Now it was back out with the Brasso and BS and I felt that I simply didn't fit in with Army life any more. Most people had no idea where I had been or what I had been doing for the last few years, and the de-militarization process I had been through didn't help the situation very much. I also couldn't talk to anybody about what I had been through, of course.

I found it quite hard to mix, work with and relate to others, as I had been totally self-reliant for far too long. My life was on a bit of a downer and it was doubly difficult for me because, being out of sight and out of mind, I had been left way behind on the promotional ladder. It was irrelevant to my superiors where I had been or what I had been doing. They had no idea, and as far as many were concerned, I had been away on some holiday.

In 1974-75, I was a corporal, pushing sergeant. Being quite well qualified in most things military, I was approaching a good position and would probably be ready to move up – to perhaps go for sergeant major (WO II) in the following few years or so.

And yet … promotion, medals and commendations during my time in the MRF hadn't been a real priority to any of us and we were usually far too busy, occupied on the streets of Belfast every day, to even think about such things. We never wore uniform and never referred to each other by rank, so all that regimental stuff had been left behind in a different life – or it had been until now.

Most of my old friends from my parent unit had already been promoted and gone off to do other things in the Army. I was left in a situation where I had to make a whole group of new friends, usually much younger and less experienced than me. Then, after a period of drifting from one job to another within my unit, and also a broken marriage, I began to feel that it was about time for me to leave the Army to pursue other interests, away from Army life.

Looking back at it – my sense of disjointedness and my difficulty in communicating, a slight air of depression – there would in modern terms probably be some diagnosis of PTSD (post-traumatic stress disorder), although I have to say that it never felt like anything so dramatic to me. I guess I had been through a lot, had killed and seen my friends killed, and been wounded myself … I was hardened but now I was alone, or at least isolated. I think my way of dealing with it was reasonable and sane. I eventually left the Army and decided to get on with my life outside it.

A year or two before my Army discharge in late 1977, I toyed for some time with an idea one of the other guys I was working with gave me. Some 'civilian' security organisation was looking for ex-forces, Army people. They were recruiting for experienced soldiers to go out to Angola on security duties, training the locals in most things military. The money seemed to be quite good and I spent a few weeks carrying around and now and again looking at the application form, seriously thinking of going. However, I eventually decided against it, thinking I'd had enough of Army life and that it was time to start thinking of a total change.

A few months later in June 1976, the TV news and Press was full of the coverage of the trial of a group of 13 mercenaries, ten of them British ex-Army, who had been captured in Angola during the civil war that was raging there.

At the end of the trial, three Britons and an American were sentenced to death by firing squad, while the others on trial received prison sentences ranging from 16 to 30 years.

It made me shudder. Obviously, I was glad that I decided not to go to Angola, especially with what sounded like a bunch of psychos running around killing each other. At the time of the advertisement, all that was mentioned was that it was security/training work in Angola. The words 'mercenary' or 'fighting' were never mentioned – but it was the same job all right.

As it turned out, a few months before my discharge I was looking forward to a new life as a civilian and getting settled into a job as a sports centre manager.

As a civilian I remained on Reserve service and did suffer a short spell of post-traumatic stress which I think did make me quite touchy, snappy and difficult. It was the subtle things that were most difficult to shake – the things that training had bred into me. I couldn't even sit in a pub with my back to the windows or door for many years. I also used to get panicky caught up in heavy traffic, constantly trying to make some space and looking for escape routes left and right, in case of an 'imaginary' attempted hijack. During the first year or so after my discharge, I was drinking quite heavily and found I had to have a few drinks before I could sleep at night. This wasn't because of night-mares, quite the contrary, it was just that I needed something to dim my mind to relax enough to drop off. My work in the MRF never gave me nightmares. But the stress didn't last too long and I managed to pull myself out of it without too much trouble. You had to in those days.

It was soon after my discharge, in 1978, that I was approached by the Military because of my infantry-MRF background. In short, I was invited to join the Reservists, which I felt might be interesting, and could include a bit of free travel together 'keeping my hand in' when I wanted to. I had to go through the entire grading process again up to Sergeant's Qualification (SQ), which I didn't particularly find a problem.

During the 1980s and 1990s, after moving on from the sports cen-tre, I spent many years self-employed, running my own company. I was again working virtually alone, or at the best with a small, select team, and generally felt much happier and contented.

I always kept up to date with the Ulster troubles and the charac-ters I used to chase after, years earlier.

However, I began to feel a little uncomfortable when quite a few years ago, the Government started letting out of prison convicted ter-rorist killers so they could spend their Christmases at home with their families. This was the government's way of trying to build bridges and creating some peace in the province. Be nice to the bad guys.

Then again, later, they decided to release all the killers in exchange for the handing in and decommissioning of weapons, in an attempt finally to bring The Troubles to an end. Years later, bombs are still going off, people are being shot and we're still waiting to see all the weapons handed in.

The Army should have been allowed to go in hard and stop it in the beginning in 1970-71. I'm sure it could have been done in those early days, before the IRA managed to properly organise themselves. Looking back to what it was like in 1972-75, I also feel sure that very many lives could have been saved, including those of three good friends of mine.

A few years ago, after selling up and closing my UK company, I decided to move abroad to Europe, where I live today. But before I left I took a couple of years off and didn't do very much except for helping one or two friends in building their own companies. I also took on a couple of home-study courses, one of which was a course in photo-journalism (I already had some expertise with cameras, courtesy of the MRF). After passing the 12-month course I worked part-time in the UK for a while as a freelance photographer, doing work for some local companies. Eventually, after moving abroad, this linked in with a variety of commercial surveillance and security work that I have been involved in, on and off, for the last ten or 12 years.

When I left the UK in 1994 I spent some time just chilling out and toured around southern France and Spain for a while, enjoying the sunshine, beer, water-sports and sailing before moving to Italy. In Italy I carried on and developed my photojournalism, finding work in both writing and photography for travel and sports magazines, covering the areas of Italy, France and Austria.

Now, during the summer months, I work around the north Italian coast and the marinas. In the winter, I spend a couple of months in Austria and France photographing skiing and other winter-sports events.

I live in a nice little cottage with a large garden in a peaceful mountain village, overlooking a wonderful lake with a majestic mountainous backdrop. It's very quiet, peaceful and idyllic, with a couple of village bars and friendly locals.

So I'm away from Britain, a country which I feel has to some extent let us all down. I dedicated many years of my life hunting terrorists and trying to protect the innocent. The Army and government used us and the best years of our lives, only to let all the terrorists free with dubious results, and I sometimes sit and think to myself, 'Why did we bother?'

In some ways being in the MRF ruined my life, but in others it made my life, even changing my personality more than once – which can be difficult to handle for some people. For sure it ruined me in my Army career, which I was originally quite happy to stay in for the full 22 years.

But on the other hand, the MRF gave me a very strong sense of loyalty, duty and determination. I used all the skills I learned in the Army when I joined the MRF, and all the skills I learned in the MRF, I often use now.

I'm sure that working undercover in a place like Belfast with only a few days' vacation in almost three years made me a better person. Thinking back, during my time in the MRF, we all had a strong sense of caring for each other. We constantly watched each other's backs, we all got along very well and none of us ever argued or got into fights within the sections. We were treated, and acted, like grown-ups. We were all like-minded, and we cared for the innocent people of Northern Ireland.

I now enjoy a trouble-free, peaceful life. I don't limp anymore, but my knee does give me a little discomfort sometimes, mainly when walking down hills or steps; but it's nothing I can't cope with.

And if ever I was approached and asked to go back and do it all again, I'm sure I would be tempted – I would go for the crack. I still have that fire in me and I doubt that I would change a thing. We had to think on our feet in those early days and it would be great to be out on the streets again with Kev, Tug, John, Colin, Dave, Ben and Mike. They were all close, good friends at that time, highly trained, totally professional and very brave dedicated soldiers.

Thinking back, it felt like we were all effectively licensed to kill for that short time, dodging in and out of the shadowy murky streets, spying on and hunting down terrorist murderers. But to be realistic, we are all far too old for that kind of thing now and I have absolutely no idea where many of the others are today, or even if they are still alive. And I don't think it would be a very good idea to call an MRF reunion … we might still get some unwelcome terrorist guests.

We were a totally new concept, a prototype test unit, in those early days. We were 'pathfinders' and 'hunters of men', during that lawless era of 1970s Belfast, developing techniques which were, over the years, fine-tuned and streamlined, and improved with the help of modern technology. It's quite possible that the MRF was the original or one of the original counter-terrorism units (CTUs) of modern times. The German police at the Munich Olympics in 1972 certainly didn't have much idea of how to handle their terrorist attack, and the SAS counter-terrorist unit was first seen to be deployed at the Iranian Embassy in London only in 1980, nine years after us in the MRF.

What was originally the Military Reaction Force appeared to later evolved into '14 Intelligence Company', '14 Company' or just simply 'The Det' (from 'detachment') – even, perhaps today by some other obscure name such as the Special Reconnaissance Regiment (SRR). Who really knows? The world of Intelligence and Special Operations is a very murky one, where nothing is totally black and white, but just hundreds of shades of grey.

The MRF was a top secret Special Operations CTU which didn't appear officially to exist on paper at that time, but was acknowledged much later in Parliament in March 1994. It was made up of specially selected volunteers from many arms of the Armed Forces and trained in covert, secret undercover operations and surveillance. The name, the faces, the training and role may have changed over the years but the basic organisation and many of the original methods are very much the same. And as far as I know, the unit is much larger now than it ever was in my day and is operational in all corners of the world.

In those chaotic early days, we were little more than a big handful of highly trained and motivated guys, armed to the teeth and sent down into the city in civilian cars, on specific operations – to kick arse. And we surely kicked plenty of bad arses.

I feel that if I ever did go back over to Ulster, one day, in the very distant future, I would take a long walk around the city centre. I would smile, thinking of that guy we chased around the City Hall square, with our cars on the pavement while everyone around us scattered and dived for cover.

Perhaps I'd pop in and have a coffee in that Hotel, perhaps sit at the same table and think back to what it was like over 40 years ago when Kev and I gave the shivers to those two RUC detectives who smugly thought they had breached our security.

Then I'd take a stroll down the Falls Road and take a look at our old Army OP, 'Oscar 1', before heading off to the North Howard Street hill. We all spent hours and hours just sitting there, waiting to get the call and race out onto the Falls Road to grab or shoot some unsuspecting bad boy terrorist.

Then I'd wander past that shop – if it's still there – perhaps buy a sandwich or coffee, thinking of the time Mike and I dashed in and grabbed the wrong guy, and then ran back in to drag out our real 'Foxtrot'.

On the Falls Road up ahead on the right, I would pass the back street where Colin dropped those two players, one of which was our 'Charlie' who was wanted for questioning.

Later, making my way further along the Falls Road, on the left, I would walk by the streets where my friend was beaten, thrown into the cellar and shot – and also the street I 'got it' in the knee and Kev lifted me up like a rag doll and carried me off. A hundred metres further, on the right hand side was where Bob was murdered while in the car with me.

Even today I can still see the big cheesy smile and bushy hair and beard of my very good and brave friend Ted Stuart, of the Four Square Laundry. I would recall, again, how he was shot to death in his van on Juniper Park, Dunmurry, on the far side of Andersonstown.

After passing the Royal Victoria Hospital I'd reach the St James's estate on the left where I fired across the face of Tug, my driver, while Kev in the back seat blasted the group of players, on the corner, through the back of the car window with his SMG.

Finally, a little further on the left, entering Andersonstown, I'd walk into Milltown cemetery, thinking of those good friends of mine that didn't make it and were murdered, left behind. I would take a long casual look around the cemetery, which is now the permanent home to so many IRA terrorists. I'd be searching for the old, familiar, notorious names – the names of those evil terrorist killers of women and babies who didn't really deserve the right to life ... and then I'd piss on them.

Appendix - Glossary

V check	Vehicle legitimacy check
IRA	Irish Republican Army (Provos - PIRA)
ASU	Active Service Unit (IRA - PIRA)
9 millie	9 mm Browning pistol
SMG	Sterling – Submachine Gun
Round	Bullet
Snap	Food
HQ	Headquarters
Players	Terrorists
SAS	Special Air Service (British Special Forces)
SBS	Special Boat Service or Squadron (British Special Forces)
Paras	Parachute Regiment
SB Boys	Special Branch
Op	Operation
OP	Observation Post
CP/CPP	Close Protection/Close personal protection (body-guard)
RV	Rendezvous (meeting point)
SIB	Special Investigation Branch (military SB)
UVF	Ulster Volunteer Force (protestant terror group)
UFF	Ulster Freedom Fighters (protestant terror group)
UDA	Ulster Defence Association (protestant group)
Mossad	Israeli secret service
Delta Force	US Special Forces

ATO	Ammunition technical officer 'Felix'
RUC	Royal Ulster Constabulary
CSM	Company Sergeant Major
OC	Officer Commanding – company commander of over 90 men.
MRF	Military Reaction Force

Images

Browning 9 millie

Walther PPK

9mm Sterling SMG - with Silencer

9mm Sterling SMG - Silenced

Outside the MRF Ops Room, 1973

Military Skills Instructor - 1990

MRF Car 'Delta' after a Shooting Incident - 1972

MRF Car 'Delta' after a Shooting Incident - 1972

MRF Compound entrance

MRF Cars & Parking area
on gravel and hard core

Flag Stone central path
with gravel to both sides

Training
Room

Accommodation
81 Section

Weapons &
Equip. Store

Stores &
Trg. Room

Operations
Room/Desk

OCs Office

Briefing
Room

Accomm.
83 Section

Accommodation
82 Section

Surround corrugated metal
fence - 12 to 15" tall

Printed in Great Britain
by Amazon